Michael Moz

GRASSROOTS POLITICS
IN AN
AFRICAN STATE

GRASSROOTS POLITICS IN AN AFRICAN STATE

Integration and Development
In Sierra Leone

Walter Barrows

Africana Publishing Co. · New York and London

A Division of Holmes & Meier Publishers, Inc.

Published in the United States of America 1976 by
Africana Publishing Company
a division of Holmes & Meier Publishers, Inc.
101 Fifth Avenue, New York, N.Y. 10003

Published in Great Britain 1976 by
Holmes & Meier Publishers, Ltd.
Hillview House
1, Hallswelle Parade, Finchley Road
London NW11 0DL

LIBRARY OF CONGRESS CATALOGING IN PUBLICATION DATA

Barrows, Walter.
  Grassroots politics in an African state.

  Includes bibliographical references.
  1. Kenema District, Sierra Leone—Politics and
government. I. Title.
DT516.9.K46B37   320.9′66′4   74-84655
ISBN 0-8649-0183-X

PRINTED IN THE UNITED STATES OF AMERICA

Preface

This book represents the final stage of an effort to explore the ties that bind the hinterland to the central political system in one African country. Since the explicit purpose of this research venture was to investigate the rural sources of politics in Sierra Leone, I was largely dependent in the countryside upon information unavailable in libraries or other convenional academic sites. Consequently, I relied extensively upon the good will and generosity of Sierra Leoneans. The lore of scholarly circles has it that research in Africa is becoming increasingly difficult, but my experience did not bear this out in the least. The people with whom I came into contact were invariably cooperative and genuinely interested in helping an untutored stranger understand the intricacies of their political life. I owe them a considerable debt of gratitude.

My fieldwork endeavored basically to exploit three streams of evidence. The most important source of information was interviews with key political actors in local—Kenema District—affairs, including Members of Parliament, Paramount Chiefs, Speakers, politicians, chiefdom clerks, and businessmen. I also interviewed a number of central administration officials, including the Minister of the Interior, who also happened to be the Prime Minister. In all, about 150 interviews were collected, each of which usually lasted over an hour, and quite often over two hours. Most were conducted in English, but some required the services of a Mende interpreter. In order to protect the anonymity of interviewees in sensitive positions, interviews have been coded by number for purposes of documentation. This is unfortunate, but the reader will understand the need to respect the privacy of informants.

Official documents constituted the second stream of evidence. I was fortunate in having received permission from the Ministry of the Interior to peruse the local government files and archives for Kenema District, which included records in the headquarters of the Provincial Secretary and of the District Officer. These proved an invaluable check on the data gained through interviews as well as an important source of information in their own right. For historical material, the archives located at Fourah Bay College were used. The Electoral Commission generously supplied me with what voting records it had available. Unfortunately, however, no detailed material for contests other than the 1969 by-elections could be located. (Even these statistics were spotty for certain constituencies.) Thus, election data is limited as an independent stream of evidence to a single event.

Third, I accompanied administrative officers on field trips into the countryside to observe their interaction with chiefdom people. Thus, for instance, I was privileged to witness the election of a Paramount Chief and of a Speaker, as well as a formal Commission of Inquiry into the affairs of another Paramount Chief.

A list of all the Sierra Leoneans whose generosity contributed to this study would be prodigious indeed. Some, however, were especially helpful. As a Visiting Research Student at Fourah Bay College I was able to tap the resources of the Institute of African Studies, particularly the experience and extensive personal networks of E. W. Blyden III and J. G. E. Hyde. Provincial Secretaries P.E.O. Taylor-Lewis and Victor Pratt most kindly allowed me to observe official procedures during a number of chiefdom elections and investigations. David Sheku's friendship, advice and encouragement was especially appreciated. Likewise, District Officers O. C. Leopold-George and W. B. Munu went out of their way to facilitate my fieldwork.

To those chiefs and Members of Parliament who spent long hours explaining the politics of their respective chiefdoms and constituencies, I am particularly grateful. Their sensitive positions caution against mentioning them by name. Also helpful were Sumalia Kuyateh, Lansana M. Kellah, Peter B. Keitell, William Smith, P. D. Musa, John Bassie, E. A. Swaray, A. H. Demby, B. S. Massaquoi, and Robert Barrow. Conversations with Peace Corps Volunteers stationed in various chiefdoms alerted me to many features of local affairs which otherwise would have passed unnoticed. Fellow scholars John Cartwright, Milton

Harvey, Tom Cox, and Abner Cohen simultaneously stimulated my thinking and checked its excursions into unreality. While the views of others have to a large extent determined the content and conclusions of this study, misinformation and misinterpretation are, of course, my responsibility, not theirs.

Research in Kenema District, which took place between July 1969 and July 1970, was made possible by a generous fellowship granted by the Foreign Area Fellowship Program. Again, the conclusions, opinions, and other statements in this study are my own and are not necessarily those of the Fellowship Program.

I owe an incalculable intellectual debt to my teachers at Yale University. To William J. Foltz in particular this debt is more than intellectual: His common sense, invaluable suggestions, and unstinting effort guided this project past more than one hazard. I am deeply appreciative.

Finally, not only did my wife, Patricia, serve as editor, typist, proofreader, bibliographer, cook, hotel keeper, mother, and loving companion —but she endured a single-minded individual through what must have seemed an interminable and thankless period of sacrifice.

W. L. Barrows
Vicenza, Italy

Contents

In Memory of My Father

GRASSROOTS POLITICS
IN AN
AFRICAN STATE

SIERRA LEONE

KOINADUGU
Kabala

BOMBALI

NORTHERN   PROVINCE

KAMBIA
Kambia

KAMBIA   KONO

PORT   Makeni   EASTERN

Port Loko   Yengema Sefadu
LOKO Lunsar Marampa
                                         Magburaka
              TONKOLILI

Freetown

WESTERN   PROVINCE
AREA
                                                      Kailahun
              Moyamba   Pendembu
MOYAMBA   BO   KAILAHUN

SOUTHERN   Bo
                                         Kenema
Sherbro Urban   KENEMA
District Council

Bonthe   PROVINCE

BONTHE   Pujehun

N THE PUJEHUN

PROVINCIAL BOUNDARY	....
PROVINCIAL HEADQUARTERS	▣
DISTRICT BOUNDARY	-------
DISTRICT HEADQUARTERS	■
MAIN ROADS	_____
RAILROADS	+++++++

0 10 20 30 40 50
MILES

Chapter 1

The Sierra Leonean Setting

"Center and Periphery" is a phrase which has in recent years acquired a number of meanings associated with development and integration in emerging nations. It brings to mind a demographic relationship between urban centers and their rural hinterlands; it also connotes a socioeconomic process involving the penetration of traditional populations by a more active modern sector; further, it draws attention to structural connections between two levels—the national and the local—of a political system. These meanings overlap, of course, for it would be difficult to discuss one to the exclusion of the others, but the latter consideration weighs most heavily in this book, which investigates political linkages between the central system of Sierra Leone and one segment of its periphery, Kenema District.[1]

The study of linkages between center and periphery is not the only way to investigate political integration and development, but it does seem an appropriate focus in the case of African politics, where generally a small well-educated elite dominates the center and the masses comprise the rural periphery. This gives rise to problems of vertical relationships, the so-called elite-mass gap. Furthermore, the rural peripheries of most African states generally are heterogeneous in composition; the central systems each must deal with plural societies, giving rise to problems of horizontal (territorial) relationships.[2] Meshing center with periphery entails, then, a dual process. On the one hand, durable links must be forged between the central system and individual communities at the local level. *Development* in this context means the growth of structures (institutions, roles, stable patterns of behavior) which provide these strong center-periphery linkages; the stronger the structural tie between the center and a particular local community, the more developed it can be considered.[3] On the other hand, a wide array of links must be established between the center and the periphery as a whole. *Integration* here refers to the distribution of connecting structures; the more widely a particular linkage pattern is distributed, the more it can be said to contribute to the integration of the political system. This distinction between the developmental and integrative sides of linkage politics may be illustrated by imagining a political net cast over the periphery and drawn toward the center. The thickness (strength) of each strand in the net corresponds to the developmental component; the number of strands as well as the extent to which they are spread across the peripheral population represents the integrative component. Were a linkage network to consist of strong ties densely concentrated upon a particular sector of the periphery, its development can be considered high but its integration low; likewise, were a net composed of thin fibers spread extensively across the political landscape, it would join a wide range of communities to the center, but its ability to "haul" would be limited.

In this context, Sierra Leone suffers from a typically African malady: the need to establish resilient connections between an urban-centered regime and its rural publics. In Sierra Leone, as in many other African territories, the towns and cities have outstripped their agricultural hinterlands in terms of economic development and political participation. Moreover, the important urban settlements have become the physical and philosophical focus of the political elites and the institutional machinery with which they attempt to govern their territories. (This is not to posit an "urban-rural cleavage" as a key feature of African politics; such claims should be empirically demonstrated, not assumed *a priori*.) This situation is particularly clear-cut in Sierra Leone, where there is only one truly urban center—Freetown, the capital city—which serves as the focal point of almost all national activities. The political system which emanates from Freetown—the "center"—occupies one level of analysis in this study; politics in Kenema District, a rural area in Sierra Leone's southeastern "periphery," represents a subsystem level of analysis. The political relationship between them is the subject of investigation.

"Social mobilization" is a concept proposed by Deutsch which

TABLE 1.1
Indicators of Level of Social
Mobilization in Sierra Leone,
c. 1965.

INDICATOR	SIERRA LEONE	SIERRA LEONE'S RANK AMONG 32 BLACK AFRICAN NATIONS
Percent Labor Force in Agriculture	75	5*
Per Capita Energy Consumption (kg. of coal equiv.)	38	19
Per Capita GNP ($ US)	150	9
Primary School Enrollment per 1,000 pop.	52	21
Secondary School Enrollment per 10,000 pop.	57	12
Percent literate (estimated)	10	19
Radios per 1,000 pop.	44	8
Newspaper per 1,000 pop.	90	3.5
Telephones per 1,000 pop.	28	13
Commercial Vehicles per 100,000 pop.	324	10
Passenger cars per 10,000 pop.	60	8.5
Percent pop. in cities of 20,000 and more	7	18.5
		Average Rank: 12.2

Source: Donald George Morrison, *et. al., Black Africa: A Comparative Handbook* (New York, Free Press: 1972), Part I.

*Since "percent labor force in agriculture" correlates negatively with social mobilization, it has been ranked from the bottom of the list.

deals with "the process in which major clusters of old social, economic and psychological commitments are eroded or broken and people become available for new patterns of behavior."[4] It is a major outgrowth of modernization and economic development, a generalized process which may in turn be thought of as being composed of a number of constituent sub-processes, such as urbanization, exposure to mass media, or growth of literacy. Table 1.1 presents a series of indicators which suggest the *level* of social mobilization in Sierra Leone compared with the rest of Black Africa.[5] Overall, in terms of the extent to which its popula-

TABLE 1.2
Indicators of Rate of Social
Mobilization in Sierra Leone:
Average Annual Percent Changes.

INDICATOR: AVERAGE ANNUAL GROWTH OF	SIERRA LEONE	SIERRA LEONE'S RANK AMONG 32 BLACK AFRICAN NATIONS
Electricity Production (1963-68)	40 %	12
Per Capita GNP (1961-68)	1.5%	8.5
Primary School Enrollment Rate (1960-66)	7.3%	18
Secondary School Enrollment Rate (1962-66)	3 %	24
Literacy Rate (1955-65)	2.5%	25.5
Radios per 1,000 (1960-66)	199 %	2.5
Newspapers per 1,000 (1960-68)	2.6%	12.5
Telephones per 1,000 (1963-67)	3.4%	22
Commercial Vehicles per 10,000 (1958-66)	15 %	5
Percent pop. in Cities (1955-65)	12.6%	22.5
		Average Rank: 15.2

Source: Adapted from Morrison, *et. al., Black Africa: A Comparative Handbook.* Part I.

tion has been activated, its old patterns of life disrupted by the forces of modernization, Sierra Leone ranks above the median in Africa. Likewise, the *rate* at which its peoples are undergoing fundamental changes is on the whole slightly higher than the majority of its African counterparts, as shown by Table 1.2. Many of these measures are inexact and the method of comparison crude,[6] but for background purposes we may envision Sierra Leone as a society being transformed through social mobilization at a rate which is likely to burden governmental institutions and strain the stability of the political system. As the socially mobilized sector of the population enlarges, demands for more political participation and public services increase correspondingly.[7]

Under such circumstances, the manner by which the central political system links up with the activating population becomes a matter of critical importance. This is especially true in the rural periphery, where the masses of people are located and where access to central institutions is problematical. Have official agencies established new ties to the countryside or have they continued with the patterns of minimal government which ' characterized colonial rule? What is the nature of party affiliation; is it based on ethnicity or class, ideology or interest, national or local issues? Do political parties sink autonomous roots at the village level or do they cling, like vines on a tree, to already-existing structures of authority? What is the role of local elites, particularly, in Sierra Leone's case, the Paramount Chiefs, who historically have performed the key linkage function between center and periphery? No regime—colonial, indigenous civilian, or military—has been willing to govern the countryside without the chiefs as the prime agent of local rule, and indeed, all major political parties have found it necessary to court chiefly support. The chieftaincy has been the basic building block of governance in Sierra Leone since the establishment of a British Protectorate over hinterland peoples in 1896, but is it an adequate linkage institution during an era of modern unsettling forces? In short, what are the consequences for political development and integration of the structures which attempt to link Sierra Leone's central system with its socially mobilizing periphery?

The Center in Sierra Leone

A glance at a map will suffice to demonstrate Freetown as a promontory on Sierra Leone's social topography. True to a pattern common among ex-colonies, the transportation and communication network funnels the bulk of commercial activity toward a main outlet to the world economy. Most of Sierra Leone's money economy is geared for export—iron and diamond mining, cash cropping of palm oil, cocoa, and similar products—and most exports exit through Freetown. The near-defunct railway, the burgeoning road system (easily the most dynamic channel for exchange in Sierra Leone), the domestic airline, the telecommunications network, the postal service—all converge on the capital city in much the same manner as a drainage system

TABLE 1.3
Ethnic Groups in Sierra Leone and Freetown.
Percentage Size in 1963.

	SIERRA LEONE (POP.: 2,180,355)	FREETOWN (POP.: 127,917)
Creole	1.92%	21.68%
Temne	29.76	23.92
Limba	8.42	14.39
Mende	30.86	9.82
Fulani	3.06	5.11
Loko	2.96	4.57
Kroo	0.22	3.49
Susu	3.09	3.02
Mandinko	2.34	2.46
Sherbro	3.42	2.39
Kissi	2.25	0.58
Kono	4.80	0.42
Kuranko	3.70	0.20
Other	3.21	7.94
Total	100.01	99.99

Source: Adapted from J. Barry Riddell, *The Spatial Dynamics of Modernization in Sierra Leone* (Evanston, Ill., 1970), p. 114.

flows toward a major river and then to the sea. Freetown historically has been the prime attraction for migration in Sierra Leone, as people from all parts of the countryside have followed the communications network towards its focal point. Table 1.3 shows the tribal composition of Freetown's population in 1963. The Creoles, descendents of liberated slaves and a unique blend of Western and African cultures, comprise the "indigenous" population of the city.[8] Note, however, that upcountry groups now far outnumber those Freetown inhabitants who identify themselves as Creoles: Tennes and Limbas, drawn by proximity and pushed by poverty, are the most important immigrants from the north; Mendes, the most numerous group in Sierra Leone as a whole, are less attracted to Freetown because of the relative prosperity of their southern homeland, but they do make up a significant portion of the urban population.

But the flow of goods, people, and information is hardly unidirectional. Freetown is also a point of dissemination.[9] It is the dispersion center for all variety of imported goods and ideas which make their way to the interior, the communications node from which the country's only radio and television station (government-owned) broadcasts to the population, the headquarters of an oft-times active press (the most important part of which is government-owned), the leading educational sector, and, more vaguely, the crucible in which the general cultural style of Sierra Leone as a whole is compounded and diffused. Historically, the spread of such "modern" agencies as schools, banks, post offices, and medical facilities has been channeled to the hinterland from Freetown along the branches of the communications network and the hierarchy of administrative centers established by the colonial authorities to rule the provincial population.[10] The greater a village's distance from this network-hierarchy emanating from Freetown, the less likely its chances for benefiting from modern amenities.

Mention of the administrative hierarchy peaking in Freetown draws us closer to our prime concern, political linkages. As the seat of national government, Freetown is the locus of all formal institutions of authority at the central level: the Presidency, the

House of Representatives, the civil service bureaucracy, and the military bureaucracy. Sierra Leone inherited from British rule at the time of Independence in 1961 a "Westminster" model of parliamentary democracy, in which a Governor-General acting in lieu of the British monarch chooses a Prime Minister, who in turn forms a Cabinet which is expected to maintain the support of a majority in the House of Representatives. But, in tune with a trend obtaining throughout Black Africa, this British-style constitution was replaced in April 1971 with a Republican arrangement, whereby remaining institutional links with Britain were severed and the Governor-General supplanted by an elected President. Indeed, the President's formal authority under the new constitution exceeds the rather circumscribed powers allotted previously to the Governor-General; virtually, as "Executive President" he now enjoys the constitutional prerogatives of the old-style Governor-General and Prime Minister combined.[11]

At the time of research (1969-70), however, the Republican Constitution was an issue under debate, not an established fact. Therefore, the accompanying "organizational chart" diagrams the way in which formal institutions of government penetrate toward the periphery from the center, using labels now outdated by the declaration of a Republic of Sierra Leone in 1971. Note that alone among the many departments which extend agencies from the capital to the hinterland, only the Ministry of the Interior has been diagrammed. This reflects its predominant role in local government and law enforcement. But it should be remembered that a number of other key ministries (e.g., Works, Mining and Natural Resources, Agriculture, and Education) penetrate toward the grassroots, sometimes to the village level.

The rhythm of politics is set by an election cycle in which the House of Representatives, unless it is dissolved early, is elected every five years. Its 62 "ordinary" members[12] are elected from single-member constituencies whose boundaries almost always (except in urban areas) include one or more chiefdoms; rarely are chiefdoms cut by constituency boundaries. The 12 "Paramount Chief" members, one from each District, are chosen not by the

FIGURE 1.1
Formal Government Structure, Pre-1971

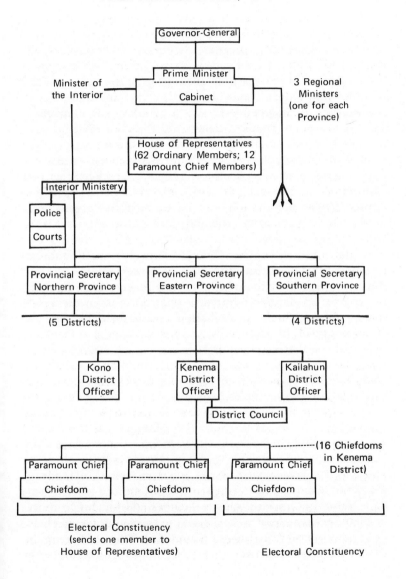

general citizenry but by local electoral colleges called Chiefdom Councils.

Rarely, of course, are descriptions of the formal governmental framework adequate for explaining the real character of politics in a system. Generally, informal institutions and processes bulk larger, and in this Sierra Leone is no exception. Political parties assumed a crucial role in the decades just prior to and immediately following Independence in 1961. The crucial period of preparation for Independence (1951-1961) was dominated by the Sierra Leone Peoples' Party (SLPP), a loosely-organized movement of hinterland peoples who mobilized politically not so much to oust the British as to assure that Independence would not bring rule by the Creole minority headquartered in Freetown. This effort to activate and unify the provincial population against Creole domination was led by Milton Margai, Sierra Leone's first "upcountry" medical doctor. Although a Mende from the south, the elderly doctor succeeded in garnering support from all sectors of the provinces, largely by aligning and accommodating two critical elites, the local chiefly hierarchies and the new men of wealth and education who were growing in influence throughout the countryside and who, in fact, were closely related to the chiefs. Both Kilson and Cartwright correctly describe the SLPP as an edifice constructed atop these basic pillars of social structure in rural Sierra Leone.[13] Mass support was mediated by the Paramount Chiefs and the new elite, a "political class" which sought to fill the positions of power left vacant by the retreating British.

The next decade (1961-1971) saw the rise to power of a new party and the decline of the SLPP. Dr. Margai (by then knighted Sir Milton) brought Sierra Leone to Independence as head of a United Front which included most important political elements in the territory, even significant Creole politicos. Missing from the grand coalition, however, was a small minority of younger, more critical politicians, mostly Temnes and Limbas from the north, who at the least were disgruntled that they had not been permitted to taste the fruits of power more fully and who at the most were prepared to launch a radical movement against what they apparently considered a "neocolonial" regime underwritten by "feudalistic" institutions of chieftaincy and rural conservatism. In late 1960, the All Peoples Congress (APC) was founded, led by Siaka Stevens, a prominent Limba politician, whose trade union background well equipped him to speak the language of popular, even radical, causes.[14] Despite its populist line and its identification with regional discontent in the north, the APC fared poorly in the 1962 General Election. Not only did it capture less than 20% of the total vote, but after the election Prime Minister Margai skillfully used the advantages of incumbency to erode what APC opposition existed.

Had Sir Milton continued in office, the APC likely would have been contained as little more than a nuisance. But his death in April 1964 brought to power his half brother, Albert Margai, whose rule proved disastrous for the SLPP and invigorating for the APC. Albert resembled Siaka Stevens more closely than he did his elder brother. He and Stevens during the 1950's had worked together as the principal spokesmen for the younger, more educated elements of the provincial elite; both served as key commoner representatives on the Provincial Assembly, an upcountry body dominated otherwise by Paramount chiefs; and both split from the SLPP in 1958 to found an opposition party critical of the conservative rural coalition and oriented toward progressive urban interests. Stevens remained in opposition, but in 1960 Albert Margai chose to repair fences with his brother and inherit power. His accession to the Prime Ministership was marked by immediate dissension within and without the SLPP, and indeed the duration of his incumbency saw increasing intraparty conflict and, as Albert sought to impose central discipline, a shift in the party's center of gravity toward its Mende core. With the governing party in disarray and increasingly identified with just one ethnic group, the opposition APC extended an organizational network throughout the north and in the urban areas, bypassing the chiefs and relying for support upon popular disenchantment with the SLPP. This strategy paid impressive dividends, for in the General Election of 1967 the APC won a bare majority of seats and the Governor-General invited

Siaka Stevens to form a new Government.

Stevens had to wait a year actually to assume the Prime Ministership, however. A military coup d'etat ousted him from office even before he had taken it. In fact, the year of military rule was marked by a series of coups, the last of which—initiated by northern rank-and-file elements within the army—reestablished civilian rule and with it Steven's incumbency.[15]

The new Prime Minister was faced with the general task of restoring authority over the army and the population at large, and the specific task of widening the APC's narrow majority in the House of Representatives. He accomplished the latter in a series of by-elections during 1969-70, in which the blunt instruments of central power—army and police mobilization, mass arrests, states of emergency, preventive detention—were used liberally and deliberately not only to quiet the countryside during times of tension but to enhance the electoral chances of the party in power. With the advantages of incumbency the APC penetrated all portions of Sierra Leone, including the SLPP's southern and eastern strongholds. No longer was it a regional party catering to regional discontent; rather its emblem was recognized and in varying degrees supported in remote villages throughout the territory. The APC was a national party in the same sense that the SLPP was a national party in 1961, when elements from every important social group were found within its fold. The SLPP's national character diminished shortly afterward, especially under the leadership of Albert Margai. But the APC so far has managed to extend its appeal throughout the periphery at the same time as its control over central government has been consolidated. General Elections in May 1973 granted an overwhelming victory to the APC: It won all 85 ordinary seats (all but 5 unopposed), and all 12 of the Paramount chiefs elected (unopposed) declared for the APC. As in most African elections, there was again strong evidence of intimidation and zealous use of governmental machinery in favor of the incumbent party.[16]

The process of party competition in the countryside, and in particular the manner by which the APC has managed to extend its appeal to groups hitherto identified exclusively with the SLPP, is an important matter which this book seeks to scrutinize.

The Periphery in Sierra Leone

The great majority of Sierra Leoneans live in villages, grow rice, and pay taxes exclusively to local chiefdom officials.

In 1963 the total population of Sierra Leone was 2,180,355 persons, of whom less than 10% resided in settlements of 20,000 or more; indeed, Freetown with a population of 130,000 represented most of the urban sector.[17] Even if we expand the definition of "urban" to include areas with 5,000 or more persons, still in Sierra Leone less than 15% of the total population could (in 1963) be considered "urbanized" (see Table 1.4).

TABLE 1.4
Size of Localities, 1963.

SIZE OF LOCALITIES	NUMBER OF LOCALITIES	NUMBER OF INHABITANTS	CUMULATIVE % OF TOTAL POPULATION
20,000 or more	2	154,530	7%
10,000 to 20,000	5	62,531	10
5,000 to 10,000	11	66,236	13
1,000 to 5,000	148	263,887	25
500 to 1,000	312	211,642	35
200 to 500	1,643	490,153	57
100 to 200	3,070	426,398	77
Less than 100	13,379	504,978	100
Total	18,570	2,180,355	

Source: Adapted from *1963 Population Census of Sierra Leone* (Central Statistics Office, Freetown, 1965), Vol. I, Table 8.

Farming is by far the most common occupation in Sierra Leone, and most farmers spend the greater part of their time growing the country's staple food, rice. A minority, particularly in the Southern and Eastern Provinces, supplement rice growing with cash crops for export, and a tiny minority relies exclusively upon cash-cropping of palm oil, coffee, cocoa, or piassava, but on the whole rice is king. About 80% of the annual rice crop is produced using the time-honored technique of shifting cultivation whereby after a certain number of harvests a cleared plot is abandoned to the forest and a new plot cleared. This traditionally has dealt with the problem of low land fertility, but particularly in a time of increasing population and rising demands for food, it now contributes to land pressure, erosion, and low productivity. In the early 1950s Sierra Leone was a rice exporter, but since 1955 domestic production has not met internal demand and valuable foreign exchange has had to be expended for imports.[18] The Government in order to develop self-sufficiency in rice production has launched a number of schemes whose success at the grass-roots level is as of yet undetermined. Mechanical cultivation of "boliland" swamps is one of the few large-scale enterprises being undertaken in the Northern Province, a region, as we shall see, which has lagged behind the rest of Sierra Leone in terms of economic development. Mechanical cultivation has so far proved too expensive to merit widespread application.[19] A method more within feasibility for local farmers—but unfortunately for Northerners, more appropriate for the Southern and Eastern Provinces—is "inland swamp" cultivation, which now accounts for about 15% of total rice production. This technique entails no drastic departures from prevailing practices and land tenure customs, although so far its success has been predicated directly upon Government subsidies and prodding from Agricultural Inspectors of the central government. Whatever the technique used, however, the important point is that Sierra Leone's performance as a national economy depends ultimately upon the efforts of small-scale farmers and the extent to which they can be coordinated by central institutions. Rice production is just one—albeit a major—instance demonstrating the need for vibrant links between center and periphery in a society undergoing widespread change.

All development schemes in the provinces—public or private, agricultural or industrial, short-term or long—must eventually receive application at the local level and must, therefore, deal with the fundamental instrument of governance in Sierra Leone, the chiefdom. This is the arena in which local political prizes are won and lost; it is where taxes are paid and justice meted out; it is the unit in which rural development schemes ultimately succeed or fail; it is the crucial emotional focus for the vast majority of Sierra Leoneans. The 148 chiefdoms of Sierra Leone vary considerably in terms of size, population, and wealth; but, for all intents and purposes, they are identical in terms of political structure. Each is ruled by a hierarchy descending from a Paramount Chief at the apex, through a number of Section Chiefs, to the Village Chiefs or headmen at the base. Each chief is assisted by a Speaker, who facilitates communications between ordinary people and their leader and who, ideally, serves as a check against arbitrary rule.

"Paramounts" are paramount only within their respective chiefdoms; there is no hierarchy among chiefdoms and so there is, officially at least, equality among Paramounts. The dynamics of local politics are in large measure channelled by the rules which govern competition for the chieftaincy, a rich source of power, prestige and wealth—and still an office prized even among the new educated elite. Paramount Chiefs are elected for life—unless deposed—by assemblies of elders and notables called Chiefdom Councils. Ordinary people are not eligible; candidates for the office must be descended from previous Paramount Chiefs. In most chiefdoms two or more "ruling families" (or "ruling houses") claim the exclusive right to supply the successor to a dead or deposed Paramount. Since the normal period of incumbency is long, the stakes are high and competition fierce. Deposition of a chief is a process carried out exclusively under the auspices of the central Government. This represents not only the ultimate source of national control over localities but it constitutes an important lever for linkage interaction: Opposition ruling families seeking to remove their incumbent Paramount Chief often petition for central intervention in chiefdom affairs; likewise, in order to secure their tenure of office, incumbents forge alliances with powerful elements at the central level.

There are subtle institutional differences among the "tribes" of Sierra Leone. Temne Paramount Chiefs are infused with more religious authority than their Mende counterparts;[20] Temne Chiefs are more remote from their people than Mende and Limbe chiefs;[21] Mende land tenure rules invest the chief with less control over land than Kono practice; the Mende and Sherbro permit females to occupy the chieftaincy, while this is unheard-of among the northern peoples; and of course each tribe has its own language, myths, religious beliefs, and customs. But in terms of basic formal structure, chiefdoms are alike throughout the country. On a continuum which ranges from highly centralized "hierarchical" states like Buganda (in Uganda) through intermediate "pyramidal" structures like the Ashanti Confederation (in Ghana) to highly decentralized "segmentary" societies like the Nuer (in Sudan), all the tribes of Sierra Leone would be located between the "pyramidal" and "segmentary" types.[22] That is, in the absence of any overarching authority, the many chiefdoms of a tribe form a decentralized system; but *within* each, chiefdom authority is relatively centralized in the hands of a Paramount Chief.

The consequential differences among the peoples of Sierra Leone are not political but socioeconomic. Unequal rates of economic development have created disparities among geographical regions within the provinces which have come to overshadow in political saliency the disparities between Freetown and the provinces. In the 1950's the crying political issue was the advantages that Creoles had over the provincial masses in terms of such valued commodities as roads, schools, hospitals, water supplies, government services, and, of course, political representation. But during the 1960's the issue turned to the distribution of goods—public and private—*within* the provinces. Whatever the index of economic development selected, the Northern Province ranked behind the Southern and Eastern Provinces.[23] For a variety of historical and geographical reasons, the spread of Western-style education, communications-transportation facilities, and general economic development was much slower in the north than in the rest of the country. This is shown clearly and systematically in Riddell's "diffusion maps" which plot the spread of "modernization" throughout Sierra Leone during the twentieth century.[24] The indices in Table 1.5 (selected more on the basis of availability of data than on theoretical consistency) present a similar picture. The major consequences were twofold: social mobilization in the 1950's and 1960's, as northerners migrated in large numbers to more prosperous regions, especially Freetown and the diamond fields of the Eastern Province; and political mobilization in the 1960's, as northerners sought in the central political system a mechanism for a more equitable distribution of goods.

Unequal rates of economic development among regions, then, underlay much of the differentiation among "tribes" in the provinces. Temnes, Limbas, and Konos (to select some of the larger groups) occupy relatively deprived areas, whereas Mendes by virtue of favorable location in the south and east have historically enjoyed greater wealth and more opportunities. These differences have been cumulative and self-reinforcing: Poor educational and transportation facilities in the north contributed to low productivity and profitability, which in turn offered a little incentive to develop education and transportation, whereas in the south and east relative availability of agricultural and mineral resources attracted social overhead investment, which in turn opened further opportunities for enterprise. Even with central government intervention aimed at reducing regional—hence, "tribal"—disparities, overcoming this inheritance from the past entails long-term programs and large-scale mobilization of national resources. This, the Sierra Leonean system has thus far been unable to accomplish. The magnitude of the task is dramatized by the predominance still enjoyed—two decades after their political demise—by Creoles in business, education, and the civil service.

TABLE 1.5
Socioeconomic Indices: Percentage
Distribution Among Regions, ca. 1963.

	WESTERN AREA (FREETOWN AND IMMEDIATE ENVIRONS)	NORTHERN PROVINCE	SOUTHERN PROVINCE	EASTERN PROVINCE	SIERRA LEONE TOTAL
Population[a]	9%	41%	25%	25%	100%
Urban pop. (5,000 +)[a]	53	13	12	21	99
School attendance (ages 5-29)[a]	33	19	26	22	100
Literacy in English[a]	46	14	22	18	100
Provincial Primary Schools (1960-1)[b]	X	24	45	30	99
Provincial Administration Expenditures (1962-3)[c]	X	31	43	26	100
Gov't Stations in the Provinces[d]	X	42	33	26	101

Cooperative Societies (1964) [e]	2	17	45	35	99
Agricultural Development Loans (1964) [f]	18	16	37	28	99
Development Expenditures: [g]					
on Electricity (1961-5)	75	25 (for all provinces)			100
on Water Supplies (1963-4)	80	20 (for all provinces)			100
on Hospitals (1963-4)	46	64 (for all provinces)			100

Sources:

[a] 1963 Population Census of Sierra Leone, Vols. I and II.

[b] Sierra Leone Government, *Provinces Handbook 1961* (Freetown, 1962), p. 53.

[c] Sierra Leone Government, *Financial Report For the Period April 1962 to March 1963* (Freetown, 1965), pp. 21-3.

[d] Adapted from *Sierra Leone Yearbook 1964* (Freetown, Daily Mail Publications), pp. 181-5.

[e] Sierra Leone Government, *A Progress Report on Economic and Social Development* (Freetown, 1965), pp. 60-1.

[f] Sierra Leone Government, *Report of the Division of Agriculture 1964* (Freetown), pp. 35-6.

[g] Sierra Leone Government, *A Progress Report . . .*, pp. 24-73.

Kenema District

Research was conducted in Kenema District, a part of the Eastern Province populated predominantly by the Mende people, who came to occupy the heavily forested southern half of what is now Sierra Leone in migratory waves which began perhaps late in the eighteenth century. Economically, it is one of the favored regions. Cash cropping and diamond mining are the prime nontraditional occupations, but manufacture of forest products, trade, transportation, and government service are common also, especially in the towns. This general prosperity and the lure of diamonds has drawn migrants from elsewhere, particularly Temnes and Limbas from the north, lending Kenema District a cosmopolitanism unusual in Sierra Leone outside of Freetown. (See Table 1.6.)

TABLE 1.6
Demographic Breakdown of
Kenema District in 1963

Population	227,428	
Population of Kenema Town	13,246	
Number of Towns with 500 or more inhabitants	89	
Total population in Towns 500 or larger	107,900	
% of population:		
engaged as farmers, fishermen, etc.		66.5%
engaged as miners, quarrymen, etc.		17.6
aged 5-29 attending schools		8.3
aged 10 and over, literate in English		5.1
aged 10 and over, literate in Mende, Temne, or Arabic		2.3
born in chiefdom of residence		58.5
born outside Kenema District		28.6
Mende		75
Temne		10
Limba		3
Creole		0.23

Source: adapted from *1963 Population Census of Sierra Leone* (Central Statistics office, Freetown, volumes I-III (1965).

Kenema Town is at once a provincial capital, a district head-quarters, and a chiefdom headquarters. As a major outpost of the central government, it houses the Resident Minister, the Cabinet's political representative for the Eastern Province; the Provincial Secretary, top civil servant in the region; the District Officer, the official most directly responsible for government matters—both central and local—in the District; and a number of other politically important ministries which have extended their bureaucratic apparatuses from Freetown. But it is also the leading town in Nongowa, the District's leading chiefdom. Kenema Town, like most of the administrative headquarters throughout Sierra Leone, is the stage where much of the drama of linkage politics is played. Not only is it the physical locale where the formal institutions of government—central and chiefdom—meet, but it is the arena for much of the informal activity which gives life to politics. From casual conversations at a local pub, to speeches by the Prime Minister to Paramount Chiefs, to party branch meetings of notables and activists from throughout the District, Kenema Town is often the site where center and periphery converge. There, an interested observer is as likely to meet a Member of Parliament as a Paramount Chief, a government officer as a chiefdom clerk, a salaried worker as a farmer carrying rice to market.

There are 16 chiefdoms in Kenema District, listed here in descending order of population:

Chiefdom	*Population in 1963*
Nongowa	47,675
Lower Bambara	30,121
Gorama Mende	25,357
Small Bo	16,998
Wando	16,403
Tunkia	14,262
Dama	14,091
Simbaru	13,895
Kandu-Leppiama	12,794
Gaura	9,614

(table cont'd)

Chiefdom	Population in 1963
Malegohun	6,858
Koya	6,318
Dodo	6,129
Niawa	4,255
Langrama	1,371
Nomo	1,287

They range in size and importance from one of Sierra Leone's largest (Nongowa) to its smallest (Nomo).

Politics in each chiefdom revolves about the Paramount Chieftaincy and the hierarchy of offices which descend from it. The power of a Paramount Chief derives from more than the formal executive authority allocated to him—or her, in the Mende case—by the central government and the "constitution" of his chiefdom. It is true that he has powers of arrest, a strong voice in budgetary and tax matters, and prime responsibility for representing his community to the outside world. But his inner authority springs from the prestige attached to his office and his personal ability to sway opinion, to form alliances within and without the chiefdom, to reward friends and reassure rivals. In short, his political skill in building support is a key factor affecting his incumbency. A Paramount Chief makes myriad decisions about matters which are intimately entwined with the daily lives of his people. The location of a school, the award of an agricultural development loan, the path of a new road to remote villages, the settlement of a land dispute, the distribution of forestry or mining royalties, housing for a Peace Corps Volunteer, permission to develop a swamp for rice production, permission to open a new market, permission to hold a meeting—these and many other day-to-day decisions ramify throughout the ordinary activities of chiefdom citizens. Hence, they take the chieftaincy very seriously.

Decisions are not, however, made arbitrarily. There is in Mende political life a strong normative call for consensus. "Hanging heads" is the way Mendes express the process of consultation and accommodation by which chiefs are expected to maintain close relations with their people, even the rival ruling families which exist in almost every chiefdom as a check against overweening power. Opposed to this premise of unity, though, is a contrary tendency. The "chiefdom palaver" is an oft-encountered phenomenon throughout Mendeland. Conflict erupts easily in community affairs, and occasionally it spirals to such an extent that all chiefdom life is swept up by the dispute. Rice is left unplanted, swamps undrained, schools unattended, roads in disrepair. Any one of a hundred issues may have touched off the feud but, as we shall see, the underlying cause is almost always competition for the chieftaincy.

The Paramount Chief occupies a prominant place in linkage politics. Not only is he the fulcrum for the see-saw battle between consensus and conflict which characterizes chiefdom affairs but he is also a key couple between center and periphery. The nature of this institution inherited from the pre-colonial past and its capacity to function in the contemporary era is an issue which carries with it more than practical import. It confronts directly our theories of how the traditional and the modern interact.

NOTES

1. There is an emerging body of literature dealing with political links between center and periphery in Africa. The usual pattern is for political scientists to view the political system from central perspective, from the top down, as it were, while anthropologists for the most part confine themselves to the peripheral populations and their relationship to the state. An example of the first perspective is Henry Bienan, *Tanzania: Party Transformation and Economic Development* (Princeton: Princeton Univ. Press, 1967); an excellent anthropological account of one ethnic group's response to contemporary politics is Abner Cohen, *Custom and Politics in Urban Africa* (Berkeley and Los Angeles: Univ. of California Press, 1969). An exception to this pattern is Audrey C. Smock, *Ibo Politics* (Cambridge, Mass.; Harvard Univ. Press, 1971), which examines local-level politics in

eastern Nigeria through the eyes of a political scientist. Center-periphery politics is the subject of an entire issue of the *Canadian Journal of African Studies*, 4, 1, (Winter 1970). For critical comments on the subject, see Martin Staniland, "The'Rhetoric of Centre-Periphery Relations," *Journal of Modern African Studies*, 8, 4 (1970), pp. 617-636; and Michael A. Cohen, "The Myth of the Expanding Centre—Politics in the Ivory Coast," *Journal of Modern African Studies*, 11, 2 (June 1973), pp. 227-246.

The field of international relations has gone further in theorizing about linkages between systems and their constituent sub-systems. James N. Rosenau (ed.), *Linkage Politics* (New York: Free Press, 1969) deals with links between actors in the international system, while Jonathan Wilkenfield (ed.), *Conflict Behavior and Linkage Politics* (New York: David McKay, 1973) treats connections between international and intra-national politics. For an explicit attempt to theorize about the connections between the international Center and its Periphery (as well as the center and periphery within each) see Johan Galtung, "A Structural Theory of Imperialism," *Journal of Peace Research*, 2 (1971).

2. For a similar distinction between horizontal and vertical relationships, see James S. Coleman and Carl G. Rosberg, *Political Parties and National Integration in Tropical Africa* (Berkeley and Los Angeles: University of California Press, 1964), p. 9.

3. By the "strength" of a linkage structure, I mean something closely akin to one dimension of Huntington's notion of institutionalization. He writes of "adaptability;" the more adaptable an organization (the greater its survival capacity), the higher its level of institutionalization. Similarly, the more resilient a linkage structure (the more it is able to withstand stresses and strains), the higher its level of development. See Samuel P. Huntington, "Political Development and Political Decay," *World Politics*, XVII, 3 (1965), pp. 386-430.

4. Karl W. Deutsch, "Social Mobilization and Political Development," *American Political Science Review*, LV, 3 (Sept. 1961), p. 494.

5. "Black Africa" refers to the states south of the Sahara which have received independence since 1956, plus Ethiopia and Liberia, making 32 cases in all. Excluded are the states of North Africa and the white-ruled states of southern Africa.

6. This use of "average rank" among indicators as an overall comparative measure of social mobilization, is based on two assumptions: 1) that the indicators intercorrelate highly; and 2) that the contributions of the separate indicators to the process of social mobilization—their relative weights—are more or less equal. The first assumption is clearly met for the Black Africa data, since factor analysis reveals a first principal component which explains nearly 60% of the variance among the indicators for level of social mobilization. The second assumption is not so closely approximated, however, since the loadings of the indicators on this first factor—"social mobilization"—range from .6 to .9. But the more sophisticated method using factor analysis to obtain composite measures yields comparative results for Sierra Leone similar to the cruder "average rank" method used here. For a more complete presentation, see my forthcoming study of "Ethnic Diversity and Political Instability in Black Africa."

7. On the destabilizing impact of social mobilization, see Deutsch, *op. cit.,* but especially Huntington, *op. cit.*

8. For treatments of this fascinating community see Arthur T. Porter, *Creoledom: A Study of the Development of Freetown Society* (London: Oxford University Press, 1963); and John Peterson, *Province of Freedom: A History of Sierra Leone, 1787-1870* (Evanston: Northwestern University Press, 1969).

9. For a discussion of such notions as "cultural centers," "nuclear areas," and "key cities," see Karl W. Deutsch, *Nationalism and Social Communication* (Cambridge, Mass.: MIT Press, 1953), pp. 36-55.

10. J. Barry Riddell, *The Spatial Dynamics of Modernization in Sierra Leone* (Evanston: Northwestern University Press, 1970), pp. 43-93.

11. The events—including an unsuccessful military coup—surrounding the declaration of a Republic were tortuous and the establishment of an "Executive" Presidency less than constitutionally punctilious. See John Cartwright and Thomas S. Cox, "Left Turn for Sierra Leone?" *Africa Report* (January, 1972), pp. 16-18.

12. The House was expanded to 85 "ordinary" seats for the General Election of May, 1973.

13. John R. Cartwright, *Politics in Sierra Leone 1947-67* (Toronto: University of Toronto Press, 1970); and Martin L. Kilson, *Political*

Change in a West African State (Cambridge, Mass.: Harvard University Press, 1966).

14. On the rise of the APC, see Cartwright, *op. cit.*, chapter 9. Siaka Stevens' ethnic identity is interesting. In politics he is usually identified as a Limba and a "northerner," but his parentage suggests a more cosmopolitan mixture. His father was a Limba, his mother is a Vai (a people closely related to the Mende), and he was brought up in Freetown by a Creole family. He speaks excellent Mende and of course fluent Krio (the Creole language). This suggests his ability to present himself as a national—as opposed to regional—politician.

15. On military politics see Thomas S. Cox, "Civil-Military Relations in Sierra Leone: A Case Study of African Soldiers in Politics," (unpublished Ph.D. dissertation, Fletcher School of Law and Diplomacy, 1973); and Barrows, "La Politique de l'Armée en Sierra Leone," *Revue Française d'Etudes Politiques Africaines,* N. 36 (Dec. 1968), pp. 54-64.

16. *West Africa,* 21 May, 1973, p. 681; *Africa Report* (May-June, 1973), p. 6.

17. Population estimates for 1971 put the size of Freetown at 187,000. *West Africa,* 2 April, 1973, p. 450.

18. Jean M. Due and Gerald L. Karr, "Strategies for Increasing Rice Production in Sierra Leone," *African Studies Review,* XVI, 1 (April, 1973), p. 35.

19. *Ibid.,* p. 44.

20. V.R. Dorjan, "The Changing Political System of the Temne," *Africa,* XXX, 2 (1960), pp. 110-39.

21. Ruth Finnegan, *Survey of the Limba People of Northern Sierra Leone* (London: Her Magesty's Stationery Office, 1965), pp. 41-2.

22. M. Fortes and E.E. Evans-Pritchard, *African Political Systems* (London: Oxford University Press, 1940), drew the original distinction between African systems characterized by centralized authority and those characterized by its absence. For an elaboration of this scheme see David E. Apter, *The Political Kingdom in Uganda* (Princeton: Princeton Universtiy Press, 1961), ch. 4.

23. For analytical purposes when discussing regional deprivation, Kono District (in the Eastern Province) may be considered part of the poorer north. See Fred M. Hayward, "Some Generalizations About a Progressive Political Organization in the Bush: A Case Study in Sierra

Leone," paper delivered to African Studies Association annual meeting, New York, 1968.

24. Riddell, *op. cit.*, pp. 13-93.

Chapter 2

Explaining Center-Periphery
Relationships

In this chapter, which attempts to establish the theoretical relevance of the questions raised in Chapter 1, two sets of conceptual models are developed. Each set presents contrasting perspectives on the relationship between center and periphery. The first considers opposing models of the interaction between modernity and traditionality, and proceeds by analyzing a concept borrowed from sociology and anthropology, the notion of "role." The second explores alliance formation by developing models based on the "rational actor" mode of analysis common in the field of economics. In both cases we have attempted to deduce hypotheses testable in the Sierra Leonean context.

Traditional and Modern

Since our overriding concern is with the relationship between the central "modern" political system and the "traditional" chiefdoms of the rural periphery, we are immediately faced with the problem of how old and new interact. This is an issue which goes to the heart of most theories of modernization, development, and integration.

Scholars concerned with the Third World by and large perceive the process of political and economic development as a clash between the old and the new, or, more commonly put, between the "modern" and the "traditional." This conceptual mode has established itself firmly in conventional, commonsensical thought; and indeed it is a major inheritance from the grand traditions of nineteenth- and twentieth-century sociological thinking. Many of those theorists who shaped much of contemporary social science dealt with change in terms of dichotomous, mutually exclusive attributes, the shift from one to the other of which represented the process of modernization. This venerable lineage includes Maine (status vs. contract), Tönnies (*gemeinschaft* vs. *gesellschaft*), Weber (traditional vs. legal-rational), Spencer (military vs. industrial), Durkheim (mechanical vs. organic), and MacIver (communal vs. associational). Parsons' pattern variables descend from the same intellectual tradition. Such thinking prescribes a zero-sum relationship between traditionality and modernity: The more a society approaches one attribute, the more it has "displaced" the other; modernization is seen as a linear movement from one set of conditions to another.

This *displacement model* of modernization can be further elaborated by specifying its basic underlying assumptions:

1) Change is holistic. Traditional societies are so tightly woven and internally so highly interdependent that change in one sector of society entails a corresponding change in all other sectors. This is what Whitaker calls "eurhythmic" change to denote its consistent, wholesale nature.[1]

2) Change is unidirectional. A modernizing innovation admitted into one aspect of a social system induces change in the same direction throughout the system. To give an illustration, if "achievement" standards based on performance and merit replace "ascriptive" criteria for recruitment into the central bureaucracy, then this same kind of change will occur in other arenas, say in local administration, chiefdom politics, and educational organizations.

3) Change entails systematic conflict between traditional roles and modern roles. Modernization proceeds to the

extent that the latter displace the former. For instance, a role prominent in the traditional order might be that of "chief," while a modern role might be "civil servant." The displacement model assumes that individuals playing the role of chief (or others like it) will inevitably resist the successful performance of the civil servant role (or others like it) whenever they interact. Implicit in this notion of persistent incompatibility between old and new roles are two further assumptions:

a) Incumbents of old roles perceive their interests threatened by the spread of new roles, and act accordingly; and

b) Old roles are not sufficiently malleable to adapt to circumstances changed by the addition of new roles into the social matrix.

The concept of "role" has gained wide currency in the social sciences.[2] Its analytical usefulness stems from the strategic position it holds at the confluence of three key dimensions of social systems: It is at once a structural, a normative, and a behavioral concept. "Playing a role" on stage involves an actor in a well-structured relationship between himself and other actors and between himself and his audience; his "part," the normative component, is laid out for him, allowing perhaps some room for individual interpretation, but basically confining his activities to the standards and expectations inherent in the role allotted to him; his behavior, the "acting," is judged by the people playing counterparts (roles), who correct or reinforce his performance with rewards or punishments (praise, applause, rotten eggs). Likewise, the person incumbent in the role of "father" is expected by people in counter-roles ("son" as well as "society") to behave in special ways towards his children, e.g., provide food, offer love, exert discipline, proffer advice, but never, perhaps, talk about sex, a behavior which is reserved for the role of "mother." *Expectations* are the key ingredient in the role concept. The expectations of others define a role not only by delimiting it through the feedback process using rewards and punishments but also by locating it in a network of roles, an array of mutual expectations and interactions which serves as the basis of the social system itself. A role *in vacuo* cannot exist; it is above all a relationship between the expectations of a role holder about his "rights" and the expectations of others about his "obligations" to them. These counterpart roles can be strictly defined, as in the dyadic relationship between father and son, or they can consist of a general "audience," as in the relationship between a leader and his public or a writer and his readers.

We can formalize these notions using symbols to denote the essential features of a role, devoid of the particularities which might come into play in any given situation. Following Nadel,[3] a role might be expressed symbolically in this way—

$$R_{12} = \Sigma\ (p, a, b, /c, d/, \ldots n),$$

where R_{12} stands for the role of actor 2 in his relationship to actor 1; the small letters (*a* to *n*) indicate the various kinds of behavior expected of him in the performance of the role; *p* indicates what Nadel calls a "pivotal" characteristic, the kind of behavior which is "basic" to the role and entails the rest of the series (*a* to *n*) except those items which are bracketed by slashes (/c, d/), indicating optional behaviors, those activities which are not necessarily built into the internal structure of the role; finally, the sign for series (Σ) simply means that the total role is the summation of all these expected behaviors.

As we have presented it, the "displacement" model of modernization assumes that the internal structure of traditional roles takes the following form:

$$R_{12} = \Sigma\ (p, a, b, c, \ldots n).$$

The network of roles in traditional society is so tightly integrated and the internal characteristics of each role so interdependent, that optional kinds of behavior are precluded. Thus, for instance, the role of "chief" in a particular society might have as its pivotal attribute (*p*) "father of the people," and from this quality would stem the other behaviors necessary in the series—e.g., (a) "be aloof," (b) "be generous," (c) "be protective," . . . (n) "placate ancestors with proper offerings to the dead." These attributes are necessary *and* sufficient according to the displacement model; additional expectations from some new source—"be efficient," "respect majority opinion"—must be excluded from the set, because individuals in counterpart roles will not permit significant deviation from what has come to be accepted as an internally consistent role, one which complements their own parts in the social drama. Innovation is resisted in traditional societies because there is little "free" (optional) choice for role incumbents. In extreme form, a traditional role according to the displacement model may even assume this internal structure—

$$R_{12} = \Sigma \ (p_a, \ p_b, \ p_c, \ \cdots \ p_n),$$

meaning that *all* its attributes take on *sine qua non* characteristics. For instance, Apter describes the Ashanti political system as one in which "means and ends are closely tied together:"

> To gather yams is not only an economic act in Ashanti, but a ceremony of fruition, expressing gratitude to gods and ancestors. Conduct is constantly scrutinized by ancestors. At the pinnacle of the hierarchy is the *omanhene* or divisional chief. Independent in his sphere of authority, he is nevertheless hedged in by restrictions. His is a religious role. . . .

> This society is in a broad sense consummatory. That is to say, the values associated with daily activity and the acts taken as a means to rendering those values satisfied are strongly ritualized and meaningful in and of themselves. The entire system, one could argue, is in the religious mode.

> The religious aspect of traditional political and social structure in Ashanti was important in maintaining the network of suitable restraints on behavior. These were easily disrupted by innovation. Disruptions involved religious problems, with attitudes towards chiefs, elders, brothers, and ancestors all intertwined. To break with tradition meant guilt, anxiety, and erratic behavior.[4]

Apter uses the term *consummatory* to depict this kind of value system, in which religiosity infuses every aspect of life. In our terms, each component of an actor's internal role structure takes on religious significance in and of itself.[5] In his role he acts out a ritual drama celebrating nothing less than society and its most cherished values.

Scholars in recent years have challenged the assumptions of the displacement model. Whitaker's penetrating article proposes "dysrhythmic" rather than "eurhythmic" change as a more appropriate characterization of political development in the emirates of Northern Nigeria.[6] The title of Rudolph's article, "The Modernity of Tradition: The Democratic Incarnation of Caste in India," highlights his objection to envisioning modernization as a unidirectional process.[7] "Misplaced polarities" is the expression used by Gusfield to register disagreement with the dichotomization of modernity and tradition, and with the assumption that they are necessarily in conflict.[8] In a characteristic *tour de force* Huntington brings together the main arguments of these "revisionists" and suggests that "modernity supplements but does not supplant tradition. . . . Modern society is not simply modern; it is modern *and* traditional."[9] Each of these scholars is dissatisfied with the displacement model and its emphasis on change at the expense of continuity; they object to the notion of development as a displacement process by which traditions fade or are crushed in whatever society joins the march to modernity. Each as in mind a more complex model which envisions the relationship between modernity and tradition as less confrontation than mutual interaction and synthesis.

The *synthetic model* posits more adaptability on the part of societies in general and "traditional" roles in particular. Change in one sector of a society need not ramify consistently and unidirectionally throughout the system. Modern and traditional traits can fuse, interpenetrate, or coexist—without systematic conflict. A role whose internal structure permits this kind of flexibility can be symbolized:

$$R_{12} = \Sigma \ (p, \ /a, \ b, \ c, \ . \ . \ . \ n/),$$

indicating that expected behaviors a to n are optional and, hence, that any combination is permissible as long as it in some way supports or is consistent with the "pivotal" attribute p. This, of course, leaves open the possibility of downplaying or altogether discarding certain behaviors and/or adopting new elements to what is expected of someone filling the role.

Again, Apter provides an example, this time from the Kingdom of Buganda. The role of "chief" in Buganda has undergone continuous transformation since well before the British colonial takeover in the late nineteenth century. At that time the heirarchy of chiefs which culminated in the *Kabaka* (king) served military and administrative roles; chiefs were territorial governors as well as leaders in battle, loyal to the *Kabaka* and dismissable by him. But during the colonial era they became literally "civil-servant chiefs," altering their roles to embrace British-style bureaucratic norms as key actors in the central administrative apparatus erected to rule the territory of Uganda. The thread which lent continuity to this changing role was service to the *Kabaka* and the kingdom. In our formula, this was the "pivotal" attribute (p) which gave significance to the other—however transient—elements of the role. As long as a new kind of behavior facilitated service to the king, it was acceptable. This pragmatism is typical of most sectors of life in Buganda, not just the chieftaincy:

> Whatever the innovated structure, whether civil-service chief-taincy, a parliament and council of ministers, modern education, or freehold tenure, it strengthened the system. The instrumental quality of hierarchical kingship was never defeated. The innovations that were most easily accepted were those that strengthened the Buganda government and also facilitated the individual's efficiency within it.
>
> . . . . All novelty came to be regarded as a device for strengthening tradition.[10]

Buganda embodies what Apter calls an *instrumental* value

system, in contrast to the consummatory nature of values in Ashanti. The two societies represent radically different relationships between tradition and modernity. In Buganda, tradition served modernity and vice versa; there was no direct confrontation between the two, but rather a mutually reinforcing synthesis. In Ashanti, on the other hand, modernism developed outside of and in competition with the traditional realm, particularly in the field of politics where the Convention Peoples Party (CPP) repudiated the chiefs and forged its own solidarity association separate from the network of roles which underlay the Ashanti system.

This comparison dramatizes contrasting modes of interaction between the emerging central systems and the preexisting "traditional" societies which now comprise the rural peripheries of African nations. A key role in each case was played by chiefs—in Uganda as servants of innovation imposed from the center, in Ghana as opponents.[11] What about Sierra Leone? We have already had occasion to note that Paramount Chiefs in Sierra Leone were thrust into a linkage position between the colonial—later, African—central administration and the peoples of their respective chiefdoms. The role of Paramount Chief came to include a new set of expectations, imposed by the central administration headquartered in Freetown and enforced by its prime agent, the District Commissioner (renamed District Officer after Independence). This *dual role* has been identified by a number of scholars as an important cause of the erosion of chiefly authority throughout Africa. This approach is in effect a form of the displacement model: The dilemma of the contemporary chief is that he is caught between two worlds, the traditional and the modern, and cannot harmonize their conflicting demands. One version of the dual role theme, historically oriented, envisioned chiefs as serving two masters, colonial regimes and their own African societies. As the two became increasingly incompatible during the era of rising African nationalism, it was not surprising that chiefs, as agents of alien rule, came to be portrayed as "symbols of resentment" and "Government stooges" by independence movements.[12] Another version is more analytical in style. It stresses the incompatibility of the modern and traditional norms to which individuals in chiefly roles must be attuned. Fallers, in his article entitled "The Predicament of the Modern African Chief," notes the particularism and functional diffuseness of traditional Soga political institutions and contrasts them with the universalistic and functionally specific behavior expected of a chief in the modern administration of Uganda. "This results in frequent conflict, both between persons and within persons."[13] Analyses similarly stressing role conflict have been advanced by Apter and Busia to explain the weakened position of the Ashanti chief in Ghana.[14]

Do the displacement model and its dual role offshoot successfully portray the contemporary position of the Mende Paramount Chief, or is the synthetic model with its stress on role adaptability the more adequate explanatory tool? We can sharpen this question by expanding our general formula for internal role structure to encompass *two* sets of expectations, one from the central system and the other from the local society. To symbolize the chief's linkage position, his role will now be characterized as embracing expected behaviors imposed from the center, indicated by capital letters (A to N), while role expectations originating in the chiefdom will retain the already-familiar lower-case signs. Thus, the role of Paramount Chief in his linkage capacity is written—

$$R_{12,3} = \Sigma\,(p, a, b, c, \ldots n, P, A, B, C, \ldots N).$$

The displacement model predicts conflict involving *whole sets,* whereas the synthetic model predicts conflict, when it occurs, between *individual elements* of sets. Further, the synthetic model allows for role adaptation, so that conflict may be dampened by (dis)appropriating individual items of role behavior. To express these notions more fully, the following list exhaust the logical possibilities for conflict within a role:[15]

Patterns of Role Conflict

1) incompatibility between the set $a, b, c, \ldots n$ and the set $A, B, C, \ldots N$.

2) incompatibility between some element(s) of the set a, b, c, ... n and the set A, B, C, ... N.

3) incompatibility between some element(s) of the set A, B, C, ... N and the set a, b, c, ... n.

4) incompatibility between some elements of the set a, b, c, ... n.

5) incompatibility between some elements of the set A, B, C, ... N.

6) incompatibility between some element(s) of the set a, b, c, ... n and some element(s) of the set A, B, C, ... N.

The displacement model stresses conflicts arising from the first three patterns, while the synthetic model envisions the more random kinds of conflict indicated by the last three patterns. We propose to compare and test the two models against the Mende experience by examining the historical development of the Paramount Chieftaincy and its position in the contemporary era. *Our general hypothesis states that if role conflict patterns 1-3 are observed, then we may infer that the displacement model is the more appropriate explanatory device for change in Mendeland; but if patterns 4-6 prove to be the prevailing modes of role conflict, then the synthetic model can be presumed to be the more valid construct.*

In concluding this section, it might be helpful to flesh in the preliminary notions of political development and integration presented earlier, using the role concepts advanced here. The greater the consensus which converges on a particular role and the more internally congruent it is, the more *developed* it can be considered. That is, a role is "institutionalized" to the extent that its content is the object of a widely shared consensus, an agreement that its characteristic behaviors are legitimate and proper.[16] Furthermore, the effectiveness of an incumbent is enhanced to the extent that his role is free of internal contradictions; his activity is hampered and the strength of the role diminished if cross-purposeful behavior is called for. Role holders in linkage positions are particularly subject to these considerations. The greater the agreement from both sides—the center and the periphery in our case—the more durable the role; likewise, the more the role coheres, the greater its capacity for concerted action in linking the two levels of the political system. *Integration* in this context simply refers to the distribution of linkage roles. The more they are concentrated in particular sectors of the society, the less their integrative capacity; the greater the dispersion throughout the population, the more likely that they will contribute to system-wide integration.

The displacement and synthetic models of modernization imply vastly different paths for the processes of political development and integration. The one sees development and integration as processes which entail the displacement of old roles by new roles, if not by revolution then by concerted pressure against the forces of "traditional reaction." The other allows for flexibility and creativity in traditional roles, so that development and integration need not necessitate radical solutions. This is the choice presented us in our analysis of the Paramount Chieftaincy in Sierra Leone. Is it a role, having outlived its usefulness, which should be excised from the body politic in the manner advocated in Ghana and accomplished in Guinea? Or does it admit sufficient adaptability to contribute to development and integration in the manner permitted in Nigeria and promoted in Uganda?[17]

Patterns of Center-Periphery Alliance[18]

Our concern here is with the formation of alliances between central actors and peripheral actors. What is the manner in which center-periphery alignments are forged? Are they based on tribal affiliation, on religion, on region, on expedience, on habit? The architecture of alliance is crucial for political development and integration. It can be built of loose bricks, uncemented by strong social adhesion, or it can bond its elements tightly, forming well-developed linkage structures. Likewise, it can be a bridge linking quite different regions and groups, or, at the other extreme, it can be built pillar-like, each separate alliance erected upon a particular community of interest, compressing rather than dispersing the ties of political affiliation.

At first glance, this concern with alliance seems opposed to our previous discussion of role conflict. Alliances join, tie together, fuse hitherto separate elements, while conflict works in contrary fashion. Yet alliance and conflict are two sides of the same coin. "When they are sufficiently intense . . . conflicts are the primary determinants of alignments. Alliances are against, and only derivatively for, someone or something."[19] Our analyses of conflict and alliance are meant to complement one another. The cleavages which cut through society provide an inventory of the available raw materials for alliance building. Similarly, alliances are constructed atop conflicts; by inspecting the nature of alliance, we gain clues which can help disentangle the important social cleavages—the main fault lines of society, as it were—from the welter of petty, derivative, and ephemeral disputes which so often seem more important to the observer than they really are. The patterns of center-periphery alignment assumed by political actors should provide at least a sketch and perhaps even a clear imprint of the underlying structure of Sierra Leone's social system.

As in the previous section, we will proceed by developing two antithetical models, designed to dramatize differing perspectives on alliance formation. Each model is composed of its own set of simplifying assumptions about the nature of alliance, which serves as the conceptual wherewithal for deducing hypotheses testable in the "real world," in this case Kenema District. It is not so much the realism of the individual assumptions which is at issue, for they are deliberately detached from the complexities of real life—oversimplified—to ease analysis. Rather, models are compared with empirical data, hence with each other, through hypothesis testing to determine which assumptions provide the best predictions of actual behavior; they are intended as surrogates for, not replicas of, the real world. Model building attempts to approximate rather than mirror reality, for to attempt to embrace all the complexity and confusion in social systems would defeat the great advantage deductive models have in the search for parsimonious theory—economy of expression.[20]

Our two models of alliance formation have in common a basic assumption traditionally posited in the field of economics and increasingly employed in political science. This is the "rational actor" assumption: Actors choose more rather than less of whatéver it is they prefer; they attempt to maximize the things they value; they attempt to adopt the most suitable means for accomplishing their goals, whatever they happen to be.[21] For our purposes, we shall assume that actors join those alliances which provide the most benefit for the least cost.

Practitioners of this mode of analysis usually take as given the preferences (values, goals) of actors; rationality consists of maximizing them. We will depart somewhat from this usage by making a distinction between two broad types of preference, utility and identity, which in turn distinguish our two models. In the *utility model* we assume that actors have preferences for "tangible" payoffs; they seek allies in order to get material rewards or means immediately pursuant to that end. This, it should be stressed, is a special meaning of the word "utility," which to the economist normally connotes whatever gives satisfaction to an actor, not exclusively commodities of the tangible sort. In our sense of the term, utility in the Sierra Leonean context might be gained from protection, money, land, a job, a rice contract, appointment to an office (e.g., the Paramount Chieftaincy), a mining license, access to information, availability of expert advice, access to a clinic, etc. More generally, four of Lasswell's eight value categories suggest what we mean by utility—wealth, well-being, skill, and enlightenment.[22] A fifth value category— power—is so wide in scope that it spills well beyond the boundary of tangibility, but it of course is a crucial utility value, either as an end unto itself or as a means to other utility values.

In contrast, the *identity model* assumes that actors' preferences are ordered on the basis of social "solidarity;" they seek to maximize satisfactions derived from similarity, likeness, commonality, community. Alliances are a means for furthering such ends. Ideological compatibility is but one species of the genus "identity alliance." Ethnicity, religion, region, class, party identification, modernity, and traditionality are other criteria upon which actors can base their alliance choices, all of which are potentially relevant in the Sierra Leonean context. Again, in more general terms, three of Lasswell's value categories— respect, affection, and rectitude—connote the quality of preferences which underlie the identity model.[23] (Power as a value is relevant too, especially as a means for furthering other identity values.) All entail satisfactions derived from *relationships* between an actor and others; they are "other-oriented" values, realized inherently through attachment to a group, in contrast to the more "self-oriented" values of the utility model, which yield satisfaction to an individual actor irrespective of his relationships with others, except as they serve as means for promoting the actor's separate interests. In the identity model, group membership has value as an end unto itself, while in the utility model it does not.

By and large, explanations of African politics in the scholarly literature and even more so in the journalistic literature, have tended to emphasize the assumption underlying our identity model. Tribe, religion, class, the "modernizers" versus the "traditionalists"—all have served in one place or another as synoptic criteria accounting for fundamental features of African politics. A "collectivist" premise runs through these accounts, an assumption that primordial attachments direct the political orientations of individuals.[24] To be sure, sophisticated analyses often envision a complex interaction between group identity as an end in itself and group identity as a means to achieving some other goal—e.g., a politician fanning the flames of tribalism to enhance electoral support from his fellow ethnics—but still the collective basis of politics ultimately prevails.[25] Moreover, ideological doctrines such as Negritude, African Socialism, and *Ujamaa* take as their point of departure the communal nature of African life.[26] Africa is not normally thought of as a bastion of individualism—quite the contrary—so it is not surprising that most treatments do not proceed from the "individualistic" premise which underlies our utility model.[27]

In order to magnify the comparative impact of these models we shall assume that in any given system either one *or* the other obtains, but never a combination of the two. That is, all actors in a system ally either on the basis of identity preferences *or* on the basis of utility preferences, but trade-offs between the two are assumed not to take place.

Clearly this is a stringent condition, one unlikely actually to exist in pure form. It permits us, however, to identify those real-world cases which lie near the ends of the spectrum which runs from situations where identity considerations predominate to the opposite extreme, where utility calculations determine the alliance choices of actors. We can at least approximate the dramatic cases. Furthermore, by formulating an extreme assumption, we highlight the issues relevant for the "mixed" cases which lie along the spectrum. Different cases will manifest different combinations of identity and utility considerations; in some systems, identity preferences will be more important than utility in alliance behavior, while other systems will reverse the priority. A major problem in comparative analysis arises when two or more phenomena occur together. How can the observer separate them in order to discover which is the more important? In any given society, which is the more basic, identity or utility calculations? Most often they interact as inextricably intertwined correlates, so the simple process of observation does not suffice to penetrate beneath surface appearance. A case in point is the nature of tribal ethnicity in Africa. Colonialists and scholars alike were accustomed to thinking of a "tribe" as a fixed group with clear-cut boundaries and a strong sense of identity which infused each of its members; in our terms, the assumption was that identity preferences carved out unambiguous groups. But scholarship in recent decades has drawn attention to a much more complex process, where utility calculations help shape the identity preferences of individuals and, in turn, the composition of ethnic groups. Wallerstein analyzes the *situational* nature of ethnicity: Migrants to urban areas shift their ethnic identity to suit their new circumstances.[28] Young writes of "super-tribalism" and "artificial ethnicity" as a response to colonialism and urbanization in the Congo, and of "emergent ethnic awareness" among decentralized peoples who had no sense of group awareness prior to the need to act in concert when an administrative hierarchy was laid atop them.[29] Cohen describes in detail how Hausas in a Yoruba city of Nigeria cultivate ethnic exclusiveness in order to assure effective control of long-distance trading networks.[30] Identity and utility preferences entangle in a welter of circular means and ends. Comparative analysis attempts to unravel such complex interactions by seeking cases where the phenomena in question are not coterminous, comparing these special cases to discover the consequences of having one or the other phenomena obtain, and then proceeding by degrees to less clearcut examples. Our extreme assumption, then, is a point of departure in the effort to penetrate complexity. It dramatizes the relevant considerations and shapes the strategy for further investigation.

Figure 2.1 depicts in simplest form a political system divided analytically into two levels, the center and the periphery. The central actors, designated C_1 and C_2, might be individuals, factions, or institutions, or in an international system they might be superpowers, but the important point is that they are in competition with each other and seek support from actors in the periphery. For our purposes, the two major Sierra Leonean parties, the SLPP and the APC, can be considered the major central actors. Central actors seek control over the system and therefore attempt to maximize support from the periphery. Support is

FIGURE 2.1

Central and Peripheral Actors in the
Political System

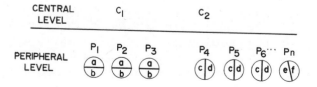

realized in the form of votes, campaign activities, and general "alignment" in favor of one party or the other. Put differently, in order to gain and retain access to governmental power, central actors seek allies in the periphery.

Peripheral actors, designated by $p_1, \ldots p_n$, can be individuals, local groups, or whole communities. They operate at the local level and seek to maximize their welfare, which is, by assumption, of either the utility or the identity sort. If communities (e.g., chiefdoms) are undivided by basic internal conflicts, the notation $p_1, \ldots p_n$ will suffice. But if communities are divided by internal cleavages, then further specification of actors is necessary. If, for instance, community p_1 is divided horizontally by class conflict, then the relevant signs become $p_1 a$ and $p_1 b$ to indicate actors representing each side of the split. Similarly, if community p_4 is divided vertically into rival ethnic groups, then $p_4 c$ and $p_4 d$ identify the relevant actors.

We assume that each peripheral actor locates himself in "issue space" and allies with the central actor whose position is least distant from his own.[31] Figure 2.2 illustrates this by showing the preferences of two peripheral actors on two "utility" issues, schools and roads. Actor p_1 prefers more school building and less road building than p_2. Since central actor C_1 is closer to him than C_2, p_1 will ally with C_1. The dotted concentric circles around a peripheral actor's preferred position represent his "indifference curves": An actor is indifferent between two central actors if they are both located on the same contour, but will ally

FIGURE 2·2

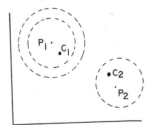

School–building

Road–building

FIGURE 2·3

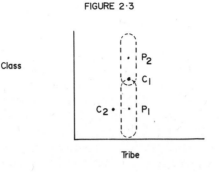

Class

Tribe

with one inside a contour in favor of one outside it. Figure 2.3 illustrates alliance choice when "identity" issues come to the fore. Peripheral actors p_1 and p_2 have preferences for the same tribe but different socioeconomic classes. In this case, however, the issue of tribe is much more salient for each actor than the issue of class; this is indicated by the elliptical rather than circular indifference curves. Actor p_1 has much less tolerance on tribal than class issues, and therefore allies with C_1 instead of C_2, even though the latter appears to be closer to his position. Actors can weigh some issues more heavily than others, and this naturally affects their alliance choices. We shall assume that all actors in a system weigh issues in the *same* way. This does not mean that they concur with each other on an issue, only that they attach equal importance to it. So in addition to our major assumption that all actors orient themselves to the same *kind* of issue— either utility or identity— we shall also take it as given that they are alike in the intensity with which they regard separate issues. The accompanying diagrams are two-dimensional, giving the impression that only two issues define the "space" within which actors make their alliance choices—but this is only for expositonal convenience. An actor can be faced with a multitude of issues, which form a multidimensional space in which he locates himself according to his preferences. There is no limit to the number of relevant issues; the only restrictions are that all the actors must be in either utility space or identity space, and within that framework they must be alike in the way they weigh issues.

There is one final assumption to be made before addressing the implications of our models for patterns of center-periphery alliance. Neighboring communities will be presumed to be closely alike in terms of internal characteristics. Differences between localities increase with geographical distance. This seems a fairly realistic assumption for upcountry Sierra Leone. If a chiefdom is poor, its neighboring chiefdoms are also likely to be poor. If a chiefdom is predominantly Mende, with a small educated minority forming the "upper class," its neighbors are likely to have similar characteristics. A natural barrier (e.g., a river) or a political frontier (e.g., an administrative boundary) increase the effective distances between communities and create regions or pockets of similarity within the periphery. In Figure 2.1, localities p_1 to p_3 are separated from localities p_4 to p_6, indicating this tendency to cluster.

We have made four basic assumptions: rationality; maximization of either identity or utility preferences; identical weighting of issues among actors; and likeness among neighboring localities. We are now in a position to survey the consequences of these assumptions for center-periphery alignments. Imagine a number of localities $p_1, \ldots p_6$ each of which is divided internally into socio-economic classes, a and b. (See Figure 2.4) Furthermore, the communities are distinguishable according to "tribe," with p_1 to p_3 and p_4 to p_6 tending to form separate clusters. If the identity model obtains and if internal cleavages are not emphasized within communities, then Pattern I will be observed. Peripheral actors will emphasize issues which do not divide the community, and thus will weigh "tribe" more heavily than "class." Tribal identities tend to cluster geographically, entailing a pattern of alliance whereby neighboring localities align with the same central actor. The clustering tendency inherent in identity-based politics assures the formation of regional alliances, with all the peripheral actors of a region in coalition with the central actor closest to them on whatever identity issues weigh most heavily ("tribe" in our illustration). Central actors will have no incentive to occupy the middle ground between the two clusters for fear of alienating both sides; an actor is likely to

FIGURE 2·4

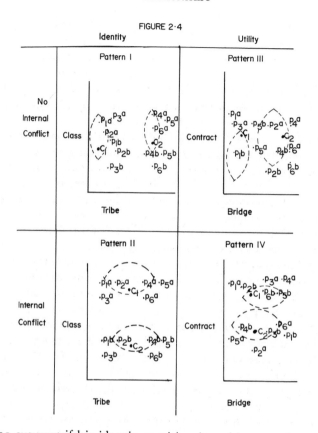

get no support if his identity position is ambiguous. C_1 and C_2 are better off by each committing himself to a separate cluster: Some support is better than no support. We can label Pattern I "alliance among neighboring localities."

If localities are internally divided rather than harmonious, then Pattern II results. In this case, local actors will weigh more heavily those issues centering on intracommunity conflict ("class" in our example). In response, central actors will position themselves in a manner designed to exploit these local splits—in order to maximize support. Again, the "lumpy" nature of identity preferences leads to a clustering of peripheral actors, but this time based on aggregations which cut through communities, rather than among communities. The alliances which emerge are systematic with respect to these basic socioeconomic cleavages: One alliance will be composed of members from one side of the split, while the other alliance(s) will be built atop a peripheral membership from the other side(s) of the split. This gives rise to the label for Pattern II: "systematic alliance."

Patterns III and IV emerge when the utility rather than the identity model prevails. If localities are unified, peripheral actors give less salience to issues which divide communities than to those which tend to hold them together. Pattern III shows actors choosing between two issues which for illustration might be (1) where to build a new bridge and (2) who shall get the contract to build it? A bridge is a "collective good," meaning that one person's use of it does not diminish its utility for all others in the community. On the other hand, the contract is a "private good;" only one builder can get the contract; his "consumption" of the good reduces its availability to everyone else. Collective-good issues are likely to be more heavily weighted in a unified community than private-good issues: It is unified precisely because its citizens emphasize the welfare of the whole rather than the interests of its constituent elements. Since, by assumption, neighboring communities are similar in most respects, they are likely to find themselves in competition for the same scarce resources from the central system. Localities p_1 and p_2 each wants the bridge built in its own territory; each will submerge its internal differences in order to maximize benefits to the community as a whole from whichever central actor offers the most—in this case, from whichever party promises to locate the new bridge in its chiefdom. Hence, alliances are built on rivalries among neighbors in Pattern III. It is entitled "alliance among nonneighboring localities."

Pattern IV considers the possibility that localities will be divided by intracommunity conflicts, in which case private-good issues are likely to be more salient to local actors than collective-good issues. In our example, actors within localities differ over which builder should be awarded the bridge contract. Perhaps one political faction wants an important supporter to get the business, as a reward for past favors; or perhaps the community divides in sectional lines, with each area pushing for its favorite son; or perhaps one ruling family backs a friendly contractor, while its rival prefers his competitor; or perhaps there is a dispute over the business practices of contractors, with bankers favoring the one who pays his debts promptly and laborers partial to the one who treats workers generously. The important point is that particularistic interests determine the alliance choices of local actors. The lines of competition for payoffs cut across basic societal cleavages such as tribe or class. In the utility model, alliance preferences are random with respect to the fault lines which divide the wider society. A peripheral actor with such-and-such class and tribal characteristics is as likely as not to find himself in coalition with actors of so-and-so characteristics; any combination is possible. The actual composition of an alliance depends on the special constellation of interest within each local community, not upon the conflicts which run through the system as a whole. For this reason, we call Pattern IV "random alliance."

A fifth and final pattern emerges when peripheral actors consider *all* the central actors so distasteful that no alliance takes place. From the perspective of the periphery, the center is in the hands of actors who are so alien or so associated with material deprivations that alliance is ruled out. The costs of alliance exceed its benefits. Indifference or even outright hostility result when the distance—in terms of either identity or utility considerations—between the entire set of central actors and the actors of the periphery exceeds a certain threshold. After that point, alienation from the system as a whole takes place. If alienation is sufficiently intense, rural revolt may erupt, as in the Hut Tax War of 1898 when much of the Sierra Leonean hinterland rose up against a colonial hegemony expanding from Freetown. If alienation is mild, it may result in a kind of "benign neglect" from below, as in the case of villagers so physically remote from the center that they can afford to ignore the national government and the posturing of its politicans. Pattern

V is entitled "alienation," signifying nonalliance between central and peripheral actors.

Unlike our other patterns of alliance, alienation is entailed by either the identity or the utility model. A single set of premises is not exlusively associated with this outcome, in contrast to Patterns I-IV, each of which is derived from only one of the two models. Thus, if we observe alienation as a persistent characteristic of center-periphery relations, we will be unable to discern from that fact alone which model offers the better explantory apparatus; either or both could suffice. On the other hand, if empirical evidence indicates unambiguously the presence of one or the other for alliance patterns, a specific model can be identified as the preferable mode of explanation. Put differently, each model implies a separate proposition about alliance behavior. *The identity model hypothesizes that Patterns I and/or II will prevail, depending on the extent of intralocality conflicts. The utility model predicts that Patterns III and/or IV will obtain, again depending on the degree of local-level strife.* If a clear-cut pattern is observed, we have persuasive evidence for accepting the set of assumptions from which it was derived.[32] Comparison allows us to adopt one model in favor of the other according to the degree to which their respective hypotheses are confirmed. Only if Pattern V emerges or if an ambiguous mixture of many patterns is all that can be observed, do we fail to establish the preferability of one model over the other. Table 2.1 diagrams our five patterns of center-periphery alliance and the models from which they are derived.

These patterns of alliance imply different consequences for political development and integration. Alliance ties which endure despite the vicissitudes and cross pressures of politics, provide well-developed links between center and periphery. When central actors have clear, predictable sources of support from the periphery, obedience can be solicited without fear that followers will abandon the alliance whenever sacrifice is required; policies can be formulated with the reasonable expectation that they will be carried out at the operational level; and power can be expanded using reliable allies as a resource for in-

TABLE 2.1
Patterns of Center-Periphery Alliance

MODEL	PATTERN
Identity	I. Alliance among neighboring locations
	II. Systematic alliance
Utility	III. Alliance among nonneighboring localities
	IV. Random alliance
Identity and/or Utility	V. Alienation

vestment in new sources of support. Development is enhanced to the extent that alliances permit the exercise of long-term authority from the center. Identity-based alliances are more likely to have this cohesive quality than alliances formed through utility considerations. They are less sensitive to minor environmental changes and more grounded in the inertia of social structure. The sense of common membership which underlies identity alliances is of course not immutable, but it is generally more stable than the environment of incentives and disincentives which sustains utilitarian alliances, in which today's ally can be tomorrow's antagonist. Hence, we can expect identity to serve as a more reliable basis for development than utility. Patterns I and II are more likely to support development than Patterns III and IV. This is speculation—stemming from the implications of the models—so empirical investigation is necessary in order to determine its validity.

The implications of our patterns of alliance for political integration run counter to their anticipated impact on development. The most widely-distributed center-periphery ties are provided by Patterns III and IV. The randomizing tendency inherent in utilitarian alliances—"politics makes strange bedfellows"—works against the concentration of links whereby a particular central actor is aligned with one region, social stratum, ethnic group or ideological tendency. Rather, utility alliances scatter linkages throughout the system, so that each political party (or other central actor) is likely to have support from portions of all groups. Put differently, cost-benefit calculations concerned with tangible commodities ignore the presence of group boundaries, cutting through those entities within the overall system which otherwise impede its integration. On the other hand, Patterns I and II, based as they are on the sentiments which underlie subsystem groups, encourage clusters of linkages instead of their even distribution. Pattern I is constituted of regionally-based linkages. Whether it is tribe, religion or some other form of identification which underlies this regionalism, the dense concentration of linkage ties in particular segments of the system hampers integration by narrowing the channels of affiliation. The system is compartmentalized into pockets of interaction, with little interaction across their boundaries. The linkages of Pattern II, although they may be evenly distributed geographically, are aggregated according to such differentia as class, caste, or religion. This contributes to horizontal—territorial—integration but creates problems of vertical—elite-mass—integration. By building upon and reinforcing forms of group identification which stratify society, Pattern II represents a higher level of integration than Pattern I, but linkages among elements of the system are still limited by the "lumpy" nature of identity affiliations. If an actor identifies with one strata, he has by necessity excluded from his alliance calculus the other strata in society, which may represent a large portion of the total population. His capacity for interaction is confined by the fact that identity groups are relatively large in size and few in number. Only a sense of identity which encompasses the entire system—such as nationalism—is capable of overcoming this exclusiveness; only when the "we" includes the whole society and the "they" other societies, does the "we-they" dichotomy inherent in identity politics contribute fully to integration. This is not to deny the possibility of multiple loyalties, but merely to state that a strong sense of nationalism—or other inclusive sentiment—is necessary for significant integration if identity is the prevailing mode of political affiliation.

In short, our models of center-periphery alliance imply that in new nations utility provides a more serviceable basis for integration than identity—in contrast to their implications for development. Again, this is speculation, inferred from the models. Verification—or rather, tentative verification—entails testing these propositions with data from the Sierra Leonean context.

A final theoretical consideration remains. So far we have made no statements about the nature of party organization; we have simply assumed that local actors align with parties according to either one of two modes of affiliation, irrespective of the organizational apparatuses which may or may not penetrate the periphery from the center. But an important issue involves the extent to which central institutions are "embedded" in local groups at the peripheral level, rather than connected with localities through autonomous structures extended from the center to the grassroots. The familiar juxtaposition of Indirect and Direct Rule can be seen in this light. The colonial regime employing Indirect Rule (ideally) built itself upon indigenous local systems, while Direct Rule (ideally) bypassed native structures of authority in an effort to penetrate directly to the grassroots level. The question is which type better encourages durable and widely distributed connections between center and periphery. Proponents of embedded ties argue that using already-existing local structures promotes readier acceptance among rural peoples, imposes fewer sharp changes, and proceeds from premises which are familiar. In contract, those who argue for building new, autonomous structures stress the need to eliminate competing authorities (e.g., chiefs) and to free local groups from traditional constraints on their direct participation in the wider process.

Eisenstadt in his analysis of historical bureaucratiç empires proceeds in the latter vein. Regimes whose support was embedded in ascriptive local groups, he contends, incurred serious constraints on their ability to develop generalized political power. The more central institutions relied upon such peripheral groups, the less the "free-floating resourses" available to leaders, the smaller their range of choice, and the more likely system breakdown.[33] Kilson in his analysis of Sierra Leonean politics makes a similar proposition. He describes the political framework in terms of an alliance between the urban educated elite and the rural traditional elite—an alliance forged according to the "principle of reciprocity," in which wealth and local autonomy were supplied to chiefdom authorities in exchange for votes and other forms of political support. The SLPP especially was heavily dependent upon Paramount Chiefs; its organization was almost nonexistent apart from the chiefdom structures which became available to it at election time. Kilson predicts breakdown of this system due to increasing reliance upon material wealth for political purposes in a country unable to afford it:

> ... [T]o persist in the modern context in utilizing traditional guideposts to political relations or behavior like the reciprocity principle is ... inevitably to court basic sociopolitical breakdown or disequilibrium, especially in view of the sizable wealth required for these guideposts to function in the modern system.[34]

Cartwright also assessed the implications of heavy reliance upon Paramount Chiefs in the governance of the rural areas, and concludes that this embeddedness did indeed have system-wide ramifications, especially as it restricted the ability and willingness of the central elite to foster basic social change.[35] These propositions bear directly upon our concern with center-periphery alliances. To what extent do the alliance links between political parties and local actors serve to constrict the boundaries of political choice in Sierra Leone? Does the basis of alliance formation—identity or utility—affect the impact of embeddedness on the stability of the system? If embeddedness does indeed "court breakdown," what is the precise relationship between it and such indices of breakdown as violence, coups d'etat, and alienation? Do autonomous party organizations mitigate the undesirable consequences of embeddedness; that is, to the extent that parties penetrate directly to the grassroots unmediated by already-established local actors, do they contribute to system stability and the ability of central leaders to exercise authority? Since party system institutionalization has been proposed in an important cross-national study as a major variable affecting political stability in Africa,[36] it will be instructive to examine the behavior and consequences of party structure from a "micropolitical" level of analysis—in order to investigate in detail its impact upon the wider political process.

Summary

The models developed in this chapter have been designed to dramatize important issues in the analysis of center-periphery relations. The assumptions from which they have been constructed are deliberate oversimplifications, distillations from the complexity of the real world which, it is hoped, capture its essence. Due to their abstract, disembodied character, the assumptions of a model cannot be directly subjected to empirical examination; they are simply too remote from the real world to be so immediately related to it. But the *implications* of a model can—and should—be tested against actual data. Thus, the validity of a model is determined by testing hypotheses deduced from its assumptions. A model's fruitfulness derives from its ability to produce propositions which stand up against efforts to disprove them. Likewise, we can accept—tentatively—a model whose implications seem to be borne out by observed experience.

In order further to highlight the issues of linkage politics, contrasting models have been presented for comparison, each built upon a set of assumptions which contradicts that of the other. One model attempts to extract the essence of what has come to represent conventional thinking about African politics, while its opposite has been constructed to express its antithesis. Hence, the displacement model is composed of assumptions drawn from the established paradigm dealing with the nature of interaction between the old and the new; it presumes systematic conflict between traditional and modern elements of societies undergoing modernization—particularly conflict within and between roles. The "modernizers" are engaged in an inevitable clash with traditional resistance to change; the battle is over only when the ancient regime has been divested of its effective power.

In contrast, the synthetic model posits considerably more adaptability among both traditional and modern elements of societies. In fact, here the distinction between modern and traditional becomes blurred, as actors fit their behavior to the immediate situation, drawing support in instrumental fashion from whichever source meets the task at hand—a process of fusion rather than fission. Social roles in the synthetic model are flexible, capable of taking on new attributes and shedding behaviors which are no longer appropriate. In a changing social drama, conflict is not inevitable because actors are not cast in rigid roles. Linkage figures such as Paramount Chiefs need not fall victim to contradictory expectations from center and periphery—and can play a constructive part in integrating them—because their role permits sufficient adaptability to avoid wholesale confrontation. The synthetic model predicts not the absence of conflict in societies, but rather the absence of thoroughgoing conflict between such characteristics of the social system as traditionality and modernity. By observing patterns of conflict within linkage roles—especially the role of Paramount chief—we should be able to compare the predictions of the displacement model with those of the synthetic model. The displacement model proposes systematic patterns of conflict between the central (modern) and peripheral (traditional) sides of a linkage role, whereas the assumptions underlying the synthetic model lead us to expect conflict, if it occurs, of a particularistic sort, unrelated to the traditional-modern distinction.

Likewise, our utility and identity models of center-periphery alliance formation are built from diametrically opposed assumptions whose implications for political development and integration differ vastly. The identity model takes as its point of departure a notion which is familiar in both popular and scholarly literature on African affairs—the "collectivistic" basis of politics, in which relatively large and relatively stable groups define the framework in which people act politically. Whether the relevant entities are tribes, religions, classes, or ideologies, actors form alliances according to their sense of identification with one or the other of the groups in question. In contrast, the utility model proceeds from an "individualistic" premise, a point of departure rarely applied fully to the African context. Here actors ally according to gains and losses of tangible goods. Especially when the environment of incentives and disincentives contains a great deal of variety—which is likely during times of change— individuals become the relevant actors, aligning and dealigning irrespective of the groups to which they otherwise belong. Collectivities such as ethnic or religious groups take on importance only as instrumentalities in the self-interested calculations of individuals. Both models assume "rational actors" who attempt to maximize their satisfactions through political action, but they differ on the nature of preferences. The identity model takes for granted the group-oriented preferences of actors, whereas the utility model presumes that political action is based on the preferences of individuals for tangible goods.

Each model implies distinct patterns of alliance between central and peripheral actors. These patterns are observable, and so by examining actual alignments we should be able to determine which model is the more applicable in the Sierra Leonean context. Were the identity model to obtain, we would expect the pattern of alliance which ensues to promote political development but hinder political integration. That is, the patterns of alliance associated with the identity model are likely to engender resilient links between center and periphery but the distribution of these links is likely to be uneven, concentrated within the membership of relatively large social groupings. On the other hand, the patterns of alliance entailed by the utility model are likely to promote integration but hinder development. Alliances which are easily made and broken enhance interaction opportunities within the system, tieing it together with a criss-crossing network of affiliations, but they serve as an unreliable base for the exercise and expansion of central authority.

These models suggest a trade-off between development and integration, a dilemma for central elites which forces them to accept risks of disintegration if they pursue rapid development and risks of inertia if they seek unity. One political resource which may ameliorate the harshness of this choice is party organization. A number of scholars have noted the debilitating consequences of center-periphery ties which are embedded in local ascriptive groups. They suggest that party organizations (or similarly autonomous structures extended to the grassroots from the center) free national leadership from restrictive sources of support, enabling the growth of central power and the formulation of innovative policies. Autonomous rather than embedded links advance the kind of flexibility necessary for overcoming the quandaries of development and integration. Since Sierra Leone has been the battleground for competition between two parties—one minimally organized, the other spreading its organizational network—we should be in a position to assess this proposition, at least in tentative fashion, by comparing their impact on the wider system.

NOTES

1. C.S. Whitaker, Jr., "A Dysrhythmic Process of Political Change," *World Politics,* XIX (January 1967), pp. 190-217.

2. "Role" as an analytic construct was first introduced by Ralph Linton in *The Study of Man* (New York and London: D. Appleton-Century, 1936). It has become to be widely used in anthropology, sociology, and psychology. Its most elaborate formulation is found as a key element in the Parsonian "general theory of action systems." See Talcott Parsons, *The Social System* (Glencoe, Ill.: The Free Press, 1951), esp. Ch. 2. The best analysis of the role concept remains S.F. Nadel, *The Theory of Social Structure* (London: Cohen and West, Ltd., 1957), a work which heavily influences our analysis. For an excellent application of the concept in an African context, see Raymond F. Hopkins, *Political Roles in a New State: Tanzania's First Decade* (New Haven: Yale University Press, 1971).

3. Nadel, *op. cit.,* pp. 31-44. The notation used here is slightly different from Nadel's.

4. David E. Apter, *The Political Kingdom in Uganda* (Princeton:

Princeton University Press, 1961), pp. 87-88, footnote 6.

5. The Latin root of the word religion, *religare* ("to tie back, tie up, tie fast") dramatizes the idea we are advancing: Each element of the role is tied inextricably with all the others; religion weaves the role into a tightly-knit bundle.

6. Whitaker, *op. cit.*

7. Lloyd I. Rudolph, "The Modernity of Tradition: The Democratic Incarnation of Caste in India," *American Political Science Review,* LIX (December 1965), pp. 975-89.

8. Joseph R. Gusfield, "Tradition and Modernity: Misplaced Polarities in the Study of Social Change," reprinted in Claude E. Welch, Jr. (ed.), *Political Modernization* (Belmont, California: Wadsworth, 1971 edition), pp. 47-62.

9. Samuel P. Huntington, "The Change to Change: Modernization Development and Politics," reprinted in Roy C. Macridis and Bernard E. Brown (eds.), *Comparative Politics: Notes and Readings* (Homewood, Ill.: The Dorsey Press, 1972, fourth edition), pp. 407-425.

10. David E. Apter, "The Role of Traditionalism in the Political Modernization of Ghana and Uganda," reprinted in William John Hanna (ed.), *Independent Black Africa* TChicago: Rand McNally, 1964), p. 259.

11. Apter generalizes from the experience of Ashanti to Ghana as a whole and from Buganda to Uganda. This probably is not justifiable, since the Ashanti comprise less than 30% of Ghana's overall population and the Baganda less than 20% of Uganda's population. Each country is highly diverse ethnically, so neither Ashanti nor Buganda can be considered "typical" of the wider population. Apter has also been critized for overstressing the conflict between chiefs and the CPP. See, for instance, Maxwell Owusu, *Uses and Abuses of Political Power* (Chicago: Chicago University Press, 1970). A Ghanaian example of close relations between traditional authorities and the "mass" party is found in David Brokensha, *Social Change at Larteh, Ghana* (Oxford: Clarendon, 1966).

12. L.P. Mair, "African Chiefs Today," *Africa,* XXVIII (July 1958), pp. 195-205. See also, David E. Apter, *Ghana in Transition* (New York: Atheneum, 1955, 1966), pp. 120 ff. J.F. Holleman, *Chief, Council*

and Commissioner (Netherlands: Koninklyke Van Gorcum, 1968), pp. 339-341; Vernan R. Dorjahn, "The Changing Political System of the Temne," *Africa,* XXX (April 1960), pp. 110-139; Audrey I. Richards, *East African Chiefs* (London: Faber and Faber, 196), p. 364.

13. Lloyd Fallers, "The Predicament of the Modern African Chief," *American Anthropologist,* 57 (1955), pp. 300-1.

14. Apter, *op. cit.,* pp. 150-158; and K.A. Busia, *The Position of the Chief in the Modern Political System of Ashanti* (London, New York, Toronto: Oxford University Press, 1951).

15. The following petterns deal with intrarole conflict, not interrole conflict. Another possibility for conflict, not treated here, exists when there is incompatibility between two or more roles filled by the same person. For instance, a man might find that his role as "chief" conflicts with his role as "husband," as in the case of a Mende Paramount Chief who preferred to have just one wife, while opinion within his chiefdom thought it incumbent upon him to take on many wives, as befitted a "proper" Paramount Chief.

16. Parsons, *op. cit.,* pp. 36-37.

17. Even after the dismantling of Buganda by Ugandan soldiers in 1966, "civil-servant chiefs" continued to be the keystone of administration throughout the country. The coup in 1971 by General Amin likewise presaged no reaction against chiefs; indeed, they probably became more essential as other national institutions were destroyed— e.g., political parties—or became disorganized—e.g., the army.

18. I would like to acknowledge the assistance of my colleague G. Wayne Peak in developing the model presented in this section. He is of course in no way responsible for its simple-mindedness or other shortcomings.

19. George Liska, *Nations in Alliance* (Baltimore: The Johns Hopkins Press, 1962), p. 12.

20. There is a growing literature on models and the strategy of model-building. See, *inter alia,* May Brodbeck, "Models, Meaning, and Theories," in Llewellyn Gross (ed.), *Symposium on Sociological Theory* (N.Y.: Harper & Row, 1959), pp. 373-407; Herbert Simon, *The Sciences of the Artificial* (Cambridge, Mass.: MIT Press, 1969); Abraham Kaplan, *The Conduct of Inquiry* (San Francisco: Chandler, 1964), Chapter VII; and Richard G. Neimi and Herbert F. Weisberg

(eds.), *Probability Models of Collective Decision Making* (Columbus, Ohio: Charles E. Merrill, 1972). A simple introduction is found in Wayne L. Francis, *Formal Models of American Politics* (N.Y.: Harper & Row, 1972). A deductive model of alliance formation is found in William H. Riker, *The Theory of Political Coalitions* (New Haven: Yale University Press, 1962). For an exposition of the view that the assumptions of a model need not reflect reality as long as it generates valid hypotheses, see Milton Friedman, *Essays in Positive Economics* (Chicago: University of Chicago Press, 1963), Chapter 1.

21. On the rationality assumption in economics, see Friedman, *op. cit.* One of the first attempts to use it systematically in political science is Anthony Downs, *An Economic Theory of Democracy* (New York: Harper and Row, 1957). James Buchanan and Gordon Tullock, *The Calculus of Consent* (Ann Arbor: University of Michigan Press, 1962) explores constitution-making from a rational actor point of departure, while Riker, *op. cit.*, analyzes coalition-formation. Some possibilities for further exploration are discussed in John C. Harsanyi, "Rational-Choice Models of Political Behavior vs. Functionalist and Conformist Theories," *World Politics,* XXI (July 1969), pp. 513-538.

22. Harold Lasswell, *Politics: Who Gets What, When, How* (Cleveland and New York: World Publishing Co.: 1958), p. 202.

23. *Ibid.*

24. On "primordial" attachments in the Third World generally, see Clifford Geertz, "The Integrative Revolution: Primordial Sentiments and Civil Politics in the New States," in Geertz (ed.), *Old Societies and New States* (New York: Thz Free Press, 1963). An important contribution to the study of nationalism which stressed tribal attachments is James S. Coleman, *Nigeria: Background to Nationalism* (Berkeley and Los Angeles: University of California Press, 1958). A common assumption among colonial authorities was that Africans must become "detribalized" in order to enter the modern world; in our role-conflict terms, Africans had to shed their "tribal" norms and behaviors in order to participate in the more individualistic life of technology and economic development. For a discussion of this see Ronald Cohen and John Middleton (eds.), *From Tribe to Nation in Africa: Studies in the Incorporation Process* (Scranton, Pennsylvania: Chandler, 1970), Chapter I.

25. For instance, one of the most persuasive accounts is Martin Kilson's "Reciprocity Model of African Politics" applied to Sierra Leone. The reciprocity model posits an exchange relationship between leaders and followers. Leaders are permitted to lead in return for something else, most often wealth, but also in Sierra Leone the central elite and the Paramount Chiefs formed an alliance based on a mutual agreement to exchange local autonomy for votes. The archetype of the reciprocity principle is the familiar patron-client relationship—but with an added feature, the "group basis" of African life. Individuals interact in the wider sphere not as social isolates but as integral members of primary groups. The authority which leaders can wield is limited by the persistence by which subgroups maintain their separate identities and continue to make demands on the alliance. We will have occasion to comment further on the reciprocity model, but the point here is simply that even in a work as cognizant of the politics of expedience as Kilson's, primoridal affiliations play an important role. Martin Kilson, *Political Change in a West African State: A Study of the Modernization Process in Sierra Leone* (Cambridge, Massachusetts: Harvard University Press, 1966), esp. pp. 259-289. For a critical examination of the model, see my "Rural-Urban Alliances and Reciprocity in Africa," *Canadian Journal of African Studies,* V, iii (1972), pp. 307-325.

26. William H. Friedland and Carl G. Rosberg, Jr. (eds.), *African Socialism* (Stanford: Stanford University Press, 1964).

27. A rare and brilliant exception is John R. Nellis, *A theory of Ideology: The Tanzanian Example* (New York: Oxford University Press, 1973).

28. Immanuel Wallerstein, "Ethnicity and National Integration," *Cahiers d'Etudes Africaines,* (July 1960), pp. 129-139.

29. Crawford Young, *Politics in the Congo* (Princeton: Princeton University Press, 1965), Chapter XI.

30. Abner Cohen, *Custom and Politics in Urban Africa: A Study of Hausa Migrants in Yoruba Towns* (Berkeley and Los Angeles: University of California Press, 1969). A useful review of much of the literature on ethnicity in Africa, as well as an excellent attempt to clear away the underbrush on the causes of ethnic conflict, is found in Robert H. Bates, "Ethnicity and Modernization in Contemporary Africa," *Social Science Working Paper,* Number 16, (November 1972), California In-

stitute of Technology. For an inventory of hypotheses on ethnicity and ethnic conflict, see Robert Melson and Howard Wolpe, "Modernization and the Politics of Communalism: A Theoretical Perspective," *American Political Science Review*, LXII, 4 (December 1970), pp. 1112-1130. A number of these issues as well as the theoretical utility of rational actor models are discussed in my review article, "Comparative Grassroots Politics in Africa," *World Politics*, XXVI, 2 (Jan. 1974), pp. 283-297.

31. "Spatial modelling" has grown progressively more sophisticated since Downs, *op. cit.*, first put forth his model constructed on a single issue dimension—ideology, running from left to right. Since then, model-builders have devised elaborate multi-issue (*n*-dimensional) models, more closely reflecting the reality of actual politics. See, for instance, Otto A. Davis, Melvin J. Hinich, and Peter C. Ordeshook, "An Expository Development of a Mathematical Model of the Electoral Process," *American Political Science Review*, LXIV, 2 (June 1970), pp. 426-448. In this section we employ the *n*-dimensional issue space concept, but shy away from the complex mathematics inherent in any complete development of its implications.

32. The choice of one of the two models does not necessarily provide a definitive explanation of alliance behavior. Better models may exist already, and no doubt more powerful explanations will emerge as the science of politics advances. All that can be accomplished here is to determine which of the two available models is more appropriate in the Sierra Leonean case.

33. S.N. Eisenstadt, *The Political System of Empires* (Glencoe: The Free Press, 1963), pp. 13-32.

34. Martin Kilson, *Political Change in a West African State* (Cambridge, Mass.: Harvard Univ. Press. 1966), p. 287

35. John R. Cartwright, *Politics in Sierra Leone 1947-67* (Toronto: University of Toronto Press, 1970), pp. 258-283.

36. Raymond Duvall and Mary Welfling, "Social Mobilization, Political Institutionalization, and Conflict in Black Africa," *Journal of Conflict Resolution*, 17, 4 (Dec. 1973), 673-701.

Chapter 3
History and Tradition

The purpose of this chapter is twofold. First, it attempts to sketch with rather broad strokes the history of the Upper Mende people.[1] Detailed knowledge about Mende society in the pre- and early-colonial eras is scanty, so no taut, complete account of its genesis is yet possible, but it may be useful to present what is known in an effort to provide diachronic perspective to our analysis of contemporary politics.

Second, it confronts in preliminary fashion the general issues of "continuity and change" raised by our juxtaposition of the displacement and synthetic models. What is the relationship between the traditional and the modern? Is social change marked by the clash of opposites or by their mutual interpenetration? We have already noted how empirical evaluation of abstract conceptual schemes can be done only indirectly, by testing the hypotheses which issue from them. Hence, the brief historical treatment provided here can serve only as a first, indicative step in comparing the displacement and synthetic models. We must await the next chapter, on the role of Paramount Chiefs in Mendeland, for a more complete investigation of the specific hypotheses on role conflict derived from the models.

Mende Societies Before 1896

Surprisingly, pre-Protectorate (i.e., pre-1896) Mende society was significantly different from what is now regarded as "traditional Mende society." An encapsulated description of traditional Mende society might read:

> The Mende are organized into many chiefdoms, each of which is led by a Paramount Chief and a Tribal Authority. The chieftaincy is hereditary, there being one or more ruling families in each chiefdom eligible to put up candidates for election by the Tribal Authority. A Paramount Chief is aided by a Speaker, who is also elected by the Tribal Authority. Chiefdoms are divided into sections, each of which is ruled by a section chief and a section speaker, who are responsible to the Paramount Chief. Each town is ruled by a chief and speaker, who are responsible to the section chief. The Mende practice shifting cultivation. Their descent system is patrilineal with matrilineal overtones. Secret societies play important parts in many aspects of Mende life.[2]

Yet this concurs in only a few points with the rough etching drawn from our knowledge of the pre-Protectorate era.

Before the establishment of British hegemony, war was the central fact of life for most Mendes. It tainted nearly every aspect of society, from residential patterns to political structures. War seemed to be an annual affair, for the "hungry season" (July and August) was looked upon as a time to supplement meager supplies.[3] Booty was not the least reason for embarking upon a campaign against neighboring towns; revenge and mercenary profits were also among the motives; but the major cause of war was likely the competition among warrior-chiefs (sing., *Komahei*) for power and prestige.[4] The spoils of war, especially slaves and weapons, were the profits by which they were able to increase their war-making capacity, which in turn added to their wealth and status. More general causes of these wars no doubt included the vast movements of refugees from the political and military upheavals in the grassland empires to the north and east during the four or five centuries prior to British rule.[5]

The war town was the central unit of existence, a direct response to the uncertainty and danger extant during pre-

Protectorate days. Within, it was built to confuse and trap an attacker; houses were constructed close together forming complicated networks of passages and culs-de-sac. Without, the town was ringed by fences, trenches, and palisades of cotton trees. Satellite villages, peopled mostly by slaves, farmed the land surrounding the town. Towns were spread further apart than they are today, "each with a vague and indeterminate sphere of influence over the adjacent countryside, and each quite independent of the others."[6] War was waged against fellow Mendes with the same facility as against neighboring peoples such as the Gbandi, the Golas, the Konos, or the Krim. There seemed to be little or no intratribal identity; indeed, by dint of propinquity, Mende towns were most likely at war with each other more than with the towns of other tribes.

Alliances were a major means by which towns could enhance their security. But alliances were for the most part short-lived and uncertain. "A town might on occasion ally itself with a powerful neighbor; but it might as easily find itself soon afterwards at war with its former ally...."[7] The nature of this alliance system is well illustrated by the plight of British administrators in their early attempts to tamp down the frequent wars which threatened the trade and profits of their customs ports on the Moa (Sulima) and Kittam Rivers. Rivalries among the local Vai and Krim towns were vastly compounded by the activities of powerful Mende warriors just inland—such as Makiah, Makavoreh, Dawa, and Mendegila—who would hire out their services to the highest bidder. Intercourse between coast and interior took the form of shifting alliances and short-lived skirmishes. The Freetown-based British, anxious for more settled conditions, in 1885 entered into direct communication with the interior peoples, but an agreement made by the Governor of Sierra Leone himself failed to keep the peace.[8] In 1886 Special Officer Peel arranged a new peace, which had the effect of aligning the British with Makavoreh and Mendegila against Dawa and his coastal allies,[9] but it soon collapsed. A year later Administrator-in-Chief J.S. Hay attempted to patch together still another peace arrangement. His reports convey an analysis of the precarious alliance system and its attendant violence:

> ... the different chiefs mistrust each other, and, doubtful of the intentions of their neighbors, each one is endeavouring to form that alliance that will best protect his own interests.[10]

> At present ... the countries in question have no paramount chief, consequently each petty headman ... is ever at variance with his neighbors, and, as there is no recognised supreme authority, on the slightest provocation recourse is had to arms. ... [E]ach anxious for supremacy engages the services of mercenaries to assist them, never calculating the cost and, at the end, find themselves saddled with an incubus they are wholly powerless to shake off as they cannot pay their warboys, who in return loot their employers should the latter not find for them fresh fields for plunder.[11]

His success in selecting a chief to rule the entire coastal area was met first by hostility from London and then by an attack on the customs port of Sulima by Dawa and Makiah. It was not until the war towns of Makiah in 1887 and Dawa in 1889 were destroyed, that what was known as the Gallinas Coast saw a semblance of peace.[12]

This alliance system, then, had the following features. (1) It was riven by distrust and uncertainty. (2) Rival neighboring towns, for security or aggrandizement, or both, sought the aid of powerful allies further afield, most often for a price. (3) Allies often turned against each other.

It must be said, however, that some warriors were more successful than others in cementing together a number of allies into an entity that was far more stable than the above account would suggest. Indeed, the more successful warriorchiefs, like Faba, Nyagua, Kailundu, and Mendegila, can be said to have built small city-states. Through their reputation as warriors, their stocks of weapons and slaves, and their skill in forming effective alliances, such figures attracted the loyalty of lesser chiefs and weaker towns. Those towns that held back were conquered. The best documented case is the rise to power of Kailundu, whose defeat of Dawa during the Kpoveh Wars (ca. 1880-1886) led to the foundation of a stable governmental system over what is now called the Luawa chiefdom in the Kailahun District of Sierra Leone plus parts of present-day Liberia.[13] A loose confederation of lineage heads and town chiefs ceded their authority to Kailundu in return for his protection. He consolidated his hold on his territory by building a network of defensive towns, coordinated by a centralized administrative structure; later he extended his suzerainty by embarking upon a series of military campaigns into Kono and Kissi countries.[14]

Such war-chiefs rarely engaged in actual combat; they were retired warriors who had made their reputations as young men. They supervised the strategy of warmaking and "subsidized the war, paying for the presents sent to other towns to solicit their assistance . . . and in return for their outlay in that and arms, receiving a neat half of all slaves and valuables captured as their share of the booty."[15] In addition, irregular exactions of tribute played a role in holding together such proto-empires, linking the warrior chief with lesser chiefs and providing resources for future forays.

Leadership was thrust upon the man who had the reputation, diplomatic and organizational skills, and wealth requisite for successful waging of war. Although kinship relations ramify through many aspects of Mende life, there is little evidence that succession to chieftaincy was based on hereditary principles. No doubt minor posts such as village headman were handed down according to rules of patrilineal succession, especially in areas remote from frequent warring or during periods of prolonged peace. And it is true that the mantle of leadership sometimes passed from father to son, as in the case of Faba, whose extensive holdings came into the hands of his son Nyagua. But by and large succession was based on the principle of expedience: A man's ability as a warrior was the prime consideration for appointment as chief. Even the case of Nyagua is not a clear-cut example of hereditary succession. He was a warrior equal to Faba in fame and ability. Some accounts claim that Nyagua was the son of

Faba, and some have him as grandson.[16] In fact, it is entirely possible that they were not related biologically but that Nyagua as a young warrior pledged his loyalty to Faba by calling himself his son.[17] The manipulation of kinship relations for political purposes is a recurrent theme in Mende society, and we will encounter it frequently in our analysis of contemporary politics. Whatever Nyagua's partpcular status, however, it appears that hereditary principles were at best secondary.

This conclusion is based on my collection of oral histories of some chiefdoms in Kenema District as well as on local archival records.[18] Moreover, it concurs with Wylie's analysis of nineteenth-century Mende history as exemplified by Luawa chiefdom. His explicit thesis is that during the nineteenth century "earlier autonomous village groups, depending on kinship and *Poro* for social control . . . gave way to large organized chiefdoms, with many tributary towns and villages."[19] Actually, there is little evidence to indicate that these incipient state-building activities did not take place prior to the nineteenth century, in cyclical fashion; but whether these large, stable alliance systems were peculiar to the period just prior to the colonial era, as Wylie would have it, or whether their recurrent rise and fall were inherent in Mende society, as is suggested by other sources,[20] the important point is that ability to wage war held sway over hereditary considerations as the basis for leadership selection.

We can infer from this account that the role of *Ko-mahei* in the precolonial period entailed expectations on the part of followers which were above all "foreign policy" oriented. A chief's prime task was the protection of his people against outside dangers. The means to this end were far less important than the end itself: War, shifting alliances, submission to a more powerful warrior, even association with an element so alien as the British—all were acceptable instruments for attempting to achieve security. Were a chief through his skills as ambassador or general able to aggrandize the community, so much the better. Put differently, we can suggest that the "pivotal" attribute of the chief's role, from the point of view of his followers, dealt with external behavior: He was expected to protect and advance their interests by manipulating the outside world in whatever fashion proved successful.

Warrior-chiefs were aided in their efforts to maintain the cohesion of their loosely-unified empires by the presence of secret societies, most notably the *Poro* society. The *Poro* cut across small-scale kinship and village groups and brought them together under an umbrella of cultural unity, for, above all, *Poro* was an educational institution. Moreover, its semireligious nature, in the form of powerful medicines and ancestral authority, gave strong sanctions to its leaders. We can speculate, along with Little, that the "more powerful chiefs had control of *Poro*."[21] This is corroborated by a remark made by one of the great chiefs of modern times, Paramount Chief Kai-Samba I, in describing a typical pre-Protectorate Mende chief:

> He was the head of the great Secret Society—the *Poro* which planned war and internal security. The state was perpetually threatened by war from the invading tribesmen of the North. . . . Adjoining chiefdoms also made . . . attacks. The chief was therefore involved in the continuous planning and execution of wars, which in most cases lasted only a few hours.[22]

If true, we can see how the corporate, mystical authority of the *Poro*—with its mechanisms for making laws, controlling trade, and policing social behavior in general—could strongly reinforce the raw rule-by-arms of such warrior-chiefs. Even if chiefly control over secret societies was less than complete, there is little doubt that they served as forces of cohesion, reducing the divisive pressures caused by the uncertainties and rivalries of war.

Poro had important functions in war. First, it served as the training institution for young warriors. Each important town had its own *Poro* "lodge" or "bush school." Periodically new initiates would be trained for as much as two to three years in the lore of the society, including preparation for military service. Malcolm estimates that *Poro* initiates spent 60% of their time on military training.[23] Second, *Poro* was a mechanism by which alliances were arranged and solidified. Those alliances sealed by a

Poro oath were more likely to last the duration of their agreed-upon purpose than those mediated by mercenary exchanges alone. This aspect also includes *Poro's* war-declaring function, for the very nature of a secret society allowed preparations for war to proceed undetected against an unsuspecting foe. For instance, the Sulima area in 1887 was attacked by forces organized by Makiah and Dawa under a war-*poro*,[24] the stipulations of which evidently included sparing certain towns but razing those allied to Chief Bockari Governor, the leading landlord and benefactor for the British subjects trading there.[25] Lastly, the *Poro* could be mobilized for peace. When a war became so destructive and long-lived that it threatened entirely to consume its practicioners, the *Poro* society became a medium for negotiations and settlement, through its common institutions and cultural assumptions as well as its power to impose sanctions. One mechanism for arranging peace was *Sar-Wuja,* a strong messenger of the society. A peacemaker—presumably a third party—would send him as an intermediary between two combatants. By *Poro* law he was not to be harmed; likewise he was enjoined to convey no false information, under penalty of death.[26] Peace-*poros* were frequent phenomena in the unsettled "Sulima District" during the 1880's. At least one was instigated by a British travelling commissioner sent to patch up alliances for ending local wars. Special Officer Peel arranged to have all the chiefs in the area meet at Sembehun in June 1886:

> Here the leaders of each side took the oath of peace according to their own country fashion. . . .
>
> I witnessed each chief individually take the oath according as the others made them swear. This ceremony lasted from morning till evening and everybody appeared quite satisfied and friendly.[27]

His efforts were in vain, for soon afterward a war broke out which was to flicker sporadically until, after the defeat of Makiah and Dawa, the powerful chief Mendegila arranged a peace-*poro* in 1889.[28] The underlying influence of the *Poro* and its ability to engender a modicum of trust and predictability served to ameliorate what otherwise would have been sheer anarchy.

Upper Mendeland was clearly undergoing considerable flux during the pre-Protectorate days. Few resilient configurations of authority and stability had established themselves for more than the lifetime of one powerful man. Fluidity rather than rigid traditionalism prevailed. That few deep-rooted political structures had taken hold is not surprising. The Mende are a relatively new people. They were the most recent in a long succession of migrant peoples to settle in the protective forests of what is now called Sierra Leone. Likely they, like their predecessors, sought sanctuary from dispersions erupting out of the grassland empires of the Western Sudan. Peter Kup puts the first entry of Mendes into Sierra Leone sometime during the mid-seventeenth century:

> This thrust, which represents the second act in the realignment of the east begun by the Krus shortly after 1600, was part of the final collapse of law and order in the Songhai empire, begun by the invasion of El Mansur, the Moroccan emperor. . . .[29]

But it was not until the end of the eighteenth century that the Mendes had penetrated deeply, pushing the Sherbros and Temnes before them in their westward and southward migration.

In addition, by the late nineteenth century Mendeland was subject to a number of new unsettling pressures: The Sofa warriors under Samori were with increasing frequency extending their raids into the Sierra Leonean hinterland; the coastal peoples with their trade in guns and palm stimulated the already skirmish-prone Mende to further battle; the Mende westward advance had ben considerably slowed by the British presence, restricting the safety-valve effect of dispersion; and European power struggles were coming to a head in Africa, exacerbating local tensions and rivalries.

Thus, a durable pattern of civil authority never coalesced. Rule was primarily by military force; authority was delegated to military viceroys or conquered vassals; tribute and protection comprised the main currency between ruler and ruled; loyalty and political identity shifted according to the power exigencies of the moment. The *Poro* society proved the most pervasive element of civility in Mende collectivities, a hidden repository of traditions and laws whose sanctions reached beyond—but not far beyond—the boundaries of each war-town or confederation of towns. It was into this milieu that the British officially stepped when they declared a Protectorate of the entire Freetown hinterland in 1896. It was only then that "traditional" Mende polities began to take form.

The British Intervention

As we have seen, prior to 1896 the British were little more than one actor among many in the almost anarchical skirmishing and jostling, alignment and realignment that marked the late nineteenth-century history of Upper Mendeland and its coastal periphery. Protection of trading facilities was their immediate goal; treaties of friendship and provision of a string of small police posts was their method; military entanglement was the result. This was a familiar pattern to the people of the region, who evidently saw no reason to resist a force whose goals seemed modest and whose mode of operation fit comfortably with their own. Even the attacks on Sulima and the police garrison at Bandasuma were far less anti-British in their motivation than the outcome of a local power struggle among blocs of warrior-chiefs, the British being unhappily allied to the losing side.

Fears of French expansion, the need to pay for a growing administrative apparatus, plans for a railway, advocacy on the part of interested groups both in London and in Freetown—all contributed to the proclamation of the Sierra Leone Protectorate in 1896. A letter circulated to all chiefs in the Protectorate explained their new situation. There would be three courts, "Paramount Chiefs" hearing only local and minor matters while District Commissioners would preside over the important cases.

Slave dealing was outlawed. Land could not be sold to nonnatives; the Crown held all mineral rights; the Queen had "rights
to take whatever land may be wanted for use by the
Government...." Beginning in 1898 every chief would have to
pay the District Commissioner five shillings for every house under his auspices. Furthermore, the Governor could depose any
chief who was "unfit for his position" and could "appoint a fit
and proper person to be chief in his place."[30] Clearly this was a
situation of a different order from the treaties of friendship and
petty alliances of former days. However, the Governor of Sierra
Leone, Sir Frederic Cardew, seems to have perceived very little
resentment during his treks of 1894-6, taken to inform the interior people of the abolition of the slave trade and to prepare
them for Protectorateship status. "The natives always appeared
to acquiesce: except Nyagua, Chief of Panguma, who was very
truculent...."[31] No deluge of protest found its way to Freetown;
there was, in fact, very little indication that the interior people
realized that anything had changed.

At least one petition of protest did, however, reach the eyes of
the administration, documenting the first, inchoate stirrings of
resentment against the British for their violation of the *modus
operandi* which had so long governed intercourse between them
and the peoples of the interior. Signed by 62 "chiefs" of the Sulima and Gallinas area, it reveals the operating assumptions of
the people with whom the British had made numerous treaties of
friendship:

> ... we consider the laws are too strong for a Native man to go un-
> der. We never were inform of such ordinance before or previous
> till we see it all on a surden, it give such a terrible cry and noise
> over the Country... [His Excellency] gave us law to clean the
> roads and not to seize ourselves, and not to fight or make any war
> or to kill wilfully; we agree to all that laws, but now we see
> ourselves in bondage, we are not free, *we know that our country
> did not take by conquest only we gave [it to] the queen to protect
> it,* we find now that she took it from us, but not only protection.[32]

As the deadline for tax payments approached, such protests increased in frequency. Many chiefs refused to pay; a number disappeared into the bush; there were rumors of secret meetings and arms cashes in the forests. Then open rebellion broke out in the Temne country around Port Loko. Bai Bureh, a Temne war chief, had evaded arrest and by early April 1898 was engaged in full battle with first the Frontier Police and then the regular soldiers of the 1st West India Regiment. The Hut Tax War had begun.

At first it looked as though the insurrection would not spread to Mendeland. A few strategic arrests of chiefs and a number of villages burned seemed sufficient show of force to assure compliance. It was discovered that under Nyagua "a large number of chiefs and warboys [had] assembled at a town called Kenama [Kenema], and they were always holding secret meetings and were collecting large supplies of arms and gunpowder. . . ."[33] But when faced with arrest, Nyagua quickly relinquished his stockades.

Then, suddenly and without warning, most of the Mendeland rose up on the morning of April 27 in an attack on all vestiges of alien rule—police posts, trading centers, British and American missionaries, and above all, Creoles. In retrospect it seems fairly certain that the uprising was planned by a few strong chiefs under the auspices of the *Poro* society. Most of the District Commissioners involved were convinced that the insurrectionary leaders met at Bumpe, where they called for and planned a *Ngoyila* (one-word) war, news of which was spread by society messengers and participation in which was encouraged by strong *Poro* sanctions. Nyagua of Panguma, Wonno of Jerihun, and Gribroh of Bumpe were said to have been the prime movers.[34] Indeed, Governor Cardew testified to his belief that Nyagua was the ringleader:

. . . it is very probable that [the Mende rising] was started at Panguma . . . for Nyagua was the most powerful chief amongst the Mendis, and exerted a very paramount influence over all the Mendi chiefs. . . . I would go so far as to say that if he had thrown in his lot with the Government there would have been no Mendi rising.[35]

Despite whatever planning had gone into the insurrection, however, the Mende were disorganized and were no match for warships, cannon, and Maxim guns. Panguma was neutralized by May 23, and Nyagua taken under arrest to Freetown. Other Mende towns which had been implicated in the war, like Bumpe, Tikonko, and Taiama, were invested and burned. By August both wars, Mende and Temne, had been substantially quelled. All that remained were the arrest of Bai Bureh and a three-pronged march through the Protectorate as a show of force, which converged on Panguma and then Kailahun (after Kailundu) in early 1899. Nyagua, together with Bai Bareh, was deported as a political prisoner to the Gold Coast, where he died in 1912.

Mende societies, conditioned upon and built for war, did not cede their political identities except by war. As a result of their defeat in the Hut Tax War, they recognized a new overlord, the "Government," and accorded it surprising loyalty and good will, permitting the colonial administration to fashion Mende political structures significantly different from their pre-Protectorate forms.

Colonial Consolidation (1898-ca. 1920)

The initial problem faced by the British was the development of an administration efficient and broad enough to maintain order and supervise the collection of taxes. Although never spelled out in one coherent document, the philosophy underlying the consolidation of colonial administration was a modification of that applied so well by Lugard in Northern Nigeria, Indirect Rule. The aftermath of the Hut Tax War was enlivened by a far-reaching debate between Governor Cardew and Sir David Chalmers, who was sent from England as a Royal Commissioner to investigate the causes of the war and to affix blame if necessary. In his report Chalmers held the protectorate administration responsible for the uprising; Cardew's house tax became the main target for his attack: "The Hut Tax, together with the measures used for its enforcement, were the moving causes of the insurrection. . . ."[36] He recommended a return to the former style of administration, in which relations between chiefs and administrative officers were loose and informal. His objective was to support the chiefs and to "strengthen the confidence of the chiefs in the English government. . . ." District Commissioners should not be "Magistrates" or "Deputy-Governors" but rather "Residents . . . whose principal duty would be to assist the Chiefs. . . ."[37]

Cardew, in rising to his own defense, denied that his house tax was a major cause of the War, and blamed instead the unsettling effects of civilizing rule on a backward people. The very purposes of the Protectorate—abolition of slave dealing, pacification of the interior, and increased trade—undermined the chiefs and their traditional prerogatives, he said; the rising was their all-too-typical reaction. He protested against Chalmers' advocacy of a return to chiefly hegemony:

> I think it would be a very retrograde step to relegate the administration of the Protectorate to the chiefs without proper supervision over them. . . . The history of West Africa under the administration of its chiefs has been all along one of slavery, oppression and wrong.[38]

None other than Sir Joseph Chamberlain acquitted Governor Cardew and his policies. The Colonial Secretary agreed that the causes of the War were multifarious and generally connected with the penetration of civilization into a reluctant territory; in his opinion, the tax was merely the "immediate or exciting cause."[39] More important for our purposes, he concurred with Cardew's administrative policies and recommendations, but not without paying homage to the principle of preserving indigenous customs and structures whenever possible:

In considering what form of administration is desirable for the Protectorate, it seems to me that the foremost consideration must be the character of the people. It is undoubtedly sound policy in West Africa not to disturb native customs more than is necessary, but to endeavour . . . to effect improvements and reforms through the native Chiefs whom the people have been accustomed to obey. The extent, however, to which this can be done obviously depends on the extent to which the Chiefs and people generally are amenable to the influence of civilising government, and open to and receptive of humanizing ideas. . . .

Taking into consideration the past history of the territories in question . . . I cannot entertain any doubt that the character of a large proportion of the natives is such as to require *firm and direct control* by the Power which undertakes . . . to rule them by civilised methods. . . .

The logical result of this view is that the framework of the scheme of administration which has been adopted is sound, i.e., that the Protectorate should be controlled by a Frontier Police, a staff of District Commissioners with both executive and judicial powers, and that local taxation to meet these expenses is justifiable.[40]

Chamberlain's pronouncements set the philosophical tone for the administration of the Protectorate, a poor man's version of the Lugardian tomes that guided policy in Nigeria. They were dualistic and somewhat contradictory in nature, calling on the one hand for "firm and direct control" but cautioning policy makers, on the other, "not to disturb native customs" and not to "diminish the dignity of a Chief in the eyes of his people."[41]

In the context of the Chalmers-Cardew debate, though, Chamberlain's report was a clear mandate to rule by direct intervention. Yet the sheer magnitude of administering the Protectorate peoples with literally only a handful of officers— most of them very young and trained as soldiers—precluded any thoroughgoing transformation of indigenous institutions. The

District Commissioners were forced by overwhelming necessity to deal with already-established institutions—that is, with the chiefs and the loosely-knit confederations they had built about themselves. In the Upper Mende region, the District Commissioners were faced with particular flux, the product, as we have seen, of frequent war and absence of firm political structures. Moreover, the administration of Sierra Leone underwent what might be called a minor degeneration during the few formative years immediately following the Hut Tax War. Governor Cardew, never fully recovered from illness and the tremors of the Chalmers investigation, seems to have failed to provide firm and detailed guidance to his District Commissioners. The archives are particularly scanty for these years. The likes of Lugard never existed in Sierra Leone. The confluence of these factors—a strong general mandate, but faltering leadership and skimpy resources for the effort to rule societies which were undergoing considerable change—determined to a large extent the peculiar nature of Indirect Rule in Sierra Leone generally and in Upper Mendeland particularly.

Present-day Mende chiefdoms and their paraphenalia are largely the creation of early decisions by British officers sent to administer the Protectorate. Nyagua's proto-empire was broken up into its component parts, the present-day Dodo, Lower Bambara, and Nongowa chiefdoms. Kailundu's territory began to shrink even before the War, at his death in 1895, when the British appointed his successor, Fabunde, in return for a promise to respect the international boundary with Liberia which happened to run through his domain.[42] Kabba Sei's falling-out with the Government led to the dismantling of his realm and the recognition of his vassals as "Paramount Chiefs."[43] The present Small Bo chiefdom formerly included Kandu and possibly Leppiama chiefdoms. Gorama Mende was once a part of what is now called Wando chiefdom. Chunks were carved out of former proto-empires to suit administrative convenience and to reward chiefs who favored the Government, whether they were formerly "paramount" or not. Almost without exception, contemporary chiefdoms are the product of these early decisions to dismantle some and to grace with Government recognition other collections of war towns. A great deal of time was spent by the District Commissioners during the first fifteen or twenty years of colonial rule surveying and recording the boundaries thus formed.[44] The vague and ever-changing spheres of influence which characterized the pre-War regimes were superceded by (relatively) clear and permanent boundaries. With pacification, the rationale for the war town disappeared and people rapidly gave life to the new units by changing their settlement patterns:

> In 1925 there were more than 1,500 large villages in Sierra Leone with between 39 and 200 buildings. Today there are only about 1,000 such settlements. During the same period the number of small villages with between 12 and 35 buildings has increased from 3,800 to 5,400, and the number of hamlets with less than 12 buildings has more than doubled, from 9,300 in 1925 to 22,800 in 1964.[45]

The war-town gave way to the chiefdom as the basic unit of social and political interaction among the Mende.

And the *Ko-mahei* (warrior-chief) gave way to the *Ndo-mahei* (literally, country chief). Ability to collect taxes and good behavior during the War seemed the prime criteria for installation as "Paramount Chief." In 1941 the Chief Commissioner noted that the Government had deposed a number of chiefs during and after the War and was faced with the problem of succession:

> Subsequent experience shows that many "successors" had no real claim and were accepted by the Government for no other reason than they would be vigorous in the collection of the House Tax.[46]

When other criteria did not apply, often a chief was appointed by virtue of descent from a signatory of an early treaty of friendship, despite the fact that a signer could easily have been a minor chief or even a messenger. Sometimes the chief who had formed an alliance with the Frontier Police was the one who was able to retain power. Needless to say, the dearth of detailed written records in the hands of the British authorities provided ample opportunity for intrigue and scheming.

In seizing upon descent as the mode of political succession, the colonial officers in effect froze the recruitment system of Mende chiefdoms, limiting future leadership to the patrilineal descendants of those who had been so arbitrarily installed in the early days of the Protectorate. Surprisingly, nothing has been written explaining why the Government chose the hereditary principle as the method of succession; the records simply do not reveal the process by which District Commissioners came to recognize only those candidates who could demonstrate membership in what came to be called "ruling families" or "ruling houses." Speculation is easy, however. Kinship is important to many aspects of Mende life, and they might simply have assumed that it carried over into the political sphere. "Ruling families" were indeed the suppliers of chiefs in Temne chiefdoms—as well as among many other peoples of Africa with whom the British had had contact, in particular the Yoruba, the Hausa, the Akan, and many tribes of South Africa—and they may simply have transferred previous experience to Mendeland. Then again, being Englishmen, they found dynastic rule more than familiar, and it may have seemed perfectly natural to impose—insinuate is a better word—this principle in place of the military principle, which was obviously unsuited to the radically changed conditions of the Protectorate. Whatever the reasons for its application, the imposition of hereditary qualifications on eligibility for leadership was by far the most important innovation of the early colonial administration. As we shall see in later chapters, contemporary local politics operates largely within the framework dictated by this stricture.

It should not be supposed that the hereditary principle was alien to the Mendes. As we have seen, it did have secondary importance as a method of political recruitment. And there is no indication in the records of adverse reaction or resentment. Indeed, the bigmen of Upper Mende chiefdoms responded with alacrity to the new rule, jostling for Government favor and dusting off—sometimes inventing—their hereditary credentials. Competition assured the acceptance of the innovation.

Yet it must be said that the British, had they known more about the Mende, could have encouraged other principles of political succession. The most obvious is what might be called a peacetime analog of the military principle. Chiefs in the past were selected mostly for their achievements and abilities in war. It probably would not have been difficult to transmute this to a selectivity based on, say, economic accomplishment or education or efficiency or service to the community. As modern parlance would have it, the administration opted for "ascriptive" rather than "achievement" criteria for local leadership. Colonial rule was consolidated at a critical juncture of Mende history, when political institutions were particularly malleable. If this analysis is correct, the British could have emphasized an achievement-oriented tendency strongly present in Mende societies which subsequently would have fossilized into a "tradition." This no doubt would have rendered today's chiefdoms considerably more modern (read: efficient, honest, wealthy, capable, democratic, etc.) than they actually are. Buganda and Busoga in Uganda are illustrative cases in point. There, as we have seen, British practice utilized the instrumental orientation of local rulers, converting them into "civil-servant" chiefs who became integral and efficient parts of the governmental machinery.[47] But in Sierra Leone, descent was emphasized as the guiding principle for succession. It quickly coalesced into a tradition which forms the core of politics in Mende chiefdoms today.

Administrative decisions had a formative influence on other aspects of chiefdom government as well. Chiefs who were formerly in a position of vassalage to those recognized as Paramount Chiefs were appointed as "section chiefs" (or "subchiefs"). Mendes had to invent a word, *Pati-mahei* (from the English "part"), to designate this innovation. Chiefs ruling a town only were appointed as town chiefs (sing., *Ta-mahei*). What is more important, they were placed in strict hierarchical order, replacing the loose, uncertain system of alliances among towns, with an ordered administrative structure emphasizing rank and (albeit limited) differentiation of function. The office of Speaker *(Lavalie)* gained autonomy. No longer directly dependent upon and ancillary to the chief, the Speaker came to be appointed by the Tribal Authority and thus was given a measure of institutional independence from the chief.

Early legislation vested official authority in the "Tribal Authorities" of the various chiefdoms. Before the colonial takeover, there were no structures of fixed membership and procedures among the Mende which could be called Tribal Authorities; the nearest analogues would be the small circle of advisors surrounding the chief and the councils of big men assembled to decide matters of peace and war *(korbanganga)*; or perhaps the inner councils of the *Poro* societies constituted the closest pre-Protectorate version of what the British meant by "Tribal Authority"—that is, a council of elders and representatives of the chiefdom who would select the new chief and share authority with him. This early legislation was vague and general:

> "Tribal Authority" means paramount chiefs and their councillors, and men of note, or sub-chiefs and their councillors, and men of note.[48]

The term gained meaning only by actual application, which, as might be expected, differed from time to time and place to place. Elections—or rather selections—of new chiefs were done by handfuls of men chosen by haphazard and arbitrary methods. All the early elections reported in the Decree Books were the "unanimous decisions" of "chiefs and elders," their unanimity less an underlying consensus than a compromise which would be acceptable to the District Commissioner. Gradually the composition of Tribal Authorities (TA's) became better defined, not as a result of specific legislation but the product of administrative arrangements. The Decree Book of Kenema District reports that:

At a meeting held at Panguma on the 28th April 1923 it was decided to constitute a proper Tribal Authority for the [Lower] Bambarra Chiefdom. . . . It was decided that the TA of Bambarra Chiefdom should consist of the Paramount Chief, the Speaker for the Chiefdom, and the sub-chief of each of the seven sections of the chiefdom.[49]

Naturally, however, in the haphazard world of the Protectorate administration, other chiefdoms had less strict—or no—definitions of their TA's. As time went on, the composition of most TA's gradually enlarged, but it was not until the 1940's that firm agreements were recorded delineating their size and mode of representation. For instance, Nongowa chiefdom agreed to the following formula for representatives from villages and towns:[50]

Over 25 houses	1 member
75-100 houses	2 members
100-200 houses	3 members
Over 200 houses	4 members

Other chiefdoms had similar but not necessarily identical arrangements, the variations presumably caused by differences in local "Native Law and Customs." Then, for a while, it became the practice to establish a 1:80 (in some chiefdoms a 1:40) ratio between taxpayers and representatives on the Tribal Authority. Finally, by the mid-1950's, administrative fiat set the ratio at 1:20 and hardened the definition of "Tribal Authority" with detailed, written instructions from the central Government.[51]

Despite the gradual evolution of TA's in response to external—that is, Governmental—requirements, the British persisted in according them an autochthonous validity which, at least among the Mende, they did not have. They were creations of the Government, but the Government looked upon them as the product of customary law. To give an example of how this worked, the administrator's bible was J.S. Fenton's "Outline of Native Law," put out in handbook form in 1932. Throughout, it perceives the Tribal Authority as part and parcel of native custom. Later administrative officers referred to Fenton for their authority on what was permissible according to native law. For instance, a paper prepared by the Chief Commissioner for consideration by the Executive Council (the predecessor of today's Cabinet) in 1953, was concerned with what to do if a TA were unable to elect a Paramount Chief because of lack of consensus. He suggested that impasse could be overcome by expanding and making more representative the TA concerned; his further suggestion was "without violating custom . . . to expand a Tribal Authority . . . to such an extent as to make it virtually a general assembly of the chiefdom." He quoted Fenton for support of its feasibility. But he rejected as "repugnant to native custom" the suggestion that the TA be *permanently* expanded to comprise the whole of a chiefdom's taxpayers.[52] In their effort to preserve and respect native law, the colonial officers sometimes invented it.

Mendes did indeed add the evolving Tribal Authority idea to their repertory of traditions. The expanded TA was accepted and absorbed just as easily as the earlier versions. Only rarely has the TA as an institution been attacked by chiefdom people, and in those few cases it has been primarily for partisan political purposes. For instance, during a tense and hard-fought electoral battle for the Paramount Chieftaincy in Lower Bambara chiefdom in 1957, the losing side petitioned the Government for direct election by *all* the taxpayers, instead of just the members of the TA:

> The Tribal Authorities are a creation of the Government and not an institution handed down from custom. While they have served their purpose they create an electoral college which can easily be influenced by corrupt practices.[53]

The Government ignored this plea, and no further complaint has been heard. By and large, the TA's today are established components of chiefdom apparatus, giving the impression of ancient venerability and backed by the weight of thoroughgoing consensus.

Not all innovations were assimilated into the corpus of traditions, however. A case in point is the idea of rotating the Paramount Chieftaincy among ruling houses, so that in time all ruling families get an opportunity to rule. An established Temne custom, it was proposed with increasing frequency as a procedure which should gain usage among the Mende. As might be expected, the most vocal proponents of this rule were the families who were out of power; incumbent families naturally argued that it was contrary to native custom. The attitude of the District Commissioners was the key determinant of the success or failure of such an innovation. Occasionally a District Commissioner (DC; "decee" is a prominent word in the Mende vocabulary) would accept the argument that alteration of ruling houses was beneficial, as in Dodo chiefdom in 1919 when the DC decided that:

> . . . Gegbai should be considered elected as Paramount Chief and that Bon should be his Speaker. Furthermore that should Bon survive Gegbai, he should be the next Paramount Chief, provided the wishes of the people, coincided with his undoubted right by Native Law.[54]

A tripartite agreement of rotation was made among the ruling houses of Leppiama chiefdom and given official sanction by means of entry into the Decree Book.[55] But in neither of these cases did the administration allow subsequent elections to be governed by these agreements. Tunkia chiefdom illustrates even more dramatically how the fate of alternating succession lay in the hands of the DC. In 1945 during an attempted Paramount Chieftaincy election, the DC turned down claims that the chiefdom's two ruling houses had agreed to alternate: "I cannot imagine . . . allowing a Temne custom to intrude into a Mende election."[56] Two years later, the DC recorded—making it official—an agreement whereby "each house should show a Paramount Chief alternately, and the house not showing the PC [should] show Speakers."[57] But five years after that a new DC disallowed the agreement as "a Temne custom" and witnessed the election of a Paramount Chief from the same family as her predecessor.[58] In most cases the administration discouraged application of the rule, and this accounts for the difference between Temne and Mende "traditions" governing rotational crowning of chiefs— which, as we shall see later, has important implications for national politics in Sierra Leone.

A post-Independence example of an innovation which failed to "take hold" is the case of Mammy Queens. The Resident Minister of the Eastern Province, Taplima Ngobeh, had started the practice of crowning important women with the SLPP cap, calling them Mammy Queens and hoping to bolster the party's position among womenfolk. Other SLPP politicians, including the Prime Minister, Sir Albert Margai, noted its political value and continued the practice. In late 1965 administrative officers, asked by the Government if it would be feasible to transform this unofficial usage into official practice, searched for precedents in traditional society—and most of them were able to find some serviceable forebear of the species "Mammy Queen." In January 1966 a directive was circulated authorizing the women of each section of each chiefdom to "gather and appoint a Mammy Queen."[59] These would then elect a Head Mammy Queen. Such ambiguous guidance plus the original partisan impulse of the idea guaranteed its rapid politicization. Some former SLPP appointees lost their Mammy Queenhood as a result of the new directive, causing District party leaders to complain to the administration. And the foundling institution became enfolded in the arms of chiefdom rivalry and revenge, as chiefs imposed members from their own factions and cries of oppression rose from women of opposing factions. By the time of the military coup in March 1967 it was generally recognized that narrow partisanship had enveloped the new position. The National Reformation Council (NRC), anxious to discredit the politics of ousted Prime Minister Albert Margai, scrapped the post of Mammy Queen entirely, ending, presumably forever, the life chances of an infant role. It is not difficult to imagine that had external factors—administrative and political—been more favorable, within less than a generation Mammy Queens would have been assimilated into the body of Mende chiefdom traditions.

It must not be assumed that all aspects of Mende life were transformed with similar ease by the colonial and post-Independence administrations. The *Poro* society is a prime example of an institution which has retained many of its precolonial characteristics. True, its war-making functions have atrophied, and, under the impact of modern education, initiates spend less and less time training in *Poro* bushes; but the society still claims remarkable and almost universal loyalty from Mende men, young and old alike. Indeed, it is enjoying something of a recrudescence, as we shall see in a later chapter. Perhaps a partial explanation for its continuity lies, again, with administrative policy. In the very early days of the Protectorate the colonial authorities apparently did not hesitate to legislate against *Poro* activities when they interfered with trade.[60] And the Protectorate Ordinance 1901, did empower the DC to "settle any matters . . . which have their origin in Poro laws, native rites, or customs, land disputes or any other disputes which if not properly settled might lead to breaches of the peace. . . ."[61] But generally the administration's attitude was one of noninterference. Once it became established that a particular dispute was of *Poro* origin, assessor chiefs who were important society members were appointed to settle the issue, in secret and with little accountability to the DC. Present policy still generally holds to this pattern. Thus, as long as a particular society kept its activities within rather generous boundaries, it received remarkably little official attention from the administration. (Unofficially, DC's were deeply curious about *Poro's* functioning; they realized its pervasive political influence in the chiefdoms and often sent Court Messengers to infiltrate secret meetings.) As a result of this noninterference the society has continued much as it did before, with no major structural changes save the loss of its military operations—at least as far as is known from the outside.

No doubt the persistence of *Poro* and other secret societies also stems from their deep-rooted connections with the Mende cosmological and religious systems. Perhaps this also explains why the Mende system of land tenure has undergone such little change in the past century: Land and ancestors are closely tied; land belongs to the dead and unborn as well as to the living. Shifting cultivation—especially of rice—is a further example of a religiously-connected sphere of life which has experienced few drastic changes in the past century, despite serious attempts by both the colonial and the African administrations to displace such ancient methods with more productive and less wasteful techniques.[62] Likewise, the Mende practice of "swearing" or taking oaths has remained unaffected by colonial overlordship. If anything, swearing has become enhanced since "the coming of Government," because the administration in order to elicit the truth—in courts, commissions of enquiry, and even during elections of chief—has had to enter into the world of strong "medicines," buying them, transporting them, and overseeing their application. Swears and medicines are very closely tied to the Mende world view, and their semireligious nature precludes their quick and easy transformation.[63]

The colonial impact, then, was greatest in the political sphere. The Mende chief is not and never has been a religious figure; as Little points out, the *Poro* society among the Mende probably fulfilled the legitimizing function performed by the chief-priests of so many other African peoples.[64] This factor, plus adventitious historical circumstances, permitted the British considerable freedom in constructing and transforming Mende political institutions. More deep-rooted spheres of life have demonstrated stronger continuity with the pre-Protectorate era.

Northern and Eastern Nigeria are often put forth as extreme examples of the varied forms which Indirect Rule could take: The Emirates of Northern Nigeria, on the one hand, were adapted with only minor reforms to the service of colonial rule, while, on the other hand, the British had to manufacture entirely new political forms in order to administer the small-scale "stateless" groups in Eastern Nigeria. The Sierra Leonean version of Indirect Rule lay somewhere between these extremes. Especially in Mendeland, indigenous political forms were not

structured enough for the British simply to graft them unaltered
to the colonial hierarchy, as in the case of Northern Nigeria;[65]
but neither were the British faced with a situation where
indigenous political institutions apparently did not exist, as
among the Ibo and related peoples of Eastern Nigeria. Rather,
Indirect Rule in Mendeland involved a process of transformation by which already-existing institutions were changed recog-
nizably but not radically to fit the colonial superstructure. The
crucial determinant was the nature of the political system
encountered by the colonial conquerors in all three cases. Mende
society simply could not boast political institutions firm and
durable enough to suit the requirements of even a rudimentary
administration, and the colonial officers felt compelled to
build—on an indigenous foundation—the chiefdom structure of
local governance that persists today.

Conclusion

Mende history makes amply clear that the rubric "traditional
society" need not imply an unchanged and unchanging entity.
Mende society has undergone considerable flux for hundreds of
years, perhaps ever since its inception. On the eve of colonial
rule political forms were fluid and, if Wylie is correct, were
experiencing a fundamental metamorphosis.[66] Further change
was imposed by colonial rule in the form of innovations which
.were easily incorporated into the body of Mende political traditions. Today's chiefdoms—traditional societies—are the pro-
geny of these changes. This corroborates Zolberg's reminder
that the colonial experience should be included in our notions of
"tradition."[67]

Models which present the process of development as a clash
between the old the new, the traditional and the modern, lose
their theoretical bite if by "traditional" we do not necessarily connote "unchangeable." Traditions that respond to new impulses
are not automatically antithetical to modernity. This suggests

that the displacement model lacks congruence with the Mende experience. In the political sphere at least, crucial Mende traditions have been inherited from the colonial era, not from antiquity. Significant portions of "Native Law and Custom" were shaped by the requisites of living in a drastically changed environment—under an administrative umbrella—and are divorced in important ways from precolonial practices. This shift, in response to modern impulses, did not result in the progressive disintegration of Mende societies, as the displacement model would predict. On the contrary, they were strengthened in many respects. These changes, moreover, cannot be viewed as a displacement of the traditional by the modern. They were adaptations to new conditions, yet could be called part of the "modernization" process only in the sense that they enabled Mende chiefdoms better to deal with a modern structure, the colonial administration. When juxtaposed with the attributes of modernity put forth by most theories—specialization of function, nonascriptive criteria for office, universalistic orientation, etc.—these changes represent little more than a step sideways, from one nonmodern system to another. Indeed, from the point of view of most development theories, the imposition of the hereditary principle on the Paramount Chieftaincy was a regressive step. Yet the fact remains that Mende chiefdoms emerged from the early colonial period as more stable and more durable entities than their precolonial forebears.

These changes resemble the "manipulated response" Whitaker notes as one reaction of Northern Nigerian leadership to modern incursions. Traditional Emirate institutions have been strengthened, he maintains, by deliberate policy, by revising and fortifying traditional patterns in order to limit the impact of change. Indeed, modernity itself has strengthened tradition in some instances.[68] But in the Sierra Leonean case the initiative was taken not by traditional leadership but by the colonial authorities and later, to a smaller extent, by African politicians and administrators. As we have seen, administrative action or inaction was a key variable in deciding the success or failure of many changes in chiefdom rules. An innovation could harden into accepted tradition were it put into practice and enforced by the administration. This concurs with Whitaker's conclusion that "a structure of social and political domination decisively influences the reception and reinterpretation of innovation. . . ."[69] In the Nigerian case the Emirates were the overshadowing institutions whereas in Sierra Leone the colonial administration was the structure of dominance. Whoever the manipulators, however, the important point is that traditions can be manipulated—at least in some circumstances. Once it is accepted that traditions are changeable, then the way is open to recognizing their manipulability. Moreover, this includes the possibility that traditions can be altered, shaped, and directed to serve modern goals.

These notions instill skepticism concerning models that envision change as a holistic process within traditional societies. As we have seen, colonialism in Sierra Leone caused significant alterations in Mende political structures and the traditions that underlay them. Yet there is little evidence to indicate that these changes have induced corresponding, congruent changes in other spheres of life. Kinship and land tenure systems, cultivation techniques, and pervasive cultural institutions such as the *Poro*—all have experienced no important radical breaks with the past. To be sure, much social and economic change has taken place in rural Sierra Leone, but almost exclusively either it has involved the growth of new towns and new institutions which lay (at least partially) outside the auspices of chiefdom administrations, or else it has been the product of direct Government intervention. Little endogenous change in other spheres seems to have been precipitated by the initial political transformation of Mende chiefdoms.

The Mende experience seems to be an example of what Whitaker calls "dysrhythmic" change, a case in which change in one sphere of life remained autonomous and failed to ramify in the other spheres. This notion challenges the assumption of interdependency among sectors which underlies "eurhythmic" change and which buttresses the displacement model. We are not yet in a position to reject with confidence the displacement model and its underlying assumptions; a direct examination of specific hypotheses from the model is necessary before its relevance can be adequately assessed. But this encapsulated historical treatment casts doubt on the notion of modernization as a displacement process, suggesting instead that change in Mendeland has resembled more the process of mutual adjustment between traditionality and modernity portrayed by the synthetic model.

NOTES

1. Roughly, the Upper Mende people, also called the Ko-Mende, inhabit the area east of the Sewa River. The adjacent coastal areas have also been included in this account because of the intimate interaction of the Gallinas (Vai) and Krim people with Upper Mendeland. This centers attention on what is now known as Kenema District, but includes Kailahun, Pujehun, and (parts of) Bo Districts. Excluded are the Lower Mende, or Kpa-Mende, who experienced an earlier and slightly different contact with the British. See the account of Madam Yoko's empire in Brian H.A. Ranson, *A Sociological Study of Moyamba Town, Sierra Leone* (Zaria, Nigeria: Ahamdu Bello University, 1968).

2. The best overall account of the Mende from an anthropological point of view is Kenneth Little, *The Mende of Sierra Leone* (London: Routledge and Kegan Paul, 1951).

3. J. Bockani, "Mende Warfare," *Farm and Forest*, VI, no. 2 (Ap.-June 1945), 104-05.

4. *Ibid.*

5. See D.J. Siddle, "War-Towns in Sierra Leone: A Study in Social Change," *Africa*, XXXVIII, no. 1 (Jan. 1968), 47-56; also Peter Kup, *A History of Sierra Leone 1400-1787* (London: Cambridge University Press, 1961), pp. 120-57.

6. J.M. Malcolm, "Mende Warfare," *Sierra Leone Studies*, no. XXI (January 1939, Old Series), p. 47.

7. *Ibid.*

8. J.J. Crooks, *A History of the Colony of Sierra Leone, Western Africa* (Dublin, Cork, Belfast: Browne & Nolan, 1903), pp. 270-71.

9. Great Britain, Parliament, *Further Correspondence Respecting*

Disturbances in the Native Territories Adjacent to Sierra Leone (London: June 1886), C-4905, pp. 22-24.

10. Great Britain, Parliament, *Further Correspondence* .... (London: 1887), C-5236, p. 35.

11. *Ibid.,* p. 34.

12. Crooks, *op. cit.,* pp. 292-93; and R.P.M. Davies, *History of the Sierra Leone Battalion of the Royal West Africa Frontier Police* (n.d.), pp. 16-17.

13. N.C. Hollins, "A Short History of Luawa Chiefdom," *Sierra Leone Studies,* no. XIV (June 1929, Old Series), pp. 10-27; and Kenneth C. Wylie, "Innovation and Change in Mende Chieftaincy 1880-1896," *Journal of African History,* X, no. 2 (1969), pp. 295-308.

14. *Ibid.,* p. 302.

15. Malcolm, *op. cit.,* p. 50.

16. Compare (Kenema Provincial Archives, hereafter designated as KPA) Lower Bambara Chiefdom, Introduction of Native Administrations (KNA/389/5) p. 8; with Dodo Chiefdom, Introduction of Native Administration (KNA/392/5), pp. 1-4.

17. Interview #98, March 24, 1970. "Actually Nyagua was a stranger. He came from Wando side. When he saw that Faba of Dodo was stronger than he was, he pledged his loyalty to him. This is according to our native custom. He said, 'You are my father.' and in doing this he pledged his loyalty to the stronger man. This is often done when a strong man sees that another is even stronger; this prevents him from being attacked by the man, who might fear an encroacher or competitor. So he will say, 'You are my father,' or 'You are my elder brother.' This shows who is superior."

18. See, for instance, (KPA) Small Bo Chiefdom (KNA/398/5), pp. 13-18; Nongowa Chiefdom (EP/111), p. 2; Lower Bambara Chiefdom (KNA/389/5), p. 8; and Dodo Chiefdom (KNA/392/5), pp. 1-4.

Oral histories were recorded for Nongowa, Dama, Gaura, and Lower Bambara chiefdoms. See also Dick Simpson, "A Preliminary Political History of the Kenema Area," *Sierra Leone Studies,* no. 21 (July 1967), New Series, pp. 52-62.

19. Wylie, *op. cit.,* p. 296.

20. Walter Rodney, "A Reconsideration of the Mane Invasion of Sierra Leone," *Journal of African History,* VIII, no. 2 (1967), 219-246. See esp. p. 236.

21. Kenneth Little, "The Political Function of the Poro," *Africa,* XXXVI, no. 1 (Jan. 1966), 68.

22. Quoted in J.M.Malcolm, "Poro and Other Secret Societies in Sierra Leone," secret mimeographed pamphlet, c. 1958. In possession of present writer. p. 2.

23. *Ibid.*

24. This follows Little's use of designating the secret society in general as *Poro,* while using lower case *poro* to indicate a specific meeting of a specific local society convened to accomplish a particular objective.

25. Great Britain, Parliament, *Further Correspondence ....* (London: 1887), C-5234, pp. 97-98. See also Christopher Fyfe, *A History of Sierra Leone,* p. 462.

26. This information is found in M.K. Comber's short mimeographed account of "A History of Mendigla" in (KPA) "The Queen's Visit—Native Dancing," (G/24/1).

27. Great Britain, Parliament, *Further Correspondence ....* (London:1886), C-4905, pp. 23-24.

28. Christopher Fyfe, *Sierra Leone Inheritance* (London: Oxford Univ. Press, 1964), pp. 246-48 reprints a fascinating report by Travelling Commissioner Alldridge on this subject.

29. Kup, *op. cit.,* p. 153. Rodney, *op. cit.,* gives somewhat different detail, but the overall interpretation is quite similar.

30. (Sierra leone Archives, hereafter designated as SLA) *Native Affairs Letterbook* (1896), Letter #459, Oct. 21, 1896, "Explanation of the Protectorate Ordinance 1896—to Chiefs in the Protectorate."

31. Great Britain, Parliament, *Report By Her Majesty's Commissioner and Correspondence on the Subject of the Insurrection in the Sierra Leone Protectorate,* 1898 (London: 1899), C-9388, Part II, p. 542. Hereafter designated as *Chalmers' Report,* Parts I and II.

32. *Chalmers' Report,* Part II, p. 573. Letter from Chiefs of Sulima and Gallinas to Sir Samuel Lewis, Dec. 18, 1896. Italics added.

33. *Ibid.,* p. 138.

34. *Ibid.,* Part I, p. 145.

35. *Ibid.,* Part I, p. 108.

36. *Ibid.,* Part I, p. 73.

37. *Ibid.,* Part I, p. 81.

38. *Ibid.,* Part I, p. 123.

39. *Ibid.*, Part I, p. 168.

40. *Ibid.*, Part I, p. 170. Italics added.

41. *Ibid.*, Part I, p. 173. For further analysis of the Chalmers-Cardew debate see J.D. Hargreaves, "The Establishment of the Sierra Leone Protectorate and the Insurrection of 1898," *Cambridge Historical Journal*, 12 (1956), pp. 56-80.

42. Christopher Fyfe, *A History of Sierra Leone* (London: Oxford Univ. Press, 1962), p. 541.

43. Little, *The Mende of Sierra Leone*, pp. 178-79.

44. (KPA) *Decree Books*, vols. II-III.

45. Siddle, *op. cit.*, p. 53.

46. (KPA) "Chiefs: Elections, Appointments, Recognitions, Amalgamations" (CONF/idential/ P/2), p. 4. July 16, 1941.

47. David E. Apter, *The Political Kingdom in Uganda* (Princeton: Princeton Univ. Press, 1961), and Lloyd Fallers, *Bantu Bureaucracy* (Chicago: University of Chicago Press, 1965).

48. Protectorate Ordinance, 1927. Cap. 2.

49. (KPA) *Decree Book*, vol. II, p. 94.

50. *Ibid.*, vol. III, p. 216.

51. *Ibid.*, vol. III, p. 287.

52. (KPA) "Procedure for the Election of Chiefs," (CCP/618/A), pp. 10-11 (Aug. 4, 1953).

53. (KPA) Lower Bambara Chiefdom: Death and Election of Paramount Chiefs (KNA/389/1/vol. I), p. 140 (Nov. 15, 1957).

54. (KPA) *Decree Book*, Vol. II, p. 48.

55. (KPA) *Ibid.*, p. 225.

56. (KPA) Tunkia Chiefdom: Death and Election of Paramount Chiefs (KNA/369/1/1), p. 62 (April 28, 1945).

57. *Ibid.*, p. 51 (June 26, 1947).

58. *Ibid.*, p. 105 (August 7, 1952).

59. (KPA) Crowning of Mammy Queens (EP/3/30/01), p. 17 (Jan. 17, 1966).

60. T.J. Alldridge, *The Sherbro and its Hinterland* (London and N.Y.: Macmillan, 1901), p. 305.

61. Cap. 101.

62. On the ritual aspects of rice farming see Kenneth Little, *The Mende Upland Rice Farmer* (London, n.d.).

63. See especially W.T. Harris and Harry Sawyerr, *The Springs of Mende Belief and Conduct: A Discussion of the Influence of the Supernatural Among the Mende* (Freetown: Sierra Leone Univ. Press, 1968).

64. Kenneth Little, "The Political Function of the Poro," *Africa,* vols. 35 and 36 (Oct. 1965 and Jan. 1966).

65. A detailed comparison of one chiefdom in Sierra Leone with one Nigerian Emirate is Kenneth C. Wylie, "The Politics of Transformation: Indirect Rule in Mendeland and Abuja 1890-1914," Ph.D. Dissertation, Michigan State Univ., 1967.

66. Wylie, "Innovation and Change . . . ."

67. Aristide Zolberg, *Creating Political Order: The Party-States of West Africa* (Chicago: Rand McNally, 1966), p. 144.

68. C.S. Whitaker, Jr., "A Dysrhythmic Process of Political Change," *World Politics,* XIX (Jan. 1967), pp. 208-217.

69. C.S. Whitaker, Jr., *The Politics of Tradition: Continuity and Change in Northern Nigeria 1946-1966* (Princeton: Princeton Univ. Press, 1970), p. 457.

Chapter 4

Chiefs in the Framework of Central Politics

Although chiefs remain the focal point of local government and politics, there has arisen in recent years throughout Mendeland—and for that matter, throughout Sierra Leone—a collective voice of regret that the "chiefs have lost the respect of their people;" that the "power of the PC's has declined;" that they have "stripped themselves of dignity;" that they have become mere "errand boys for Government." While Chieftaincy in Sierra Leone has eroded to a degree far less than its counterparts in many other African nations, it nevertheless has declined in stature and authority. This chapter attempts to describe and explain the present position of Paramounts in Sierra Leone generally and Kenema District in particular. Further, it examines patterns of role conflict in an effort to test the contrasting hypotheses derived from the displacement and synthetic models of change.

Laissez-Faire (ca. 1920-1937)

Whereas the era of colonial consolidation involved considerable intervention from the Government in erecting the chiefdom edifices of rural Sierra Leone, the period that followed was marked by a willingness to allow peripheral peoples considerable internal freedom. The second stage of colonial rule was characterized by what Crowder calls a "policy of laissez-faire."[1] Few formal changes took place in the chiefdoms; little attention was given by the administration to the activities of the chiefs; supervision from the center was minimal. In central perspective, the role of Mende chiefs resembled closely Finnegan and Murray's description of Limba chiefs:

> From the governmental point of view not much was expected of chiefs. In their eyes the chief's main role was to supervise tax collection, keep the peace in his chiefdom and act as a link in what communication network there was.[2]

There were limits to this posture of laissez-faire, however. Paramount Chiefs in some instances were deposed or forced to

TABLE 4.1

Depositions and Resignations of Paramount Chiefs, Kenema District, 1904-1966

NAME		DATE	CHIEFDOM
Madam Mabundu	(I)	?	Leppiama
Malondo	(I)	1904	Leppiama
Madam Nemahun	(I)	1905	Togboma (Malegohun)
Landoh	(I)	1913	Leppiama
Bundu	(I)	1914	Kandu
Madam Humonya*	(I)	1919	Nongowa
Bockari Kekura	(I)	1924	Nongowa
Siaffa Kebbie	(L)	1938	Dama
Momo Vangahun	(?)	1939	Nongowa
Joe Quee Nyagua	(L)	1948	Lower Bambara
Brima Bunduka Dassama*	(I)	1951	Gaura
Vandi Sama*	(I)	1951	Tunkia
James Jombo*	(L)	1951	Small Bo
Kai-Samba II**	(L)	1966	Nongowa

I	=	Illiterate	*	Resignation
L	=	Literate	**	Pensioned for sickness

Source: Kenema District Decree Book, Volumes II and III.

resign as a result of gross maladministration or exploitation. The most famous case was that of Madam Humonya of Nongowa chiefdom. She was coaxed into resigning in 1919 as a result of an inquiry which found her guilty of forced labor, illegal levies, failure to appoint a Speaker, and failure to consult with her advisors. Significantly, yet another deposition took place in Nongowa during this period, while chiefdoms farther removed from Kenema, the District headquarters, incurred less supervision and interference from the administration. In general a wide range of behavior was permitted, as much by default as by the deliberate policy of bolstering chiefly authority.

Government policy enhanced the position of the chief vis-a-vis his subjects. In many chiefdoms agreements were signed arranging for a local tax in services, kind, or coin which would provide incomes for the chiefs, regularizing the unpredictable and intermittent payments of tribute which characterized the old regime. In return, ordinary people were promised immunity from labor obligations on *manja* ("state") farms. Paradoxically, however, these "treaties" served to support with Government legitimacy and power the claims that chiefs could make upon their subjects. Regularization and formalization had the effect of reducing the commoners' option of withholding payments and labor as a sanction against overdemanding chiefs.

The 1920s and 1930s marked the apogee of power and authority for chiefs in Kenema District and for chiefs throughout Sierra Leone as well. There was little external restraint on their use of courts, of labor services, of monies public or private; internal restraints were actually diminished as a result of the weight given to chiefs by Government recognition.

The Role of Chiefs Under Colonialism: The Reform Era (1937-1961)

Unharnessed chiefly rule enjoyed a longer reign in Sierra Leone than in most other British African colonies because the system of Native Administrations was not introduced until 1937.

This marks the beginning of the third stage of colonial rule, which can be called the period of reform. The Native Administration (NA) system was embodied in a series of ordinances which provided for improvements upon and more systematic supervision of chiefdom institutions. The Chiefdom Tax Ordinance (1937) and the Chiefdom Treasuries Ordinance (1937) allowed for revenues and funds from which chiefs were to receive fixed salaries according to established procedures. The Tribal Authorities Ordinance (1937) defined more clearly the duties and rights of TA's and specified procedures for the election and deposition of Paramount Chiefs. The Forced Labour Ordinance (1932) set limits to the labor that chiefs could commandeer, one effect of which was, incidentally, to legalize further the exactions which could be made in the name of chiefly rights. And the Protectorate (Amendment) Ordinance (1945) made legal provisions for local governmental institutions outside the chiefdom framework, i.e., District Councils and a Protectorate Assembly.

As Lord Hailey contends, the Native Administrations did not comprise a sharp shift from previous practice:

> . . . [T]he procedure inaugurated in 1937 did not signalize a material departure from the principals on which administration had been conducted from 1901 onwards, for during that period indigenous authorities had been utilized, though in an unsystematic manner, as agencies of local rule. The change lay rather in the fact that the Ordinance of 1937 reflected a fuller recognition of the need for the development of the Protectorate area and of a much closer attention to the methods followed in its administration.[3]

Institutionalization of the new reforms was a very gradual affair at best. Chiefdoms were reformed a few at a time, so that by 1946 there were only 120 NA's out of a total of some 200 chiefdoms.[4] Kenema District at that time had only 10 of its 16 chiefdoms organized into NA's; indeed, even today two chiefdoms (Nomo and Langrama) in the District remain "unreformed." The pace of reform was such that its cumulative impact in most chiefdoms was felt only by the late 1940's and early 1950's. In the more advanced chiefdoms, those which were established as NA's earliest in Kenema District, however, this impact was realized in the late 1930s. In both sets of cases the result was a spate of violent demonstrations against chiefs and the subsequent resignation or deposition of many of them. For Nongowa, Lower Bambara, and Dama, the advanced chiefdoms, the pattern of protest took the form of accusing unpopular chiefs of involvement with what the British called Fetish Murder Societies* and the formation of "anticannibalism" movements which pressed for their deposition. It is not clear in retrospect which chiefs, if any, were actually implicated in crimes of ritual murder, but the effect of the atmosphere of fear and vigilantism was detrimental to them. Paramount Chiefs in Dama and Nongowa were deposed and P.C. Joe Quee (grandson of Nyagua) of Lower Bambara was nearly deposed.

In the remainder of the District, among those chiefdoms which were organized later, the pattern of violence and protest took a different form and was manifested in the postwar years. In these cases bands of youngmen** attacked chiefs and their compounds, demanding their resignation or the destoolment of their Speaker. Petitions flowed into the District Commissioner's office complaining especially of forced labor and illegal levies. In 1948 disorders in Baoma chiefdom (in Bo District but adjacent to Kenema District) led to the resignation of its Paramount Chief.

---

*"Cannibalism" in this context involves murder of a victim for certain parts of his body which are thought to be key ingredients of powerful medicines. Generally it is associated with the Leopard Society and the Alligator Society. A major work on this subject, by Milan Kalous, is forthcoming.

**"Youngmen" is an oft-used category in Mendeland. It refers to males who hold no position and little power in chiefdom affairs. A youngman need not necessarily be young in age, although there is a clear tendency in Mende societies for age and power to coincide. "Elders" are those who hold power, position, and respect. It is quite possible for an "elder" to be fairly young in years, as is the case for a number of Paramount Chiefs.

In Kenema District P.C. Joe Quee-Nyagua was deposed. The next year saw serious disturbances take place in eight of the district's sixteen chiefdoms, all of them involving complaints against the chiefs. In 1950 this pattern of violence was repeated, and in neighboring Kailahun District disruptions involving thousands of people led to depositions in Luawa and Kissi Tungi chiefdoms.[5] Similar events took place in Pujehun District. By 1951 in Kenema District three additional Paramounts had resigned and a Speaker was deposed.[6]

These demonstrations against incumbent chiefs were not unique: Mendes had often ousted chiefs who had outlived their usefulness or popularity. What was unusual was the frequency and virulence of the disturbances. There are a number of factors which contribute to an explanation of this rather sudden flurry of antichief behavior.

1. Dynastic struggles underlay most of the chiefdom disputes. On the surface these disturbances appeared to be confrontations between youngmen and elders, that is, between commoners on the one hand, and those who held power and position, on the other. But actually they were less a manifestation of "rural radicalism"[7] than a violent extension of ordinary ruling house compztition. The colonial records are replete with references to the manner in which members of the chiefdom elite manipulated youngmen for their own purposes. For instance, an unsuccessful aspirant to the Paramount Chieftaincy in Small Bo succeeded in directing popular agitation against first the Speaker and then the incumbent chief, both of whom were removed from office, opening the way for a new election. In Simbaru, an unsuccessful candidate "allied with the youngmen and threatened violence and to burn down Boajibu" unless the Speaker were removed.[8] In Niawa in 1953 a cannibalism charge fabricated by the opposition house against the Paramount Chief was accompanied by "crowds of youngmen used in an attempt to instill fear."[9] The colonial officers generally concurred that it "is the youngmen who do the shouting and the demonstrating and the rioting. But it is their fathers who, if they do not direct them, at least support them. Behind every 'youngmen' trouble is a group of elders."[10]

People interviewed also made unmistakably clear the relationship between youngmen and elders. One example is this statement made by a Paramount Chief:

> The tactic of using the youngmen is very common in this country. It has been used for a long time. If ever you see the youngmen aroused and politically active, you know that some bigman is behind them. The common people in this country would never do anything without the backing of a bigman. A bigman is always behind the activities of the youngman.[11]

In most cases, these protests against chiefs were planned and instigated by men of influence in the "out" ruling houses. Almost all chiefdoms have an opposition minority, centered usually on a second (and/or third, fourth, etc.) ruling house but occasionally on an unsuccessful candidate or a section historically opposed to the headquarters town. It is this built-in competition, most often structurally defined by ruling-house rivalries, which underlies and sustains almost all conflict at the chiefdom level. It is not unique to the "period of reform," but no explanation of local politics—violent or nonviolent—can be initiated without bringing forth this crucial factor.

This suggests strongly that rural violence during this period was not so much a popular upwelling against an exploitative system as it was a technique for removing opponents. It was rebellion, not revolution. This should serve to qualify the interpretations of Kilson and Cartwright, who have portrayed rural revolt in Sierra Leone as conflict between chiefs and commoners. Chiefdoms in the Northern Province have indeed erupted into generalized revolt against ruling elites, particularly during the 1955-6 disturbances when large numbers of Temne and Susu chiefs were besieged by popular forces.[12] But in Mendeland popular violence typically has been channeled by dynastic conflict. Thus, in addition to a distinction between revolution and rebellion, we can further differentiate between two types of rebellion: (1) where insurrectionary activity is to a large extent stimulated by conflict within the ruling elite; and (2) where elite and commoners come into violent conflict directly.[13]

This contrast between modes of rebellion in Mendeland and Temneland has certain parallels with traditional Burundi and Rwanda. Rebellion in Burundi derived largely from dynastic struggles, whereby nonelite participation in violence was mobilized by rival elite groups. In Rwanda, on the other hand, rebellion took the form of direct confrontation between elite (Tutsi) and nonelite (Hutu).[14] Just as in Mendeland, rebellion in Burundi occurred frequently and seemed derivatively to strengthen the society through release of built-up pressure and renewal of ties between leaders and followers—in the manner described by Gluckman.[15] In Temneland and Rwanda, however, rebellion occurred relatively less frequently but involved widespread eruptions which precipitated repressive measures and accretions of central authority. This type of conflict in the Rwanda case shifted into a form of outright revolution which of course was not replicated in Temneland, but the disturbances which swept Northern Sierra Leone in 1955-6 were far more serious in scope and effect than the numerous but limited outbursts which intermittently occur in Mendeland. Rebellion seems to have a greater safety-valve effect in Mende chiefdoms than in their Temne counterparts.

2. As reforms were institutionalized, opposition factions within chiefdoms were given new issues with which to appeal to the administration in their campaigns to unseat chiefs. If an opposition ruling house were too impatient to wait until the incumbent died, then the only recourse was to have him deposed. The administration—"Government"—was the only means to this end. Opposition strategy took the form of a search for issues which not only would attract the administration's attention but which would be deemed sufficient grounds for deposition. As reforms were legislated and put into practice, the range of issues available to an ambitious opposition expanded. Forced labor, illegal levies, improper use of chiefdom funds, extortion, failure to consult with the TA—all became the subject of petitions and demonstrations. The Commissioner of the Southeast Province described the process by which dissatisfied elements searched for effective issues. Noting how "palavers" had become a regular feature of public life, he predicted that the administration could:

... expect a continuous series of events, now to a sterotyped pattern:—a sudden flaring up of opposition; mass demonstrations by the young men; the throwing up of leaders in the opposition; the framing of accusations, varying until they find one which catches the fancy of Government (át the moment it is cannibalism as a first tryout; there are signs that, as this has failed, offenses against Bundu and Porro will be the favourites. Past successes have been Porro offenses, forced labour, forced levies, manja farms and sexual depravity).[16]

Moreover, by "legitimizing" a number of these issues, the reforms written into the NA system gave voice to what apparently were deep-felt complaints on the part of commoners against their leaders. That is to say, the effect to reform was not exclusively an expanded opportunity for opposition leaders cynically to get an audience for their antichief charges; genuine grievances did indeed exist, forced labor being prime among them, and the new reforms advertised that it was not only permissible but possible to protest effectively against chiefly behavior.

3. This point leads directly to a third factor contributing to the heightened tempo of attacks on Mende chiefs. This is simply that some of them were losing popularity among their people, due primarily to an impoverishment of the personal ties between ruler and ruled. To an extent greater than most African societies, the Mende chief owed much of his authority to personal qualities rather than to religious status or to institutional position. The individual chief who judged cases fairly, who reciprocated the tribute given him by his followers, who listened to what they had to say, who ate with them, married their daughters, protected and helped them—this chief was likely to enjoy widespread support in this chiefdom. This inheritance from the precolonial era is clear: Followers gravitated to the leader who could provide what was needed at the time, most often protection. The role of chief had changed from its precolonial incarnation substantively but not structurally. Military security was of course no longer the *sine qua non* of chiefly success. But its functional equivalent was an expectation on the part of followers that their chiefs should

act instrumentally to secure concrete benefits for them. This "pivotal attribute" was accompanied by few additional role requirements other than a general expectation that chiefs act in friendly and generous fashion toward their people. The role did not countenance the kind of remote imperiousness embodied in the highest offices of some other West African societies, such as the *Mogho Naba* of the Mossi or the *Obas* of the Yoruba. Chiefs were expected to forge direct connections with their subjects, through friendship, clientship, kinship, marriage, or whatever other relationship contributed to close contact. Personal ties underwrote the relations between leader and follower in a manner reminiscent of the big-city bosses in America between the Civil War and ca. 1930.[17] In both cases, rule was, following Weber, of the patrimonial sort.[18]

In Mendeland, these personal ties became attenuated as a result of the reforms embodied in the NA system. A fixed slary replaced the tribute (whether regularized or not) paid directly to the chief by individuals and families. The Treasury—keystone of each Native Administration—inserted an institutional buffer between a chief and his individual supporters, enabling at least a nominal distinction between public funds and a Paramount Chief's private purse. The Chiefdom Clerk became less a private secretary to the chief and more a public servant. Prior to the reforms many chiefs hired clerks—often from their own ruling family—to handle their business with the wider world. The introduction of NA's changed this by providing for a civil servant responsible for the NA treasury and court records. In the past many chiefs were themselves clerks prior to their election; this afforded them valuable experience in local administration and widespread contact with local political forces. But the reforms brought central supervision which attempted, often unsuccessfully, to discourage such entanglement in local affairs. And in the spirit of reform, the administration encouraged the election to chiefship of literates, especially those educated at the Bo School for the Sons and Nominees of Chiefs. At least temporarily, this proved disastrous. Young, literate, and presumably enlightened chiefs led considerably more precarious lives than the "old greybeards" during this period. They grew more aloof and private; left their chiefdoms more often; conversed directly, in English, with British officials; and acquired friends from outside among lawyers, politicans, and intellectuals. The less perspicacious among them flaunted their good fortune. In short, education put chiefs out of touch with their people, imposing a cultural barrier. By 1957, the last seven chiefs to have been deposed in Sierra Leone were literate. The unsettling effects of education have, however, declined in recent years as literacy has spread throughout the countryside, reducing the gulf between the enlightened and the unwashed.

Further, a rupture of far-reaching consequence took place in the field of judicial reform. Section 8 of the Protectorate Ordinance (1933) authorized the Provincial Commissioner, if he saw fit, to appoint a President of the Chiefdom Court, to sit in place of the Paramount Chief. The power to replace the PC with a Court President was used at first only rarely, but by the late 1950's the administration increasingly applied its option of removing judicial functions from the chief's perquisites, and by the time the Chiefdom Courts Ordinance (1963) was enacted, in all chiefdoms Court Presidents rather than Paramount Chiefs controlled local courts. The effect of this reform should not be underestimated. Chiefdom people looked to the Paramount to settle their differences; he was the man who had the power to reward or punish them; the judge of cases very much affected the fortunes of the litigous villages and towns of Mendeland. To have this removed from the chief cut sharply into his prestige. Interviewees, in responding to my questions as to why the chiefs now seem to command less respect than in the past, were almost unanimous in pointing to the imposition of Court Presidents as a major cause. The following is a sample of their explanations:

> Originally the chiefs were protectors of people and leaders in war. Indirect Rule took over these original duties of chiefs; the army and police did these things. Then the courts were taken over by Government, another important function of the chiefs. This was a very significant change. It was the beginning of the end.[19]

Paramount Chiefs have lost a great deal of power because of Court Presidents. Court Presidents now have the power to fine people and make decisions. This has meant that people now go to the Court President rather than to the PC. It has also taken away income from the PC.[20]

The main reason for the decline in the authority of the PC's has been the introduction of the Court Presidents. People in this country respect the man who makes important decisions for them, or against them. Once the PC no longer ran the court, he no longer had that power over people. Their respect for him has gone way down.[21]

4. In addition to reducing the vibrancy of the personal ties between chiefs and people, Court Presidents also represented a competing pole of power in each chiefdom. This latter can be viewed as another factor associated with the reform period and its deleterious effect on chieftaincy in Mendeland. Not only Court Presidents but politicians, Members of Parliament, lawyers and Ministers appeared on the local scene as a result of constitutional changes at the national level paralleling local reforms. Each cast himself as lawmaker and potentate, and in doing so at the local level each represented a separate pole of power at least potentially competitive with chiefly power. This is how one Paramount Chief put it:

It is true that the authority of the PC's has declined. Since the coming of politics, the PC is no longer the only source of advice and law for the common people. Members of Parliament come to the people and say that they make laws and that they are the supreme authority. Ministers say that they are in charge. And chiefs are boxed in by political parties. The common people no longer can be swayed or forced to vote as the PC says.[22]

The policy of reform, including constitutional changes, restructured chiefdom politics, replacing the unipolar (chief) and bipolar (chief-opposition ruling house) system of the laissez-faire period with a multipolar (chief-opposition-Court President-politician-lawyer, etc.) constellation of power.[23]

This vastly increased leverage against the chiefs. Chiefdoms no longer were isolated units visited twice yearly by the District Commissioner. Alliances with powerful elements operating at the national level became possible. This was crucial for center-local relations because, as we have seen, chiefdom politics are determined ultimately by factors which originate *outside* the chiefdoms, most particularly administrative decisions.

During the 1950's, the British administrators became increasingly and painfully aware of lawyers and politicians as direct competitors with themselves. DC's in their secret reports frequently complained of outside intervention in chiefdom affairs.[24] Lawyers, especially those from Freetown, saw chiefdom disputes as a profitable source of clients; lawyerly intervention greatly complicated deposition proceedings; and, as "upcountry" people entered the law profession, there was indeed a conscious effort to constrain the arbitrary authority of British administrators, as exemplified by the career of Albert Margai, who made no secret of his distaste for District Commissioners.

Politicians played a similar role in multiplying the loci of power at the chiefdom level. On the surface, politics appeared to be a force favorable to chiefly interests. The dominant political movement of the 1950's was the Sierra Leone Peoples' Party (SLPP), which was closely allied to the chiefs, who also had the option of reaching for allies at the national level to buttress their positions at the local level. In supporting the SLPP, individual chiefs made themselves more secure in office. It is significant that the initial flood of violence and depositions during the late 1940's and early 1950's abated suddenly. This abatement coincided with the appointment for the first time of SLPP leaders to ministerial posts. Dr. Milton Margai's installation as Chief Minister in 1953 was particularly important; henceforth, most high-level policy was nonantagonistic if not favorable to chiefly interests. As Kilson contends, the SLPP leaders, in exchange for political support, guaranteed the chiefs a large measure of control over local affairs.[25] Yet the reverse side of the coin is often neglected by SLPP watchers. The chiefs had suffered a major depletion of their autonomy. Their relationship with the SLPP was indeed a reciprocal affair. No longer beholden to the administration alone, chiefs became dependent upon politicians as well. If it is true that individual chiefs derived a strengthened lease on their incumbencies, it is no less true that the institution of chieftaincy was rendered less secure, contingent as it had become upon the vagaries of politics. "The coming of politics" is an oft-heard phrase in Mendeland; it refers precisely to this new incursion from outside the chiefdoms.

5. A fifth factor can be labeled "administrative deficiency." British officials were inclined to give administrative explanations for the uprisings. They saw rapid turnover, inadequate personnel, and insufficient supervision over chiefdom affairs as matters which contributed significantly to the volatile conditions in the troublesome localities. And indeed during this period the administration was experiencing substantial flux, as Table 4.2 shows. Writing in early 1950 one DC put it this way:

The troubles in this District have been due to recent frequent changes more than to any other single cause. Each new DC has to

TABLE 4.2
Kenema District, Turnover of
District Commissioners

YEAR	NO. OF DC'S
1949	2
1950	4
1951	5
1952	1
1953	3
1954	5
1955	5
1956	4
1957	2

Source: (KPA) U/2/2. Kenema
District, Annual Reports, Volume II.

discover afresh who are the constitutional minorities in each chiefdom; sometimes he fails to do so, with serious results.[26]

This condition, plus the fact that the average chiefdom was visited only about twice a year,[27] meant that in general DC's were operating on less than intimate knowledge of the people whom they were charged with supervising and protecting. Violence in the chiefdoms was in part simply a means of demanding the attention of overburdened and otherwise unresponsive administrative officers.

Perhaps, however, officials were apt to exaggerate their own importance. There is no direct relationship between local disturbances and impaired administrative *rapport* with chiefdom people, as a glance at Table 4.2 will suggest. The more peaceful mid-1950s experienced the same high rate of turnover as did the period of disturbance. Generally the reforms of the 1950s had the effect of removing the DC's monopoly of communications and control, reducing his role as sole link between the central and the chiefdom levels. At their inception in 1947, the District Councils were intended as modern, democratic bodies which would eventually take over most of the DC's functions. Furthermore, the DC lost his prime, persistent link with the chiefdoms when the Court Messenger force was abolished and replaced by regular police organizations in early 1954. The proliferation of new government departments thinned his hitherto multifarious contacts with localities. And perhaps most importantly, as we have seen, politicans and lawyers began to rival the DC's as men of consequence for chiefdom people. The precise effect of these changes on the institution of chieftaincy is difficult to assess. Clearly, however, the institutional links between center and locality became more complex and more numerous. A multiplicity of roles and a multiplexity of power poles emerged during the reform period, competing with the simple, paternal relationship between DC and PC which had so long characterized government and administration in the provinces.

6. This final consideration takes into account the social mobilization extant during the postwar years. Works of a general

nature are already available and are adequate for describing the overall effects of new towns, new associations, new classes, and new schools.[28] The years 1945-1960 were a period of social and economic ferment in eastern Sierra Leone. The return of servicemen from duty in Burma, the spread of a moneyed class, and the expansion of commerical and administrative centers like Kenema, were among the causes and symptoms of postwar social mobilization. The 1950's were years of particular prosperity for Kenema District, fed at first by high prices for cash crops and then by a diamond boom. Large-scale migrations, especially to and from the mining areas, produced a "floating population" far less susceptible to social control than the more inert elements which had so long comprised the foundation of stability and order in the area. The construction of roads to almost all chiefdoms facilitated this mobility, enabling rural people not only access to trading centers but, for the more restless among them, egress from the **limitations** of small-scale communities. The impact of new schools is analogous; among other things, they represented an avenue of escape from rural conditions.

The direct effect of this mobilization upon chieftaincy is difficult if not impossible to postulate in specific terms. In general, however, it can be said that its influence complemented the political effects of reform discussed above. That is, economic development as well as the political changes imposed by reform contributed to an alteration of the structure of choice. Just as the chief was no longer the only powerful man in his chiefdom, he was also no longer the only man of wealth. Just as increasing complexity multiplied local channels of access to political and administrative power at the center, so too burgeoning economic activities enhanced the opportunities for a livelihood outside the chiefdom structure.

In short, increasing complexity and specialization during the reform period introduced new roles and new sources of power which sometimes complemented but more often competed with the Paramount Chiefs. (See Figure 4.1) Similar phenomena circumscribed the role of District Commissioner. The crucial center-local link of the old regime, the relationship between DC

Figure 4.1
Proliferation of Roles and Poles of
Power During the Reform Period

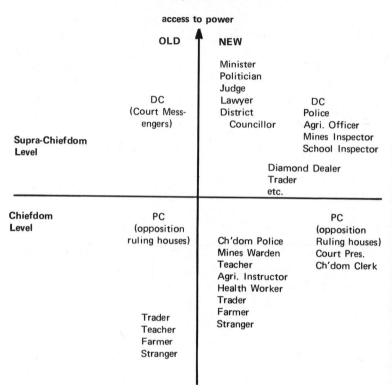

access to power

	OLD	NEW	
		Minister	
		Politician	
		Judge	
	DC	Lawyer	DC
	(Court Mess-	District	Police
	engers)	Councillor	Agri. Officer
			Mines Inspector
Supra-Chiefdom			School Inspector
Level			
		Diamond Dealer	
		Trader	
		etc.	

Chiefdom	PC		PC
Level	(opposition		(opposition
	ruling houses)	Ch'dom Police	Ruling houses)
		Mines Warden	Court Pres.
		Teacher	Ch'dom Clerk
		Agri. Instructor	
		Health Worker	
		Trader	
	Trader	Farmer	
	Teacher	Stranger	
	Farmer		
	Stranger		

and PC, was infringed by a proliferation of competing links. This expanded the opportunities for center-local alliances and rendered less dominant the position of Paramount Chief.

But the role of Paramount Chief was supplemented not supplanted by these new roles brought by modernity. Its authority declined in a relative, not absolute sense. Moreover, there was no systematic conflict between its internal attributes and the new expectations aroused by the reform era. Conflict abounded, it is true. Politicians, lawyers, civil servants, and of course oppositon ruling houses all found themselves from time to time at odds with individual chiefs. But, with the exception of opposition ruling houses, this was not a result of thoroughgoing incompatibility between role sets but rather a product of particular circumstances. As often as not, these same role holders were in alliance with chiefs when other circumstances obtained. The behavior of opposition houses was, as we have discussed, not an attack on the *role* of Paramount Chief but merely a symptom of their desire to substitute themselves for the incumbents. In large measure the overt conflict associated with chiefs during the reform era was the product of these "out" groups. Far from representing an assault on a traditional institution from modern forces, this kind of conflict attested to the vibrancy and desirability of a role inherited from the past.

Further support for this interpretation is discovered in the nature of the Sierra Leone nationalist movement, which reached its height, if it can be called that, during the reform era. Anticolonial nationalism in Sierra Leone never took on the mass proportions of, say, Ghana or, to a lesser extent, Nigeria. The British simply did not resist what they had come to accept as an inevitable movement toward eventual independence. If anything, they hastened the schedule through self-government and then Independence by proposing constitutional advancements before mass opinion had been aroused to demand them. As a result, the process of transition from colonial to independent status was an elite affair.[29] It was not, moreover, a matter of the "modernized" African elite struggling against a coalition of colonialists and chiefs, as the conventional version of emerging nationalism in the Third World would suggest. Rather, once it became clear that the British were about to evacute, three African elites—the Creoles, the educated men of wealth in the provinces, and the chiefs—came into conflict with each other in the scramble to take power and to shape the structure of future politics. In its twilight years, the British colonial administration played much more the role of mediator than antagonist in its relationship with these three elites.

By and large during the formative 1951-61 decade before Independence, the two provincial groups managed to coalesce against the Creoles, who had threatened to dominate the peripheral majority from its minority stronghold centered in Freetown. This is not to say that the chiefs and the new elite formed a "natural" alliance. Especially in the years immediately after WW II the new elite, composed mostly of teachers and professionals, objected strenuously to the predominate role allotted to chiefs in the new provincial institutions brought by the reform era. Parallelling the advancement at the chiefdom level embodied in the Native Administrations were such supralocal innovations as the Protectorate Assembly and the District Councils, and both were heavily saturated with chiefly participation. The educated elite in response founded the Sierra Leone Organization Society (SOS) in July 1946 as a means for protesting the subjugation of the "Progressive and younger elements" to the "present monopoly over Protectorate representation which Chiefs hold in the District Councils, the Protectorate Assembly, the Legislative Council, and the Executive Council."[30]

The chiefs and the new men were clear competitors for power and influence among the hinterland masses, but for a number of reasons the gap between them was narrowed substantially in 1951 when the founding of the SLPP allied them in an overt political movement. First, and most important, both chiefs and the educated elite had common cause in the effort to staunch the Creole bid for hegemony which surfaced during the extended (1947-50) debate over the new "Stevenson" constitution. Differences within the protectorate elite paled in comparison with their mutual distaste for such political groups as the National Council for the Colony of Sierra Leone (NC), which stood for perpetuating Creoledom's privileged position. Second, the conflict between chiefs and the educated elite was not so much a matter of hard-and-fast principles as it was a problem of sharing power. The SOS did not want to eliminate chiefs and the rural institutional apparatus which underlay them; they simply wanted a greater voice in protectorate affairs, one commensurate with their status as a special—educated—elite.

Likewise, the chiefs presented no united front against sharing power. Indeed, the more articulate and influential among them, such as PC Julius Gulama, PC Bai Koblo, and PC Kai-Samba I (of Kenema District), spoke in favor of colonial proposals for opening up provincial institutions to a wider range of participaton. Third, the two elites had much in common beyond their desire to advance protectorate interests vis-a-vis Creoles. Many chiefs were educated, having attended the same prestigious secondary schools (Bo School, Albert Academy) which launched their protectorate brethren into the new elite. Many chiefs prior to their election took jobs as teachers, druggists, health workers, clerks, and traders—precisely the occupational characteristics which lent the new elite its "modern" cast. And of course members of both elites formed a network of kinship and friendship ties, since most of the new men belonged to ruling families or owed their success to chiefly favor early in their careers. To speak of them as two separate elites is to obfuscate the myriad socioeconomic threads which drew them together into a loosely-knit class capable of taking concerted political action when necessary.

Fourth, the chiefs should not be envisioned as having been a brake on the movement towards greater national self-assertion. The chiefs were not drawn reluctantly into the fold by an activist new elite bent on mobilizing against colonialism. In many respects the opposite sequence took place in the Sierra Leone case. In 1940 the first Chiefs' Conference assembled chiefs from throughout the Protectorate. Unlike most other developments during the reform era, it was not an institution delivered unsolicited by the colonial administration to the African population. Rather it was convened in response to demands from chiefs for a forum to discuss Protectorate-wide issues and to advise the administration of opinion among chiefs and their people. Chiefs did not hesitate to exercise their advisory function, often to the point of sharp criticism of colonial policy. The Conference met such a need that it became an annual affair until 1946 when its essential features were absorbed by the newly-founded Protectorate Assembly and the District Councils. Chiefs were also the most instrumental element in reviving the Protectorate Educational Progressive Union (PEPU), an organization which pressed for equalizing the educational status of hinterland and Freetown youth. It was only after PEPU became active again in 1946 that the SOS was formed by the new elite as a counterweight to chiefly initiative. The educated chiefs especially proved themselves to be anything but "Government stooges." Chiefs in general avoided the kinds of "dual role" conflict— incompatibilities between colonial and popular expectations— prevalent in other African colonies, primarily because mass expectations remained largely unaffected by nationalist currents but also because chiefs themselves were among the vanguard elements of whatever nationalist movement existed.

Finally, Dr. Milton Margai represented precisely the kind of leadership which could unite the two elites. The grandson of a chief and son of a wealthy merchant; a founder of both PEPU and SOS; a medical doctor who worked through secret societies like *Poro, Wunde,* and *Sande (Bundu)* in a manner which brought him into contact with "big men" throughout the provinces; a leader who had encouraged chiefs to assert themselves against the colonial administration—Margai was a true synthesis of both camps. When in 1951 the SOS decided to convert itself into a political party and to join forces with PEPU, the SLPP was born and Dr. Margai was chosen leader in the effort to sweep the upcoming election.

> Among the Protectorate men, there was little doubt that Dr. Margai should lead the new party. He was the oldest among the educated men, and age produced deference. Equally important, as the principal advisor to the chiefs, and a man of highly conservative inclinations, he was the most acceptable to the leaders who still held the confidence of the bulk of the Protectorate population, and who more immediately controlled the **election of all** representatives from the Protectorate.[31]

A movement almost completely devoid of organizational muscle, the SLPP became beholden to local power structures and "bigmen"—especially chiefs—throughout the provinces for electoral support. It was at this very early state in its development that the SLPP evolved the tacit agreement which was to sustain it in power for a decade and a half: The chiefs would lend their support to the new elite at the central level in return for a freer hand at the local level. "Pa" Margai was perfectly suited for overseeing such a *modus vivendi.*

The interests, then, of the chiefs and the modern elite were neither identical nor antagonistic, but rather converging. In the vocabulary of role·theory, new expectations and new roles associated with the rising educated elite introduced incompatibilities within the role of Paramount Chief. But this represented a challenge neither to the entire role nor to any of its essential attributes. The new elite came into conflict with chiefs only with regard to certain peripheral and transitory elements of their evolving role, e.g., domination of the Provincial Assembly and other Protectorate institutions—matters which were easily adjusted through compromise and sharing. This kind of role conflict is an example of Pattern 6, whereby the incompatibilities which do exist are characterized by limited and intermittent conflict between some expectations from the central level (e.g., the new elite) and some expectations from the peripheral level (e.g., chiefdom elders), but not wholesale confrontation. In similar fashion we can depict the antichief violence which took place at the local level during the reform era as role conflict which approximates Pattern 4, incompatibility between some expectations arising from local society (e.g., a desire for less corruption) and some elements of chiefly behavior (e.g., extortionary levies). Again, this represents a pattern in which the Paramount chieftaincy *qua* role was not under challenge. In Mendeland, the attacks on chiefs and their property were motivated by a desire to rectify specific abuses and, even more so, to replace incumbents. There was little impetus during this period to relegate "the N.A. system to the rubbish can of history where it belongs," as Kilson would have it.[32]

Post-Independence (1961-Present)

Most of the reform-era tendencies discussed above persisted into the next stage, the post-Independence period. There is no sharp dividing line separating the two periods. Independence was more a formality than a major shift in power, since Africans by the late 1950's had control of most ministries. Moreover, the program of reform embodied in the NA system was continued after Independence, although perhaps at a slower pace. Yet politics in Sierra Leone as it reached fuller expression following the departure of the British, brought into stark relief the nature of the pressures and contradiction to which chiefs were subject. Paramount chiefs in Mendeland—and to a large extent, throughout Sierra Leone—have been subject to cross pressures largely because they lack a well-defined and widely accepted role in the *central* system. Expectations which issue from the center are contradictory, being composed of three separate tendencies any one of which would provide chiefs with a reasonably clear-cut position in the national framework, but which in combination make for ambiguity and conflict. For the sake of expository convenience, these tendencies will be presented as if they represent separate roles, but it should be remembered that they form a composite which defines the chief's role from central perspective.

THE ROLE OF NEUTRAL FIGUREHEAD

The colonial administration had strived to inculcate the notion that chiefs should remain aloof from politics, that as life-long rulers they had no need for partisan involvement. This norm persisted, perhaps with increased strength, after Independence. It is common to hear that Paramount Chiefs are "natural rulers" and that they should be "above politics" or "independent of politics" in order to maintain the dignity of their office. This standard is a common inheritance from British colonialism and has subjected chiefs in many places to what Whitaker calls "The Myth of Neutrality" in writing about Northern Nigerian

Emirs.[33] For similar reasons, the norm of neutrality in Sierra Leone as in Nigeria was contradicted by structural and political factors which drew chiefs deeply into the partisan fold.

Most important was the sheer fact that the Government was crucial for the future and security of each Paramount Chief. Deposition was a matter initiated and conducted *outside* the chiefdom structure, so a chief looked first to the Government for assurance that his tenure of office was secure. (Although PC's are elected by the Tribal Authorities, they are in the last event appointed by the Government.) Depositon or the threat of deposition was used by the British as the ultimate means of control over the "natural rulers" they so solicitously protected. Independence brought no change in this basic relationship between center and periphery.

The norm of neutrality was strained by the fact that Paramount Chiefs became integral parts of formal institutions at all levels of government. The Sierra Leonean political framework endows chiefs with considerable official power and influence not only in their chiefdoms but in the District Councils, in the House of Representatives, and in the Cabinet as well. This heavy participation in the day-to-day business of government vitiates the notion of chiefly independence from narrow politics.

At the local level, Paramount Chiefs remain the principal figures in the Native Administrations*, empowered with considerable executive and administrative authority, even though their judicial functions have been officially rescinded. Their position at the lowest rung of the administrative hierarchy which eminates from Freetown places in their hands the kind of regulatory and budgetary powers most subject to debate among rural folk. Chiefdom finance is among the most prickly issues. Peculation, illegal levies, incompetence, inordinate expenditures devoted to "hereditary" institutions (e.g., chiefs' salaries), and declining capacity to promote local economic development pro-

*At Independence, Native Administrations were renamed Chiefdom Administrations; Tribal Authorities were renamed Chiefdom Councils; and District Commissioners were renamed District Officers.

jects are among the charges aimed at chiefs and their rural administrations.[34] Recent efforts to intensify central supervision have improved the situation, but the fact remains that Paramount Chiefs are heavily involved in the spending of local funds. "Neutrality" is hardly the appropriate expectation for a position so critically located in the heart of politics.

Similar comments apply to the district level. A core theme in the genesis of the District Councils has been the role of Paramount Chiefs. District Councils evolved from the conferences of chiefs that took place during the 1940's, and while there has been a *de jure* trend to increase popular representation, chiefs *de facto* have been able to preserve their position as the most powerful element in the Councils.[35]

In Sierra Leone generally and Kenema District particularly, the District Councils since Independence have miscarried as instruments of local government and regional development. They have failed to engender within themselves a sense of corporate responsibility and identity; corruption and laxity have tainted them in the eyes of local populaces as merely another layer of governmental tax collection; their affairs have been infused with minimal popular participation; they have failed to sustain a capacity to provide needed services at the district level—the many functions which had been assumed by the Councils during the reform era were, by 1965, being *returned* to the chiefdoms and the central administration as tasks too burdensome to be performed at the district level; and they have failed spectacularly to exert control over their own financial resources. The pathology of their degeneration is reflected in their budgetary accounts. Kenema District Council offers a particularly striking example. At one time KDC was the wealthiest District Council in Sierra Leone. By the late 1960s it was able neither to pay its staff on time nor to cover many of its outstanding debts. Its General Reserve Fund diminished from Le 61,780 in 1961 to Le 2,906 in 1967/8, a result of persistent deficits in annual accounts.[36]

The military government (NRC) during its year in office suspended the District Councils and established Committees of Management in their stead. The APC government continued this practice of appointing chiefs and "bigmen" to serve as Council members rather than allowing popular elections. But at least in the case of Kenema District, little improvement has ensued. Structural factors remain unaltered, the same problems extant. The same staff is employed; the same unsatisfactory sources of income continue to frustrate efforts to improve services; favoritism and **corruption** persist and irreducible current expenditures still consume the bulk of revenues.

Kilson argues that the poor performance of the Councils stems from the heavy participation of chiefs in their institutional makeup.[37] For Kenema District, this is in one sense accurate, but in another sense it begs the question. True, Paramount Chiefs have been thoroughly immersed in the corruption, irresponsibility, and mismanagement associated with KDC; there is no gainsaying their culpability, although more "modern" elements of the elite have been equally blameworthy. But on the other hand, chiefs have lent stature to the Council. There is serious question whether it would have succeeded at all had there not been this institutional connection between Council and chiefdom, particularly since the Council had to perform its actual services at the grassroots level, where the cooperation of chiefdom authorities was essential. Early leaders like PC Kai-Samba I lent their imprimatur during its fledgling years. And Paramount Chiefs continue to command and transfer to higher levels the psychological support of the population at large. There is no movement to exclude them from any form of local government; of all the interviewees who expressed themselves concerning the District Council, only one—himself a PC's son—thought that Paramount Chiefs should be removed from its membership. Rather than being the more "rational" form of local government, as Kilson contends,[38] the District Councils have proved to be inferior to the Chiefdom Administrations. They have been institutional stepchildren, parasitically dependant upon higher and lower levels of government for the bulk of their economic and political resources. KDC and most of the other District Councils throughout Sierra Leone have failed primarily because of this inability to generate their own sustenance. The chiefdoms, on the other hand, for all their deficiencies have remained the bedrock of local governance. The APC Government has apparently taken this point of view, because recently President Stevens abolished all District Councils (and their Committees of Management) and declared that in the future *greater* reliance will be placed on Paramount Chiefs and chiefdom institutions to fill the void.[39]

Paramount Chiefs did not represent a fundamental cause of the Council's demise. Rather, their involvement in the seamy side of KDC affairs was symptomatic of a general institutional fault which strained all the elements, not only chiefs, which were brought in to shore up an unsound structure. More to the point for purposes of this chapter, by deliberate institutional design Paramount Chiefs were placed in positions upon which conflict and controversy were centered. As members of the KDC they were drawn unavoidably into the partisan fold simply because of the Council's importance for the day-to-day political and economic affairs of the district. Having been placed in these institutional positions, the chiefs were hardly well-suited for enacting the "neutral figurehead" role expected of them first by the British and then by many members of the central African elite. Instead of encouraging them to be "above politics" the District Councils thrust chiefs into the thick of the fray.

Finally, Paramount Chiefs have been assigned institutional positions at the central level of government. We have already mentioned how the Constitution provides for one Paramount Chief from each of Sierra Leone's twelve districts to be elected to the House of Representatives. This has had a number of consequences, all of them working against the norm of chiefly independence from narrow politics:

1. A PC wishing to sit in Parliament must campaign among the Tribal Authorities of his district. This brings him into competition with other chiefs desiring the position.

2. The twelve Paramount Chief Members of Parliament cannot act as autonomous legislators. They bridge the separation of legislative and executive powers, for they are paid by, supervised by, and beholden to the executive branch of government. This has led to a convention by which Paramount Chief MP's always

vote *en bloc* in favor of the party in power. This removes a considerable decision-making burden from their shoulders, but does not erase their identification with the policies and politics of the party in power. The chiefs are the most disciplined members of the Government party, guaranteeing its leadership 12 votes out of 72 even before it begins the process of mustering support in Parliament.

3. This identification of chiefs with the Government of the day is enhanced by the practice of bringing PC's into the Cabinet, usually as Ministers Without Portfolio.

4. During periods of **leadership** succession, however, there is, almost by definition, ambiguity about who forms the Government of the day. These transitions put unusual pressure on chiefs because their rule of thumb—"support the party in power"—does not apply. The Constitution is singularly silent concerning the role of chiefly MP's during leadership crises. Should they be counted when forming a new Government, or is their status as clients of the old Government sufficient to disqualify them as full voting members of Parliament? Lack of agreement on this question contributed to the crisis and coup d'etat following the General Election of March 1967. The Governor-General decided that the PC's should not be counted and consulted in the process of appointing a Prime Minister. The military junta disputed this, claiming that it was necessary to wait until the results of the Paramount Chief elections were available.[40] Whatever the merits and demerits in this particular issue, under the present Constitution chiefs are likely to come under strong partisan pressure whenever the future of the party in power is in doubt.

The concatenation of these institutional factors at the local, district, and central levels has drawn chiefs deep into the political vortex. It is difficult if not impossible for a PC to assume the role of "neutral figurehead" in more than passing fashion because his *de facto* and *de jure* powers as well as his dependence upon the Government induce him and the royal dignity into the partisan world. For such a role to prove noncontradictory, it would be necessary for chiefs to give up most of their day-to-day involvement in the business of government. This in turn would entail replacing chiefs and chiefdoms with other institutions of government, especially at the local level. No such development is in sight. State and party apparatuses in Sierra Leone presently are simply too weak to penetrate deeply enough into rural society to absorb the functions now performed by "traditional" rulers.

THE ROLE OF PARTY AGENT

The myth of neutrality was further corroded by the advent of party activity. As long as "Government" and "administration" were synonymous during the colonial era there was little difficulty with the notion of being "above politics." But as Independence approached and as "Government" became comprised of elected representatives and party leaders, neutrality became a dilemma. The structure of competition at the central level changed, replacing a system with no—or muted—competition with rivalry between at least two political parties. A chief came under strong pressure to "pledge his loyalty"—a commonly-uttered phrase in Sierra Leone—to the Government. This connotes more than mere service as a good chief. It has come to mean that chiefs are expected to support and work for the Government of the day, that is, the party in power. Little distinction is made between Government and party. Norms of disinterestedness are rarely applied to the behavior of chiefs in this context. Indeed, a counternorm prevails: It is the duty of a PC to support the holders of power lest they make trouble for him and his people; also, the good will of people in power can be useful for the chiefdom. Perhaps this norm is an inheritance from pre-colonial days, when chiefs were expected to make alliances with more powerful warriors in order to preempt attack and gain protection. Whatever the antecedents, their dependence on the Government makes chiefs vulnerable to partisan manipulation at the hands of the party in power. The position of Paramount Chiefs becomes especially untenable when a new party gains control or, to a lesser extent, when the party in power splinters. New loyalties must be generated rapidly.

Perhaps it would be well to quote some PC's and their relatives concerning this subject:

As the Paramount Chief I automatically support the Government in power. If it loses I don't worry. I just go to the new side—and the new Government won't disturb me. I fear the Government more than my own people.

I will work with the APC just like I worked with the SLPP—because it is the law and regulation of the country. I won't force anyone to support the party in power. But automatically my chiefs will support the Government. The party in power and the Government are the same thing.[41]

My father [a deceased PC] long ago devised a policy that no matter how people felt in their hearts, they would make it appear that they supported the Government of the day. This policy is still carried out. Everyone proclaims his loyalty to the APC even though most people in their hearts favor the SLPP.[42]

Some chiefs did not interpret "loyalty" as requiring outright partisan action in favor of the party in power:

I support the Government 100%—and I support the APC. Party is Government and Government is Party. But this does not mean that I will sell party registration cards or be on some party committee. After a while I would be petitioned for being involved in politics.[43]

And one PC interviewed by me explicitly made a distinction between party and Government, allowing himself room to support the Opposition SLPP while remaining a good chief:

A Paramount Chief has no trouble if he supports the party in power; but if he is identified with the Opposition, the Government makes life difficult for him. There is [however] a difference between supporting a party and a Government. . . . People should not know me as a hypocrite, jumping from one party to another, depending on who is in power.[44]

It is interesting to note that this independent-minded chief was induced, under threat of a Commission of Inquiry—prelude to deposition proceedings—to swing in the direction of the party in power shortly after making this statement. In general, central administrative and political authority over chiefs is such that they can afford to remain "neutral" only under risk of duress.

We have already on a number of occasions discussed the intimate relationship between chiefs and the SLPP. Less clear-cut, but no less important, has been the relationship which the APC has developed with chiefs. Initially, when the party was struggling for recognition in 1960, its spokesmen adopted an antichief stance in order to attract youngmen and other elements excluded from the cozy alliance between chiefdom authorities and the SLPP which had ruled for almost a decade. The APC leadership was younger, less tied to ruling families, less wealthy, and more ideologically-inclined than were the SLPP politicians.[45] Moreover, during the 1962 General Elections, chiefs used threats and intimidations to impede APC campaigning, especially in the Northern Province.[46] In the 1967 General Election the SLPP leadership again encouraged local authorities to negate APC gains through force and repression, but this time the APC was able to capitalize upon widespread disillusionment with the SLPP Government and to convert it into electoral victory. The APC, unlike all previous opposition parties, campaigned on a platform which sought to reduce the role of chiefs. Its original "class" approach had by 1967 become a "tribal" appeal which sought to attract support from northerners alienated by the Mende-dominated SLPP Government, but the chiefs, as agents of that Government, were opponents, not allies, in the eyes of APC leaders.

The apogee of SLPP-inspired violence against the APC and its supporters occurred during by-elections in 1968 and 1969. Not only did the intensity of force increase, but an additional traditional institution—the *Poro* Society—was mobilized against the spread of APC activity into areas which had once been SLPP monopolies. This occurred in a number of localities in the Southern and Eastern Provinces, but its most dramatic manifestation was in Kenema District.

The *Poro* was converted by SLPP adherents into an instrument for intimidating APC voters in Lower Bambara, Small Bo, and Nongowa chiefdoms. *Poro* initiation ceremonies in conjunction with feared "devils" were used to terrify strangers and non-members. For example, in Blama, Small Bo chiefdom, the Society launched a full-scale terrorization campaign. The period immediately prior to the by-election was marked by frequent daylight appearances of the Kimei devil—who is not seen but heard—and the crowds which customarily accumulate about him. On hearing the high-pitched whistle of the *Poro* devil, non-members abandoned their work and fled to their homes. A number of market women—Temnes and other northern strangers—were caught by the crowd, stripped and robbed, and their wares destroyed. The crowd went on to stone and burn houses belonging to suspected APC stalwarts. Some women claim to have been raped. Even an army unit stationed in Blama was attacked, resulting in five injuries.[47]

It was the large-scale campaign against strangers in Kenema District which provoked Prime Minister Stevens into declaring a State of Emergency, postponing the by-elections, and detaining in Manfanta Prison almost 300 SLPP leaders and followers.

The *Poro* Society in electoral politics was a relatively recent innovation. Other "traditional" institutions had had a longer history of involvement during campaigns. Better described as coercion than outright violence, chiefs often took steps to discourage opponents from canvassing in their chiefdoms. A varied selection of techniques served to make campaigning difficult for party workers not allied to the local incumbents. They could be arrested for holding "illegal meetings" or "undermining the authority of the chief." Permission to campaign or even to enter the chiefdom might be refused. "Swears" might be administered obligating participants to vote for the chief's party. Or the chief might simply threaten loss of office to any subordinate who encouraged the opposition. These practices were especially common in the North, and had the effect of driving the APC undergound.[48] They occurred in Mendeland on a less blatant scale, but likewise—at least until 1968—placed severe obstacles before APC campaigners.

Once the APC took office, however, the tables were at least partially turned. Some SLPP candidates claim that in the by-

elections Paramount Chiefs—allied to the new party in power—
had misused their influence for partisan purposes. For instance,
this was a key allegation by Joseph Borniea in his election petition against Joe Quee-Nyagua. He testified that chiefdom elders
enjoined him to renounce his candidacy, and when he refused
they mounted a "massive campaign" to hamper his activities in
all three chiefdoms in the constituency.[49] As we have repeatedly
stressed, local authorities were under considerable pressure to
support the party in power; some of them felt obliged to
demonstrate loyalty to the new Government by working against
the SLPP.

The SLPP has also charged that during the by-elections the
Government condoned and even encouraged large-scale intimidation of local people. Party thugs, the army, and the police
were used, they say, to frighten voters from the polls and to cow
chiefdow authorities into supporting the Government party. It is
difficult to assign motives in this case, but it is an observable fact
that the *effect* of intensified official activity during and after the
State of Emergency was to give advantage to the APC. Soldiers
and policemen were brought into service in response to and
possibly in retaliation against the emergence of the *Poro* as a
political weapon. Almost immediately they were thrust into the
same role as the elements they were sent to suppress. They
became agents of intimidation.

Mass detentions during this period lent official coercion its
greatest impact upon electoral politics. Commencing November
21, 1968, SLPP members and chiefdom elders throughout
Mendeland were rounded up by the army and police. In all, about
300 people were detained for at least two months. Again, the
justification for these arrests was the need to impose order
following the *Poro* disturbances. Yet in terms of consequences
and implications, preventive detention in this case represented
more than a mere return to tranquility. Its effect upon political
competition was threefold: it temporarily eliminated the Opposition while permitting the Government party to campaign
unhampered; it demonstrated the power of the Government,
drawing vacillating elements to the APC side; and it enhanced

the prestige and influence of the APC's local allies, who were able to present themselves as big men powerful enough to have chiefs incarcerated.

Given this background of strife and intimidation, "One could suspect that while it might preserve the institution, an APC government would reduce chieftaincy to a largely ceremonial role."[50] But this has not materialized. No basic changes have reduced the role of Paramount Chief; it continues under the APC in much the same manner as it did under the SLPP, as an ambiguous but powerful political position; indeed, if anything, its stature has been enhanced since the days of Albert Margai and his self-destructive policies. The APC has not sought to dismantle the chieftaincy for three basic reasons. First, once it assumed the mantle of governmental power, it took on the responsibility of ruling the countryside. In the absence of anything to replace the chiefdom administrations, the new regime had no choice but to work through them. This became all the more apparent with the realization that the District Councils had to be scrapped. President Stevens has committed himself to the chiefdoms as the basic units of development in upcountry Sierra Leone. Second, the APC in its effort to consolidate itself as a national party necessarily had to penetrate the Southern and Eastern Provinces. Much of its success in achieving this is due to the alliances it forged with ruling families and Paramount Chiefs in Mende chiefdoms. This theme will be elaborated in following chapters, but it should be mentioned here that the organizational apparatus built up by the APC in the north and Freetown did not extend to the Mende areas of the south and east. To attract immediate support and to cultivate fertile soil for planting party roots in these areas, the APC joined forces with "traditional" elements in almost every chiefdom. Third, as government employees, Paramount Chiefs came under enormous pressure to declare their support for the party in power, converting to APC advantage what had been an SLPP monopoly. Those chiefs who have proved recalcitrant have felt the force of central governmental power, including the threat of deposition or even outright deposition itself. In Kenema District, for instance, those chiefs who had strongly supported the SLPP and did not switch allegiance when the APC took power in 1968, came under irresistible pressure from both the Government and their own intrachiefdom oppositions. Violence has forced two Paramount Chiefs to live outside their chiefdom headquarters. In addition, one PC was suspended twice and subjected to proceedings preliminary to a Commission of Inquiry into his administration, which were abandoned midway through when he promised to suppress his pro-SLPP inclinations. Another was threatened with the release of an incriminating report if her chiefdom were not reconciled in a manner favoring the APC. Others came under constant petitioning from local oppositions. Those who have avoided such pressures have either come out strongly for the APC or have maintained a posture sufficiently ambiguous to escape censure. The impact of this pressure has been to push virtually all chiefs into the APC camp. Once assured of at least their nominal support, the government had taken steps to solidify their position among the rural populations. President Stevens has on a number of occasions bolstered chiefs against dissident elements within their chiefdoms; for instance, in a recent speech to PC's in Kenema District he "warned people against challenging the authority of chiefs. He assured the Paramount Chiefs that as long as they worked amicably with their people, they would have nothing to fear."[51]

Establishment of a one-party state, especially if it were supported by wide consensus throughout the countryside, would do much to relieve the role contradictions presently experienced by Paramounts. The conflicts between "neutral figurehead" and "party agent" would be ameliorated were party competition eliminated. President Stevens apparently had something like this in mind when, during the 1973 General Election campaign, he spoke repeatedly of conducting future elections in a manner akin to what he interprets as the "traditional" style, whereby leading citizens in local communities are "sounded out" until opinion coalesces on a single choice, thus avoiding the corrosiveness of an open contest.[52] Apparently, then, he envisions a one-party state built, among other things, upon consensus and cooperation from chiefdom elders. The chiefs, in this arrangement, would assume a role similar to the one which had evolved during the colonial era.

THE ROLE OF CIVIL SERVANT

Occasionally in Sierra Leone the opinion is put forth that chiefs should play the role of civil servant. This, it is felt, would shield them from the partisan arena but would permit active involvement in the administrative and developmental problems of their chiefdoms, in a manner analogous to the role of District Officers at a higher level.

A number of conditions have contributed to this growing expectation that chiefs conduct themselves according to standard procedures under the umbrella of administrative law and regulations. By virtue of their position as paid government agents, chiefs in effect comprise the lowest level of the central administrative apparatus and are subject to a number of its rules. The reform era, especially in the field of chiefdom finances, introduced norms of responsibility and proper procedure which were reinforced by an increasing inclination towards central supervision and, on occasion, intervention. We have already discussed the numerous steps taken by both the colonial and post-Independence administrations to induce a sharper sense of public service and public finance at the chiefdom level. Civil service norms were further disseminated by the the deeper penetration of more and more administrative agencies from the center. Health, education, police, public works, mining, agriculture—these and a number of other functional areas of government became increasingly relevant to chiefdom people as additional ministries launched operations in the countryside. Bureaucratic norms spread in their wake.

Finally, intrachiefdom oppositions have seized upon civil service norms as a convenient weapon with which to attack incumbent chiefs. The growing expectation that chiefs act like administrative officers provides opposition factions with additional political ammunition; their willingness to bring these issues to bear reinforces the norm, spreading it further. The entire Ministry of the Interior, from the lowest Assistant District Officer to the President himself, is the target of this form of "interest articulation." Formal written petitions and delegations of protesters are the preferred methods for voicing complaints against chiefly incumbents. The governmental offices in Kenema Town are intermittently beseiged with villagers from one chiefdom faction or another waiting to gain audience with the District Officer or the Provincial Secretary or the Resident minister. In Freetown, high officials, especially the Prime Minister (now President), continuously receive delegations from aggrieved upcountry factions seeking relief from the "improper" activities of their chiefdom authorities. The list of complaints often includes non-civil-service issues like *Poro* infractions or deviation from tradition, but invariably it covers an array of bureaucratic sins: misuse of authority, misuse of funds, improper arrest, failure to consult, inadequate bookkeeping, improper levies, and, most frequent, involvement in partisan politics. The official who hears these complaints—in particular the Prime Minister/President—in effect takes on the role of "superchief," receiving delegations of elders in much the same fashion as Paramounts traditionally heard cases in the chiefdoms. It is he who decides whether the norm is important enough and the violation serious enough to warrant punishment. So far since Independence in Kenema District, no Paramount Chief has been deposed (although PC Kai-Samba II of Nongowa chiefdom was "pensioned for sickness;" see Chapter 5). The government— under both the SLPP and the APC—has been more interested in using the threat of deposition as an instrument for assuring party loyalty among chiefs than in enforcing civil service norms. Hence, both chiefdom oppositions and the government itself use the civil service role as a self-interested means for pressuring chiefly incumbents. This further politicizes the chieftaincy and assures continued conflict between the "neutral figurehead," "party agent," and "civil servant" roles.

Even if central actors were genuinely to emphasize norms of

disinterestedness, competence, and service for Paramount Chiefs, the civil servant role still suffers from a basic internal contradiction. Chiefs in Sierra Leone simply by virtue of structural conditions cannot operate fully in the normative framework of a civil administration. Unlike the civil-servant chiefs of, say, Buganda, whose traditional unit is large and unified and who are appointed rather than elected, chiefs in Sierra Leone draw their authority from the people and customs of small territories. Hiring and firing, transfer and promotion are not compatible with the geographically-based chieftaincy of Sierra Leone. (Assessor Chiefs come close to assuming a civil-service role in Sierra Leone. They are appointed by the administration to accompany and advise officials during elections and disputes in other chiefdoms. They are selected on the basis of their knowledge of native law as well as on their ability to govern their own chiefdoms. An Assessor Chief, however, is employed only intermittently, and once a task is completed he returns to the chiefdom from whence his authority is drawn.) Finnegan and Murray are correct in maintaining that chiefs were allocated a genuine economic development role for only a short time, during the early reform era, and that had this continued longer in conjunction with an increased flow of resources from the center to the periphery through the chiefs, they might well have taken on a greater developmental capacity than they now possess.[53] But for the chiefs to become full-fledged civil servants they would have to be moved from the small-scale networks of personal relationships and locally-oriented institutions (e.g., secret societies) which give authority and meaning to their role from the standpoint of chiefdom people.

It is interesting to note that the military government during its short year in power seems to have offered chiefs their clearest opportunity to assume a non-contradictory role in the national scheme of things. The military junta envisioned the PC's as one link in the chain of command which reached from the NRC to the lowest village headman. This comes close to the "civil servant" role; the "party agent" role was abolished with the liquidation of party activity; the "neutral figurehead" role was inadequate for a regime so heavily dependent upon civil authorities to carry out military-style orders:

> [Major B.I. Kai-Samba] said it was necessary to maintain a Chain of Command for smooth running of the administrative machinery and that it was improper for anyone to sidestep the Paramount Chiefs and the DC's. . . . "Such an action," he said, "is disrespect for authority, and the NRC would not encourage it."[54]

A regime so ill-disposed toward civil strife as the NRC offered few incentives and many disincentives for grassroots confrontation, and evidently chiefdom oppositions responded accordingly, since throughout the District the frequency of overt conflict decreased sharply from its premilitary level. The NRC's method for dealing with lawlessness was to call the leaders of rival groups before the relevant miltary official in Freetown. For instance, it simply ordered the two antagonists in the Dama dispute, PC Dassama and Speaker Lansana, to cease feuding—and the chiefdom did indeed settle down.[55] One exception to this general tendency was communal conflict in Wando chiefdom. The Temne community under the leadership of one Kemoh Kamara—alias "Kamara Thousand," who was originally an SLPP propaganda secretary but who became affiliated with the APC by 1967—had come increasingly at odds with the chiefdom elders. Threats upon chiefs' lives, tax discrimination, inciting tax evasion, undermining official authority, intimidation on the part of gangs of youngmen—all were among the charges and countercharges which stimulated the palaver. Then the PC's car was ambushed in February 1968, allegedly by a gang of Temnes. The District Commissioner recommended that Kemoh Kamara be immediately removed from the chiefdom, but the NRC demurred. Rather, it issued several directives for both Kamara and the Paramount Chief to appear before the NRC Secretariat in Freetown, but neither hastened to comply. Dilatoriness was rewarded in this instance, because the military regime was overthrown before it could enforce its command. This case was unusual, however; normally chiefdom factions paid at least lip service to the NRC's authority and made motions to comply with its orders for peace.

Whether, given more time, the military would have been able to forge a consistent role for Paramount Chiefs, is, of course, a matter of speculation. In all likelihood, as Cox implies,[56] the NRC's impolitic penchant for issuing orders and expecting instant compliance regardless of circumstances, would have undermined through a general process of alienation whatever advances it might have taken in rationalizing the role structure of traditonal authorities.

If this analysis is correct, the plight of chiefs especially since Independence stems primarily from inconsistent expectations which issue from the center. Three separate role concepts converge to produce a contradictory part to play in the national scheme of things. This is illustrated in an interview statement by Prime Minister Siaka Stevens:

> If the chiefs can come up with progressive things . . . then there is a place for them. But many chiefs are backward and confused. Of course there are good chiefs too.

> We in the APC try to coax the chiefs to get them on our side. This helps in an election. And the chiefs have to move in line with the Government. No, [in answer to my question] chiefs are not like a Mayor of a city, who can be a base of opposition. Provincial people are just not that sophisticated. They are not really civil servants either, I don't know what you would call them.[57]

The kinds of conflict we have been describing are not due to incompatibility between central expectations and locally-originated expectations about the role of chiefs. Nor are they a result of a clash between "modern" norms and "traditional" behaviors. It is largely in the "modern" sector that crosspurposeful behavior is called for, the product of (a) expectations inappropriate for the institutional framework into which chiefs have been placed, and (b) expectations which conflict with each other. (Were the role of "District Officer" so ambiguously framed, it too would have undergone deterioration; indeed, under the Albert Margai and Siake Stevens regimes many a District Officer's career has foundered because of an inability to reconcile "civil servant" norms with pressures from the center to act as "party agent;" politicization of the civil service has been part of the same general process which has embroiled chiefs in partisan politics.) True, chiefs have been the object of severe criticism from some of their subjects, who have persistently drawn central attention to chiefly departure from "neutral figurehead," "party agent" and "civil servant" expectations. But their motives have been largely opportunistic. Like the behavior of chiefdom oppositions during the reform period, this represents not so much spontaneous outrage at the obsolescence of a traditional role in a modernizing era as a manipulative search for issues with which to discredit role incumbents. Their aim has been to fill the role, not abolish or emasculate it.

In short, Pattern 5—incompatibility among elements of the central set of expectations—best approximates the kind of role conflict experienced by Mende chiefs during the post-Independence period. This in combination with Patterns 4 and 6, which reflected the prevalent conflicts during the reform period, provides solid evidence for preferring the synthetic model of modernization to the displacement model, reinforcing the more impressionistically-based conclusion of Chapter 3. If Kenema District is at all indicative, the nature of change in Sierra Leone is a matter of fusion between modern and traditional elements. The role of Paramount Chief has not been an obstacle to modernization but rather an ever-present actor in a shifting social drama, sometimes inducing change but more often simply adapting to it. Its potential as a developmental and integrative link between center and periphery will never be fully realized until the central elite works out a more coherent set of expectations about its place in the national framework.

NOTES

1. Michael Crowder, *West Africa Under Colonial Rule* (London: Hutchenson, 1968), pp. 221-26.

2. Ruth Finnegan and David J. Murray, "Limba Chiefs," in Crowder and Ikime (eds.), *West African Chiefs,* (N.Y.: Africana, 1970), pp. 407-436. Incidentally, the remarks made by Finnegan and Murray regarding Limba chiefs in the nineteenth century closely resemble our characterization of Mende chieftaincy. See especially pp. 407-419.

3. Lord Hailey, *Native Administration in the British African Territories,* Part IV, p. 33.

4. Sierra Leone, *The Protectorate Handbook, 1947,* (Chief Commissioner's Office, Bo), p. 30.

5. Sierra Leone, *Annual Report of the Sierra Leone Protectorate for the Years 1949 and 1950* (Freetown: Government Printer), p. 5.

6. (KPA) U/2/2, Kenema District, Annual Reports, Vol. II, p. 145.

7. Kilson, *Political Change . . . . ,* p. 60.

8. (KPA) CONF/INT/5 Intelligence Reports. January 1950-November 1953.

9. (KPA) U/2/2 Kenema District Annual Reports, II, 172.

10. (KPA) CONF/P/3 Memorandum on Chiefdom Palavers (1954).

11. Interview #81. Feb. 23, 1970.

12. Sierra Leone, *Report of the Commission of Inquiry into Disturbances in the Provinces (November, 1955 to March, 1956)* (Freetown, 1956).

13. This distinction is suggested in Rene Lemarchand, "Political Instability in Africa: The Case of Rwanda and Burundi," *Civilisations,* XVI, No. 3 (1966), pp. 307-35.

14. *Ibid.*

15. Max Gluckman, *Custom and Conflict in Africa* (New York: Barnes and Noble, 1956).

16. (KPA) CONF/P/3, Memorandum on Chiefdom Palavers (1953).

17. See Fred I. Greenstein, *The American Party System and the American People* (Englewood Cliffs, N.J.: Prentice-Hall, 1964), pp.

37-53. Mario Puzo's *The Godfather* vividly and dramatically draws in the network of personal relations which forms the core of a slightly different type of organization.

18. Max Weber, *The Theory of Social and Economic Organization* [translated by A.M. Henderson and Talcott Parsons], (New York: The Free Press, 1947), pp. 341-347.

19. Interview #145. June 23, 1970.

20. Interview #115. April 16, 1970.

21. Interview #91. March 9, 1970.

22. Interview #81. Feb. 23, 1970.

23. For somewhat more elaborate attempts to use "polarity" and other concepts from the field of International Relations in analyzing center-periphery politics, see my "Rural-Urban Alliances and Reciprocity in Africa," *Canadian Journal of African Studies,* V, iii (Summer 1972), pp. 307-325.

24. See especially (KPA) CONF/INT/5, Southeastern Province, Intelligence Reports, Jan. 1950-Nov. 1953. One newly-arrived Commissioner wrote that his impression was "that the Administration in Sierra Leone is far more arbitrary than either in Nigeria or the Gamba. . . . [and] to a far greater extent than has been my previous experience or than would ever be tolerated by the litigous Yoruba or Ibo. It leaves the gate wide open to lawyerly intervention, an intervention which is very difficult to counter." Sept. 1952.

25. Kilson, *op. cit.,* p. 216.

26. (KPA), CONF/INT/5, . . . Intelligence Reports, . . . Feb. 2, 1952.

27. As indicated by replies to a questionnaire administered by Lord Hailey. See *Annual Report of the Sierra Leone Protectorate for the Year 1947* (Freetown, Government Printer), p. 8.

28. See, for example, Thomas Hodgkin, *Nationalism in Colonial Africa* (New York: N.Y.U. press, 1957); also, Kenneth Little, "Structural Change in the Sierra Leone Protectorate," *Africa,* XXV (July 1955), 217-233.

29. Much of the following material on nationalism in Sierra Leone is based on Kilson, *op. cit.,* chapters 9 and 10; and John R. Cartwright, *Politics in Sierra Leone 1947-67* (Toronto and Buffalo: University of Toronto Press 1970), parts II and III. Both Kilson and Cartwright in-

terpret the prelude to Independence in Sierra Leone as basically an elite phenomenon.

30. Albert Margai and F.S. Anthony, *Memorandum to the Secretary of State for the Colonies on the New Constitution,* Secessional Paper No. 48 of 1948 (Freetown), quoted in Kilson, *op. cit.* p. 157.

31. Cartwright, *op. cit.,* p. 56.

32. Kilson, *op. cit.,* p. 202.

33. C.S. Whitaker, Jr., *The Politics of Tradition: Continuity and Change in Northern Nigeria 1946-1966* (Princeton: Princeton Univ. Press, 1970), pp. 303-307.

34. For more detail see Martin Kilson, *op. cit.,* chapter 12; and Barrows "Local-Level Politics in Sierra Leone: Alliances in Kenema District," (unpublished Ph.D. dissertation, Yale Univ., 1971), chapter 4.

35. More detailed accounts of the District Councils than will be presented here can be found in Kilson, *op. cit.,* chapter 13, and Barrows, *Ibid.*

36. *Sierra Leone Gazette* (1966), pp. 806-7; and (KPA) KDC/B/10, Statements of Account.

37. See Martin Kilson, "Sierra Leone Politics," *West Africa,* June 25, 1960, pp. 708-09.

38. Kilson, *Political Change . . .,* pp. 202 and 212. By "rational" Kilson is referring to the Weberian notion of a specialized structure fitted to serving needs in a complex society.

39. *West Africa,* March 31, 1972, p. 403; and Dec. 25, 1972, p. 1717.

40. Compare the remarks of the Dove-Edwin Commission and the Government reply in *Report of the Dove-Edwin Commission of Enquiry into the Conduct of the 1967 General Elections* (Freetown: Government Printer, 1967).

41. Interview #110. April 11, 1970.

42. Interview #82. Feb. 22, 1970.

43. Interview #117. April 22, 1970.

44. Interview.

45. Cartwright, *op. cit.,* p. 132.

46. *Ibid.,* p. 152.

47. The source of this account is confidential. Its veracity is confirmed by other sources, including official files and interviews.

The Government formed a Commission of Inquiry into the affairs of Small Bo chiefdom during the 1968 by-election attempt. It was composed entirely of *Poro* members, comprising in effect a Government-sponsored *poro* meeting, called to judge the "society" of one chiefdom.

48. See Cartwright, *op. cit.,* pp. 151-156. A number of interviewees explained how intimidation from the local establishment forced the APC to build a strong organizational network in the North:

> "Another reason why the [Northern] chiefs were unpopular was that the Government had ordered them not to allow any political meetings other than SLPP. This forced the APC to campaign on a small scale: they would go to individuals and say it was time for a Northerner to head the Government, that they were tired of a Mende in charge."

Interview #113. April 15, 1970.

49. From the text of Justice S.C.W. Betts' judgement, reported in *Daily Express* (Freetown), Sept. 29, 1969.

50. Cartwright, *op. cit.,* p. 134.

51. *West Africa,* April 30, 1973, p. 577.

52. *West Africa,* Dec. 25, 1972, p. 1717.

53. Finnegan and Murray, *op. cit.,* pp. 424-5. The authors are writing about Limba chiefs, but their comments apply with remarkable comparability to Mende chiefs as well.

54. *West Africa,* June 10, 1967, p. 770.

55. Interviews #81 (Feb. 23, 1970) and #87 (March 4, 1970).

56. Thomas S. Cox, "Civil-Military Relations in Sierra Leone: A Case Study of African Soldiers in Politics," (unpublished Ph.D. dissertation, Fletcher School of Law and Diplomacy, 1973).

57. June 23, 1970.

Chapter 5

Constituency Politics

This chapter and the one that follows are concerned with documenting and analyzing the patterns of center-periphery politics which emerge from contemporary electoral activity. The case studies presented here dwell on the interrelationships between cleavages at the local level and national party competition in four of Kenema District's seven Parliamentary constituencies:

Kenema South (Dama, Gaura, Tunkia and Nomo chiefdoms);

Kenema East (Lower Bambara, Dodo, and Malegohun chiefdoms);

Kenema Central (Nongowa and Koya chiefdoms); and

Kenema Town (part of Nongowa chiefdom)

The three neglected constituencies (Kenema West, Kenema North, and Kenema Northeast) resemble in most ways the important features of the units examined in the case studies, so no crucial aspects of center-local politics have been ignored by the decision to sacrifice breadth for depth.

The prime purpose of this chapter is to provide a detailed and contextual source of data for the more analytical chapter on patterns of center-periphery alliance which follows. But ancillary aims are served as well. Kinship as an idiom of Mende politics is introduced as a recurring motif; land as an important stake in the political game is described especially in the section on Nongowa chiefdom; and the impact of diamonds upon public affairs in up-country Sierra Leone receives attention in a number of case studies, most particularly the account of politics in Lower Bambara chiefdom. Finally, for strictly archival purposes, these case studies provide documentation for events which otherwise would have remained either unrecorded or lost in the welter of poorly-kept official files.

Kenema South Constituency

Political contests in Kenema South constituency are particularly important because it is the home and power base of Salia Jusu-Sheriff. As his star has risen, from Member of Parliament to Cabinet Minister to Leader of the SLPP Opposition, so too his constituency has taken on added importance. His ascent has vastly increased the stakes—central and local—involved in competition for this seat in Parliament.

Jusu-Sheriff narrowly won the 1962 General Election in a field of five candidates. All five had strong ties with long-standing political groups in the four chiefdoms which make up the constituency. *J.K. Taylor* was from Dama, and was related to its incumbent ruling family, but he had close contacts with Paramount Chiefs in other chiefdoms as well. In particular, he had acted as envoy for the PC of Tunkia, writing letters for her and interceding with the central government on her behalf. As a teacher and later as an Inspector of Schools for the District Council, he was in an especially advantageous position to act in this role as intermediary. *A.M. Lansana* also had a strong power base in Dama chiefdom, where his ties to prevailing political and social structures were manyfold. His father was Chiefdom Speaker; his paternal relatives held power as village and section chiefs; he married into an important ruling family; and as a former chiefdom clerk and sanitary inspector he had gained extensive experience with local government and widespread contacts with local notables. *B.S. Bunduka* was a leading member of

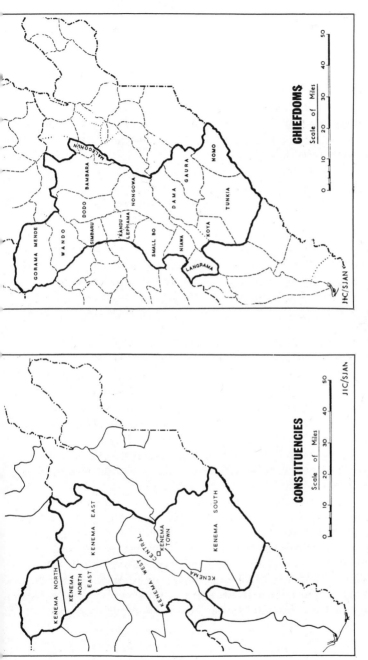

CONSTITUENCIES

KENEMA NORTH

KENEMA NORTH EAST

KENEMA EAST

KENEMA CENTRAL

KENEMA WEST

KENEMA TOWN

KENEMA SOUTH

Scale of Miles
0   10   20   30   40   50

JIC/SJAN

CHIEFDOMS

GORAMA MENDE

WANDO

DODO

BAMBARA

MALEGOHUN

SIMBARU

KANDU-LEPPIAMA

NONGOWA

SMALL BO

DAMA

GAURA

NIAWA

LANGRAMA

KOYA

TUNKIA

NOMO

Scale of Miles
0   10   20   30   40   50

JIC/SJAN

Adapted with permission from *Sierra Leone in Maps* by J. I. Clarke (London and New York: University of London Press and Africana Publishing Company).

an important ruling house in Gaura chiefdom, who was "put up" as its candidate for Parliament. *Amara Njavombo* was a leader of the opposition ruling house in Tunkia chiefdom. *Jusu-Sheriff* himself belonged to a family whose historical ties with Tunkia chiefdom were well known throughout eastern Mendeland. His own words incisively denote that connection:

> My ancestors were Muslims from Guinea who originally settled in Dama chiefdom, then moved to Tunkia to found the town of Damawulo [small Dama]. Traditionally, big Alphas such as they were, formed close associations with ruling families. They became very close to the Sama family. Ever since, there has been a reciprocal relationship between them, with the Sheriffs perhaps supporting the Samas with their learning and influence, and the Samas helping them perhaps financially. The Njavombos have always identified the Sheriff family with the Samas—quite rightly.[1]

His influence was not restricted to Tunkia, however. His maternal uncle (*Kenya*, a very important figure among the Mende) was Taplima Ngobeh of Luawa, a leader of the SLPP and Resident Minister of the Eastern Province. Moreover, Jusu-Sheriff had just returned from England and Kings College, Durham, where he had been President of the Sierra Leone students organization of the United Kingdom and Ireland.

In the 1967 General Election the field had been narrowed to two major candidates, Jusu-Sheriff (who was supported by Taylor) and Lansana (supported by Njavombo). A minor candidate, Yankay Sesay, was a Temne competing under the APC banner. Jusu-Sheriff by then had become the (albeit reluctant) leader of an insurgent faction of the SLPP. Lansana had been elected in 1964 to succeed his father as Speaker of Dama chiefdom, and he enjoyed the surreptitious support of Prime Minister Albert Margai, whose intra-SLPP intrigues included an attempt to undermine Jusu-Sheriff's home base. Despite this intervention from the center, however, Jusu-Sheriff was victorious:[2]

KENEMA SOUTH CONSTITUENCY, GENERAL ELECTION, 1967

1. Salia Jusu-Sheriff	(SLPP)	11,602	Elected
2. Yankay Sesay	(APC)	311	
3. A.M. Lansana	(Independent)	8,863	

Following a year of military government, the judiciary under the new APC Government disallowed the election in Kenema South and ordered a new contest. At this point Lansana switched to the party in power. In the by-election which was finally held in March 1969, Jusu-Sheriff (SLPP) again won over Lansana (APC), although by a considerably reduced margin.

This sequence of elections and its aftermath (1962-70) forms the basis of our case study, which is most usefully presented on a chiefdom-by-chiefdom basis.

DAMA CHIEFDOM

For almost a decade Dama has been the seat of intense intrachiefdom conflict, the bulk of it inspired by antagonism between the Paramount Chief and his Speaker. Underlying this personal dispute has been the more common rivalry between ruling families.

The historical roots of Dama's difficulties reach back to the deposition of Paramount Chief Siaffa Kebbi in 1939, when he was accused of participation in cannibalistic activities and convicted by a Commission of Inquiry. PC Kebbi was installed in 1917, the first graduate of the Bo School (for the Sons and Nominees of Chiefs) to attain chiefly office. His rule was progressive, in the sense that under him Dama experienced unusual economic development, especially in the field of agriculture, and it became the first chiefdom in the district to establish the paraphernalia of a Native Administration. Likewise, his rule was harsh, due, at least in part, to the demands made on chiefdom people for development of coffee and cocoa plantations, rice swamps, roads, and the like. By the early 1930's petitions were received by the Government accusing him of membership in a cannibal society; by the late 1930's his detractors were so common and the chiefdom in such turmoil that he was deposed and banished to a nearby chiefdom. His influence persisted, however. Even in exile he was able to interfere with the administration of his successor, PC Bobor Dassama. It is said that he participated in a "revolting ceremony" calculated to "scatter" Dassama's mind and to induce the TA to beg for his return to Dama.[3] The chiefdom was kept in periodic ferment by his machinations and by rumors of his return. Finally the administration lifted his banishment, just in time to allow his embroilment in the 1957 General Election. Ex-PC Kebbi exhorted his supporters to vote for A.H. Demby, while PC Dassama was behind J.K. Taylor. Demby became the Hon. Member of Parliament for Kenema South, and as might be expected, Dama chiefdom became further immersed in its own feuding. The PC became involved in a serious dispute with the town of Diamei, in which, among other things, he was convicted of grave offences against the *Poro* Society; shortly after, petitions flowed into the District Commissioner's Office accusing him of a wide—but usual—assortment of infractions. Only his death saved him from the indignity of a formal Commission of Inquiry.

Two general comments help elucidate this dispute. First, competition between the two major ruling houses, Dakowa (of which Kebbi was a leading member) and Dassama, underlay the aforementioned events. It is generally recognized that the Dassamas were in the vanguard of the campaign to depose Kebbi; likewise, elements connected with the Dakawas contributed to the ferment during Bobor Dassama's rule. Second, in Mendeland accusations of cannibalism and of *Poro* infractions may or may not be true. They frequently arise when a chief becomes unpopular, and most likely involve varying mixtures of genuine indignation and cynical manipulation. Such charges have often been effective in reducing or even eliminating the power of a chief or politician.

The election of Vandi Dassama in succession to his father in 1959 seemed to allay further disquiet. The District Commissioner reported that the new chief had foresworn attempts "to fall on his peoples or to recoup his [election] expenses by methods which used to be only too common."[4] And for a few years the chiefdom was indeed quiet.

Again, however, a national political contest had ramifications in Dama detrimental to its tranquility. The 1962 General Elections put unusual pressure on PC Vandi Dassama: He was related to four of the five candidates. Jusu-Sheriff and Lansana had particularly strong ties to the Dassama family. Not only did Jusu-Sheriff and Dassama go to Bo School together, but when the former's ancestors settled in Dama they built close bonds with the chief's family. Lansana, of course, was a native of Dama and as a member of one of its powerful families expected unstinting support from the Paramount Chief. Both candidates say that they were promised backing but did not receive it.

Lansana's resentment was compounded in 1964 when he ran for Chiefdom Speaker following the death of his father. The PC said he would remain neutral during the election, but Lansana interpreted his actions as hostile. Ever since his successful campaign for Speaker, Dama has undergone the sporadic disruptions associated with what in Sierra Leone is commonly known as a "chiefdom palaver." Paramount Chief and Speaker have waged war upon each other. The Speaker was suspended for six months for "swearing" the chief. The local court's business was held up because the Speaker refused to nominate his two members. Complaints flooded the District Officer's desk concerning elections of chiefdom councilors, apportionment of rice swamps, and use of land for diamond mining—all of which were directly tied to the growing animosity between the two highest officers in the chiefdom.

With the approach of the 1967 General Election, the local dispute gained in intensity as its national implications became clear. Speaker Lansana again declared as an Independent candidate, and was covertly supported by Prime Minister Albert Margai, who was engaged in an effort to unseat a number of his own Cabinet members, including Salia Jusu-Sheriff. PC Dassama and Jusu-Sheriff by this time had become natural allies, if only because they shared the same rivals.

Apparently the Prime Minister had advised Lansana to revive the old palaver that had racked the chiefdom in previous decades. Lansana is a consummate politician, able to communicate easily and effectively with ordinary people, and he used his talents to undermine support for the PC while at the same time mustering votes in his own campaign for Parliament. His skill in manipulating kinship affiliations was particularly helpful in mobilizing support:

> Lansana is effective because he knows how to talk to native people. He will learn the history of a family; then he will try to connect its trouble or its backward position to something the Dassamas did. He has connected himself to the Dakawa family in this way. He has convinced them that it was the Dassamas who were responsible for [the deposition of] their chief, PC Kebbi. Since the Dakawas are a large family, extended into many villages, a great number of people are brought to his side in this way. Lansana has also married into the Dakawa family.[5]

Lansana's family itself is large, extended not only throughout Dama but into strategic parts of neighboring Gaura chiefdom as well. In addition, as a former Sanitary Overseer and Court Clerk in Dama he has had contact with almost every village in the area. As a farmer himself, he appealed to fellow tillers of the soil to vote for someone who is close to them rather than someone like Jusu-Sheriff who spends most of his time in Freetown.

In this fashion the Speaker has weaned the ordinary people away from the Paramount Chief. Both sides agree that Lansana controls the youngmen, while most bigmen continue to support the chief. In a democratic era numbers become important, and Lansana's influence over the youngmen gave him a clear majority of the votes. Even though—officially, at least—he lost Kenema South as a whole, in his own chiefdom he was victorious.

The coup following the 1967 elections muffled the dispute. The NRC was keenly interested in Dama and took deliberate steps to eliminate further friction. Both protagonists were ordered by NRC officers to cease their palaver. Lansana was called before Chairman Juxon-Smith and told to cooperate. In the absence of encouragement from the central level, the palaver cooled during the period of military rule. It revived, however, immediately upon the re-inauguration of civilian government.

The new APC Government was friendly to those who had opposed SLPP candidates. Lansana's petition for a new contest was granted. He joined the APC prior to the by-election. As we shall see in other case studies, *it became common for strong but unsuccessful Independent candidates in the 1967 General Elections to be absorbed into the APC for the by-elections which followed.* Lansana's ties with the APC and Prime Minister Stevens became especially noticeable. This identification with the party in power greatly enhanced his chances for winning.

The attempt to hold by-elections in November 1968 was accompanied by violence and disruption. Nomination Day witnessed a serious attack on Lansana by a mob in Kenema Town, and subsequent reprisals against the PC sacked his compound and forced him to live permanently outside of Giema, the chiefdom headquarters. A national State of Emergency was declared. PC Dassama and a number of his allies were placed for two months in preventive detention. SLPP supporters claim that is was Lansana who sent to Freetown a list of those to be arrested in Dama. Whether true or not, it was generally perceived to be at' least approaching the truth, imbuing Lansana with added influence and prestige, i.e., with the reputation of one so close to the seat of ultimate power that he could have chiefs incarcerated. Lansana's new-found alliance improved his electoral performance considerably. When the by-election was finally held, he carried Dama by a majority especially impressive when the stature of his opponent is taken into account:[6]

KENEMA SOUTH BY-ELECTION, 1969		
	A.M. Lansana	*S. Jusu-Sheriff*
	(APC)	*(SLPP)*
Dama Chiefdom	5,489	2,174
Gaura Chiefdom	1,235	3,362

	(APC)	(SLPP)	
Tunkia Chiefdom	2,248	5,217	
Nomo Chiefdom	493	52	
Total	10,065	10,805	Elected

In Dama, Jusu-Sheriff gained a majority at only 4 of 19 polling stations. Two of these were in the town of Kpandebu, a heavily Muslimized area and the place where Jusu-Sheriff's ancestors first settled. Numerous kinship ties connect its residents not only with Jusu-Sheriff but with PC Dassama. The other two, Loppa and Baraka, are towns located in Lower Dabo section, whose section chief is an "uncle" of the Paramount Chief. Lansana's greatest victories were achieved in Upper Dabo, his own section. Madina, his home town, gave him a 393 to 8 advantage over Jusu-Sheriff.

The postelection period was more peaceful only in the sense that the intermittent violent clashes that accompanied the campaigning had ceased. The administration received petitions protesting the PC's alleged maladministration, favoritism, forced labor, improper levies, seizures of land, and infringement of *Poro* laws.[7] In response, Dassama has adopted a policy of withdrawal, living outside of Giema and generally remaining inactive so that there would be few grounds for deposition proceedings.

Lansana has filled this void. His close relationship with the party in power has earned him further dividends in his local struggle. Central decree substituted him for Dassama as Chairman of the Forest Industries Corporation, a seminationalized operation headquartered in Kenema Town. He was also appointed as a member of the Board of Governors for Kenema Government Secondary School. These positions provided him with leverage in helping youngmen find jobs and educational opportunities, highly valued goods in rural Sierra Leone. The administration did not object when he erected a new market at Giema to compete with the traditional market at Gofor, politicizing even petty trade. The backers of each party patronize the different market places:

It is true that the market at Gofor is used by the supporters of the PC, and can be called an SLPP market, while the Giema market is APC, used by the Speaker's supporters. The reason why Lansana had the Giema market built was to impress upon people his power, and his influence with the Government. People will flock to support someone if they know that he is in favor with the Government. Also a market is a place where people gather, and it is easy to talk to them.[8]

Reinforcing lines of cleavage make politics in Dama particularly acute. The basic rivalry between the chiefdom's two leading ruling families has been sharpened and sustained by the personal antagonism between its two leading executives, which in turn has activated conflicts between youngmen and elders. Competition at the central level has further exacerbated the dispute, linking local protagonists with the two national political forces and raising the stakes as well as the resources of grassroots politics.

GAURA CHIEFDOM

Politics in Gaura revolves about rivalries among four ruling houses, each identified with a particular town:

Mendigila	(Joru Town)
Gbatekaka	(Kpuabu)
Bunduka	(Sandaru)
Bakoi	(Kokoru)

Jostling among these families provides a particularly interesting example of how, among the Mende, kinship relations are used instrumentally for political purposes.

After the death of Paramount Chief Musa Mendigila (descendant of the great warrior-chief mentioned in Chapter III), Brima Bunduka was elected in 1944. The Englishman who presided noted that Bunduka belonged to the "Sandaru-Kokoru" house— i.e., Bunduka-Bokoi—and that it "is indeed one house, not two" as Provincial Secretary Fenton had recorded in 1933.[9] More to the point, which the presiding officer apparently missed, was the fact that an alliance had formed under an umbrella of putative kinship ties. It was for political purposes that the two families fused. As time went on, and as PC Bunduka proved himself a tyrannical and unpopular chief, the family broke apart into its original elements. Bunduka resigned as PC in 1951.

In the next contest another principle of alliance apparently operated to build a coalition large enough to elect a PC. That is, the principle of fusion by creating one family from two or more was replaced by a temporary alliance based on a principle akin to Riker's "minimum winning coalition."[10] The rules of the game set down by the administration helped to determine the behavior of the players. To win, a candidate had to receive at least 60% of the votes. If on the first ballot nobody won, a second ballot would be held in which minor candidates could realign themselves by supporting another candidate who had a greater chance of winning. This would be repeated until one candidate received at least 60%.

For the 1952 election there were nine candidates. Before the voting began there was an initial process of alignment which narrowed the field to four candidates. (Direction of support is indicated by arrows in the following table.)

PARAMOUNT CHIEF ELECTION, GAURA CHIEFDOM, 1952

Candidates

Siaffa Bunduka   (Sandaru)
Musa Gbatekaka   (Kpuabu)
Madam Tiange Gbatekaka   (Kpuabu)
Madam Soweh Mendigila   (Joru)
Fofi Sayo Kallon   (Sandaru)
Mara Kallon   (Sandaru)
Ama Mendigila   (Joru)
Nomo Kallon Sayo   (Sandaru)
Baimba Bokoi   (Kokoru)

Family loyalty had very little to do with most of these reshufflings. The votes received in the first ballot did not produce a candidate with the required 60% majority. Realignments in the second ballot gave Madam Tiange Gbatekaka slightly more than 60% of the votes cast.

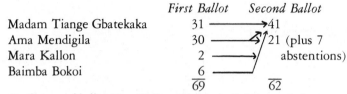

	First Ballot	*Second Ballot*
Madam Tiange Gbatekaka	31 ——→41	
Ama Mendigila	30 ——⌐/21 (plus 7	
Mara Kallon	2 ——→ / abstentions)	
Baimba Bokoi	6 ——	
	69	62

(In the second ballot, Mara Kallon and Baimba Bakoi gave their votes to Madam Gbatekaka; of Mendigila's votes, 2 went to Gbatekaka and 7 abstained.)

It seems clear that Riker's pattern of coalition manifested itself in this case, since an alliance comprising (almost) the smallest possible number of winning votes was formed.[11] The Bakoi family claim that they were promised the Speakership in return for their crucial support, but this did not materialize.[12]

The death of PC Madam Gbatekaka in 1964 was the signal for a return to the kinship principle of coalition-formation. In this case the Mendigilas and Gbatekakas fused to become one family, and a petition was sent to the government by the "Right Family of the Gbatekaka and Mendigilas" nominating Madam's son as a candidate. There was protest from some members of all four families about his eligibility, but a Cabinet decision ruled that he was a legitimate candidate. He won the election without difficulty, and became officially known as PC Alhaji Brima Mendigila Gbatekaka IV.

To outsiders the newly-conceived family presented a united front, as did a group of elders in two collective interviews:

The Gbatekakas and the Mendigilas are one family. They have agreed to rotate the Paramount Chieftaincy, although exceptions to this can be found in the case of people wanting the son of a popular PC to succeed him (her). This was the case with the present PC. The other two ruling houses are not nearly so united.[13]

There are four ruling houses. But the Joru house is really one, composed of the Gbatekakas and the Mendigilas. They are one family. Mendigila was a famous warrior. His son was Gbatekaka. So they are one family.[14]

Actually, these are *post hoc* justifications. Since the alliance was made only in 1964, to speak of historical ties reaching back to the pre-colonial era is clearly inventive. Indeed, it is most likely true that Gbatekaka was *not* Mendigila's son since Alldridge uses Gbatekaka's installation after Mendigila's death for proof that "primogeniture is not a *sine qua non* to a succession in Mendi law, and that chieftainship is not hereditary."[15] But this is precisely the point. Kinship relations, real *or* imagined, are employed as an ideational and emotional underpinning for alliances, the purposes of which are primarily political.

Behind the facade of family unity, the new Paramount Chief has experienced some difficulty in keeping the coalition together. Some elements of the Mendigila side have complained that he devotes undue attention to his own primary group, i.e., the Gbatekakas of Kpuabu, and that he has not kept the promises that originally induced the Mendigilas to join forces.[16] This partially explains why PC Mendigila-Gbatekaka has been a strong supporter of Jusu-Sheriff and the SLPP. A.M. Lansana is related to the Mendigila side, and it is said that the Chief feared that a victorious Lansana would perhaps give them enough encouragement to sever the bonds of coalition in order to try for the chieftaincy themselves.

There are additional, more compelling, explanations for the close relationship between the PC and the SLPP. The Gbatekakas historically have had ties to the Samas, the ruling house in Tunkia Chiefdom, and thus to Jusu-Sheriff. Indeed, PC Mendigila-Gbatekaka grew up in Tunkia, not in his own chiefdom. His mother supported Jusu-Sheriff in 1962, not only because of close family friendships but as well because the rival Sandaru house had put up B.S. Bunduka as its candidate for Parliament. In the 1967 and 1969 elections, A.M. Lansana was strongly identified with the Bunduka cause: Sandaru and Madina (his home town) are close physically as well as socially. And he has three sisters in Kokoru. So the PC had even more reason to back Jusu-Sheriff.

In short, national party alignments in Gaura followed almost invariably the lines of cleavage drawn by intrachiefdom politics, in turn determined by the structure of competition between leading families. The following diagram illustrates this pattern of linkage:

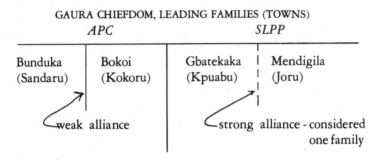

GAURA CHIEFDOM, LEADING FAMILIES (TOWNS)

APC		*SLPP*	
Bunduka (Sandaru)	Bokoi (Kokoru)	Gbatekaka (Kpuabu)	Mendigila (Joru)
	weak alliance	strong alliance - considered one family	

Election data lend support to this model. For the 1969 by-election the polling stations in Gaura chiefdom voted in the following manner (major towns are given in italics):[17]

Polling Station	A.M. Lansana (APC)	S. Jusu-Sheriff (SLPP)
Sandaru	488	59
Nyandehun	102	315
Mendekema	189	233
Koulowaila	39	311
Sembehun	95	172
Lelehun	15	263
Joru I	19	329
Joru II	31	283
Kpuabu	24	450
Perri	294	149
Kokoru	492	149
Tikonko	22	323
Baoma	25	326
Total	1,835	3,362

As expected, in each important town, large majorities were given to the party politician allied to its ruling family. A glance at the table on p. 152 will show that Jusu-Sheriff's success in Gaura was crucial for his victory in the constituency as a whole.

The period prior to the election witnessed occasional flurries of violence, much of it the result of growing friction between Sandaru and Joru. The unrest climaxed in January 1969, when the national army laid seige to Joru with tear gas and unruly soldiers. Most of its inhabitants fled into the bush, leaving Joru a ghost town for a few days. SLPP supporters claim that the destruction was inspired by elements from Sandaru as well as by A.M. Lansana. An independent observer confirms that it was most likely calculated to bolster APC support and to "demonstrate the iron fist of Government power."[18]

Disquiet continued even after the election skirmishing had ceased. PC Mendigila-Gbatekaka has been petitioned for offenses involving *Poro* bushes and for swearing the chiefdom to vote for Jusu-Sheriff. The PC in turn has sent a stream of complaints to the administration against Lamin Kallon, the leading APC stalwart in Gaura. In July an old land dispute was revived between Gaura and Dama chiefdoms. Gaura's PC complained that people from Dama destroyed fruits and pasted APC symbols on trees in the disputed bush. Speaker Lansana accused the Gaura people of similar destruction as well as displaying palm leaves, a *Poro* symbol.[19] The case is still unresolved. Beyond this, the chiefdom court has been ignored by most people, most likely because a Sandaru man was appointed by the Government as Court President.

In a manner considerably more distinct than in Dama, politics in Gaura is clearly based upon ruling house rivalries.

TUNKIA CHIEFDOM

Since 1958 Tunkia has been severely divided by the congruence of ruling house, geographical, and religious cleavages. This schism has been further reinforced by national politics.

There are two ruling families in the chiefdom, Sama and

Njavombo. The Samas are centered in Gorahum, the chiefdom headquarters and the leading town of Lower (southern) Tunkia. The Njavombos, who really are a collection of families,[20] have concentrated in Gegbwema, the major town of Upper (northern) Tunkia. This north-south split coincides loosely with a religious differentiation, since Gorahun and the small towns surrounding it are considered a seat of Muslim learning and Ahmadiya orthodoxy, whereas in the northern section is found the amalgam of animism and Islam (or Christianity) more commonly practiced in Sierra Leone. It was in Lower Tunkia that the ancestors of Jusu-Sheriff settled, building their reputation as powerful Alphas and aligning themselves with the Sama house.

In 1958 one Baba Keita, a trader from Guinea, persuaded PC Madam Mamawa Sama to lend him or sell him—depending upon the version—47 masks of the Bundu Society. He disappeared with the sacred objects; it is said that he sold them in Spain. Thus began the famous "*Soi* Case," the effects of which still paralyze the chiefdom.[21] Upper Tunkia, where secret societies are particularly strong, rose up against the chief and took her to the Magistrate's Court in Kenema. Big-name lawyers became involved: Albert Margai, Berthan Macaulay, L.A.M. Brewa, and S.T. Navo.* The case, dragged in and out of courts, reached its denouement when Baba Keita was caught and testified that a number of the complainants were among those who had plotted with him to obtain the Bundu masks. Both he and PC Madam Sama were acquitted.

Moinina Kallon, however, did not let the case die. A youngman whose mother ranked high in the Bundu Society, he gradually assumed the position of spokesman for the insurgent

---

*Berthan Macaulay was Attorney-General under Sir Albert and played a significant role in the maneuvering just prior to the first 1967 coup; as a result of his alleged involvement in the takeover he was tried for treason. L.A.M. Brewa during Sir Albert's premiership was a vocal member of the insurgent wing of the SLPP; his critical role in the electoral downfall of Sir Albert will be mentioned later in this chapter; he switched to the APC in 1968 and has served as Minister of Health and as Foreign Minister. S.T. Navo became a leading member of the SLPP Opposition.

elements of Tunkia. Despite attempts by the Government to reconcile the chiefdom, he persevered in collecting monies from Upper Tunkia people for hiring lawyers and firing the dispute in general, which, if anything, had increased in intensity since the high court's decision. As the Commissioner of Police wrote, "The chiefdom is now divided into pro-Madams and anti-Madams, with both sides frantically rushing in and out of Poro and Bundu bushes."[22] Disturbances continued to wrack the chiefdom during 1961, with Upper Tunkia accused of holding illegal meetings under the cloak of the *Poro* Society, and Kallon in turn refusing to accept compromises arranged by Assessor Chiefs until court expenses incurred during the *Soi* Case were paid to him and his faction by the Paramount Chief. In 1962 he was convicted by the Supreme Court of inciting people not to pay taxes. Finally, an inquiry held under the auspices of Resident Minister Taplima Ngobeh (Jusu-Sheriff's uncle), concluded that there would never be peace in Tunkia if Moinina Kallon remained in the chiefdom. He was banished in June 1963.

Had Prime Minister Milton Margai lived longer, the *Soi* Case and its concomitant chiefdom dispute would probably have slowly receded into the fog of half-forgotten history. But he died less than a year after Kallon's removal. The new Prime Minister, Albert Margai, soon began to chafe against the independence of some members of his Cabinet, one of them Lower Tunkia's favorite son. As part of his attempt to unseat Jusu-Sheriff, the Prime Minister lifted Moinina Kallon's banishment, thus assuring that the chiefdom dispute would be resumed in force by the time the 1967 election campaign was under way.

During the 1967 General Election, Kallon and the Njavombo ruling house allied with the Albert Margai faction of the SLPP, supporting the Independent candidacy of A.M. Lansana for the Kenema South seat against Jusu-Sheriff. But for the 1969 by-election they switched allegiance to the APC. There was, however, more continuity than change in this conversion: They remained consistent in supporting not only Lansana but the national politicians in power as well. A simple pattern of linkages had emerged whereby Upper Tunkia, led by Kallon and the Njavombos, became staunch adherents to the APC coalition while Lower Tunkia, under Jusu-Sheriff and the Samas, upheld itself as a stronghold of the SLPP movement.

The results of the election illuminate this pattern in detail. The following table designates each polling station as either "U" Upper Tunkia) or "L" (Lower Tunkia):[23]

1969 HOUSE OF REPRESENTATIVES BY-ELECTION, TUNKIA CHIEFDOM

Polling Station		A.M. Lansana (APC)	S. Jusu-Sheriff (SLPP)
Gorahun Town	(L)	7	810
Golawoma	(L)	14	719
Damawulo	(L)	13	895
Daru	(L)	60	355
Buluma	(U)	251	54
Taninahun	(U)	162	282
Jenneh	(L)	53	338
Gegbwema I	(U)	318	193
Gegbwema II	(U)	149	103
Ngiewahun	(U)	108	397
Jao Town I	(L)	90	364
Jao II	(L)	95	283
Kuawuma	(U)	428	70
Kongahun	(U)	262	116
Belebu	(U)	59	137
Gbaama	(U)	175	101
	Total	2,248	5,217

Lower Tunkia gave majorities (most of them overwhelming) to Jusu-Sheriff while Upper Tunkia's towns, with a few exceptions, supported Lansana. In order to explain the exceptions additional ad hoc factors must be introduced. Taninahun is the seat of a splinter faction of the Njavombo coalition of families. In recent years, it has been loosely identified with the Paramount Chief. In addition, its inhabitants were seriously bloodied by a joint police-army unit sent from Kenema during the State of Emergency. A number of people were killed and others jailed or detained, including B.M. Kamara, a candidate for Paramount Chief in 1952 and a ranking officer in the Sierra Leone Police who was never recommissioned following imprisonment during the 1968 coup. Their support of the SLPP was in part a reaction to what they considered an abuse of Government power. Ngiewahun is a town which in recent years has become embroiled in a number of "bush disputes" with neighboring villages, both in Tunkia and in an adjoining (APC-led) chiefdom. Hence, it has sought support from the Paramount Chief in its fight to farm surrounding land.

As in Dama and Gaura, unrest continues to plague Tunkia despite the lull in electioneering. PC Madam Sama has been petitioned for alleged victimization, infringement of laws of secret societies, favoritism, improper taxation, and refusal to allow the appointed (APC) Court President to conduct sittings. (The reader will note the similarities between this and petitions against the PC's of Dama and Gaura.) In keeping with the symmetry of such feuds, Lower Tunkia's people have retaliated with protests of their own. Moinina Kallon in particular has been the target of their attacks. He has been accused of opening without permission his own market in Gegbwema, setting himself up as a customs inspector on the Liberian border, and acting as mines warden, policeman, and magistrate. There is little doubt that he profits from a perpetuated chiefdom dispute, since he collects contributions from supporters to fight cases in court and in the hustings. In general these complaints accuse him of abusing his position as a local APC leader by translating his connections with the governing party into exploitative power.[24] In addition, interaction between the overall chiefdom dispute and localized bush palavers has led to further crop destruction and reported deaths.

Tunkia never has been a tightly-knit chiefdom. Contemporary events have rendered the fabric of unity even more tenuous by perpetuating divisive issues (e.g., the *Soi* Case) and exacerbating existing cleavages. National leaders have been as responsible as local factions for the persistence of unrest; indeed, their mutual reinforcement provides the most economical explanation for the patterns of political conflict now extant in this part of Kenema South.

NOMO CHIEFDOM

While in most cases internal division determine center-local politics, in Nomo *inter*chiefdom suspicions seem to contribute most to an explanation of its voting behavior in 1967-69. As Sierra Leone's tiniest chiefdom, Nomo is understandably wary of her larger neighbors.

Occasional proposals have been put forth recommending that it be amalgamated with either Gaura or Tunkia. A major difficulty, however, is that Nomo is composed of Golas, a Liberian people, whereas its neighbors are Mendes. As well, to merge such a small area with considerably larger units would relegate the Nomo people to permanent subservience. In view of this, the Chief Commissioner in 1955 argued against amalgamation, recommending instead that Nomo "be recognized as an uncharacteristic corner of Sierra Leone."[25]

Rumors of amalgamation have not ceased to worry the people of Nomo, however. This is a major reason why the chiefdom's voters were nearly unanimous in rejecting Jusu-Sheriff in the 1967 and 1969 elections. Paramount Chief Karmoh feared that the Tunkia and Gaura chiefs wanted to annex Nomo with the help of their powerful SLPP ally.[26] Beyond this, Nomo and Tunkia had become engaged in a dispute over forestry lands which sharply curtailed the flow of royalties into both chiefdoms.

On the other hand, the Njavombos have strong family connections in Nomo and were able to communicate intimately with its PC. As well, like many chiefs, Karmoh's policy was to support the party in power, which during the by-elections, meant the APC.

There is little internal dissention within Nomo. Elections of Paramount Chiefs normally provide overwhelming majorities for the winner.[27] Being small and remote, it has experienced little social and economic mobilization; migrations, strangers, rising social groups, inflated ambitions, and geographical mobility are not among the problems threatening the order of the regime. Opposition factions are miniscule, as is suggested by the results of the 1969 by-elections:[28]

NOMO CHIEFDOM

Polling Station	A.M. Lansana (APC)	S. Jusu-Sheriff (SLPP)
Faima	390	28
Dambara	103	24
Total	493	52

Given such cohesion, the chiefdom faces the outside world as a unit, contrary to the common pattern in Mendeland, where opposing segments ally with rivals at a higher level.

Kenema East Constituency

Kenema East has been a persistent source of political turmoil since the 1967 election, due in large measure to a long-standing dispute which has torn Lower Bambara, the largest and wealthiest chiefdom in the constituency. The remaining parts of the Kenema East, Dodo, and Malegohun chiefdoms, are considerably more peaceful, but their tranquility is occasionally disrupted not only by the antagonisms which spill over from their larger neighbor but as well by the effects of the diamond mining which is common to the entire area.

In the 1967 General Election there were five candidates, three from Lower Bambara and two from Malegohun. The results published by the NRC indicated that the SLPP candidate gained a plurality:[29]

KENEMA EAST CONSTITUENCY, 1967

1. Joseph G.M. Borniea	– (SLPP)	6,560	Elected
2. Joe Quee-Nyagua	– (Independent)	4,796	
3. Allieu Koroma	– (APC)	1,250	
4. James R.M. Gendemeh	– (Independent)	1,225	
5. Alfred Saffa Yajo	– (Independent)	1,491	
	Total	15,322	

The winner, *Joseph Borniea,* is an educated member of a family usually associated with the Speakership of Lower Bambara chiefdom. His father had been the Speaker for Alimamy Farma, the Paramount Chief who succeeded Nyagua following the latter's arrest and deportation during the Hut Tax War. He has maintained a similarly close political relationship with Farma's grandson, A.M. Farma, the present Paramount Chief. Their major rival, *Joe Quee-Nyagua,* is himself a grandson of the famous warrior-chief. As a former Paramount Chief, he is the leading member of the "out" ruling house of Lower Bambara. (See Chapter 4.) The APC candidate, *Allieu Koroma,* is a Temne connected with the diamond industry which predominates in Lower Bambara. *James Gendemeh* is the son of Malegohun's Paramount Chief. *A.S. Yajo* is a prominent member of an opposition ruling house in Malegohun.

Following the restoration of civilian Government, Joe Quee-Nyagua joined the APC and successfully petitioned for a fresh election in Kenema East. The courts upheld his claim that undue influence had been exerted by the Government and the chiefdom administrations in favor of the SLPP candidate. For this by-election, naturally he enjoyed the support of the former APC candidate, Koroma. A.S. Yajo also lent his backing, while, in keeping with the pattern of local opposition, Gendemeh supported Borniea. The results reversed the outcome of the General Election, giving Joe Quee-Nyagua a majority in all three chiefdoms:[30]

KENEMA EAST, BY-ELECTION. 1969		
Chiefdom	Joe Quee-Nyagua	Joseph Borniea
	(APC)	*(SLPP)*
Lower Bambara	4,633	3,483
Malegohun	1,121	497
Dodo	1,886	425
Total	7,640 Elected	4,405

As in Kenema South, a strong Independent candidate was absorbed into the APC; likewise, with party and Government backing his electoral performance improved remarkably—in this case enough to unseat the candidate who ostensibly had won in 1967. Joseph Borniea in turn petitioned for a reelection, claiming duress on the part of the police, army, Government, and APC members. By July 1970 (when this research ceased) a final decision by the Supreme Court was still pending, giving rise to tensions and uncertainty which became an integral part of local politics, especially in Lower Bambara.

LOWER BAMBARA CHIEFDOM

Peaceful politics in this chiefdom has been a scarce commodity. Fierce competition between its two ruling houses, Nyagua and Farma, has been exacerbated and complicated within the last fifteen years by the introduction of intensive diamond mining by both a European extractive company and individual African diggers. These two factors—family strife and diamonds—in large measure account for the pattern of politics in Lower Bambara.

In a remote sense, the origins of politics in Lower Bambara extend back to the defeat and deportation of Nyagua during the Hut Tax War. As a matter of historical fact, the events connected with installing a successor established the two-family recruitment system which prevails today. Alimamy Farma replaced Nyagua and ruled until 1933, and no additional family has sought rights to supply the Paramount Chief. This much is clear. Yet uncertainty surrounding Nyagua and his successor has supplied the propaganda mills of both sides with plentiful raw material. Politics takes the form of disputing the hereditary qualifications of the opposing side. The Nyagua family in particular has adopted this mode of adversary politics.

The political activists of the Nyagua family claim that Alimamy Farma was really Nyagua's servant and that he was simply appointed as a caretaker for the chiefdom during the latter's exile. For instance, during a hotly disputed election for PC in 1954, they wrote to the Provincial Commissioner that Nyagua "handed [the chiefdom] to his drummer-boy Farma who he brought from Sherbro, to take care of it, and Farma in one way or other became Paramount Chief of the Lower Bambara Chiefdom."[31] The purpose of this lesson in history was to prove that "the Nyaguas owned the chiefdom" and that their claim to the chieftaincy was far more legitimate than the Farmas. During the same election turmoil the Nyagua spokesman sought to prove to the Administration that the Farma candidate, Dauda, was merely the "houseboy" of the late Alimamy Farma and not a kinsman in line for political succession. The same tactic was used in 1958 when they tried to disallow Moriwai Farma's eligibility with the claim that he was not the real son of Alimamy.

For their part, the Farmas maintain that it is the Nyaguas themselves who are the "strangers" to the chiefdom. Their version emphasizes precolonial times, when Nyagua was supposed to have come from the east to attach himself to a more powerful warrior, Faba of Dodo. (See Chapter 3.) Since the British broke up the warrior empire after the Hut Tax War, the Farmas claim that the real ties of the Nyaguas are with Dodo chiefdom while the founders of Panguma, Lower Bambara's headquarters town, were they, the Farmas.

The historical accuracy of these claims is not germane from the standpoint of political analysis. The true facts have been long lost amidst the moving dialectic of charge and countercharge. The important point is that political competition takes place within the idiom of hereditary legitimacy. Political rivalry becomes translated into a particular language, one in which controversy over kinship credentials becomes a means for expressing other, wider issues and conflicts. Controversy about family—political—qualifications is not the root cause of the long-lived dispute in Lower Bambara; it is simply a medium for expressing partisanship in "familiar" terms, a propaganda mechanism.

Persistent conflagration in the chiefdom has stemmed rather from the election to Paramount Chief of Joe Quee-Nyagua, his deposition and banishment, and the subsequent skirmishing surrounding his return to Lower Bambara and to prominence. He became Paramount Chief under unusual circumstances. In 1936 he contested for the chiefship against his father's brother, Quee Gboli, and emerged with only a slight majority. Ordinarily such an election would have been declared unsuccessful and another attempt made at a later date in the hope that a broader consensus could be achieved. But in this case the administration suddenly discovered that Quee Gboli twenty-five years earlier had been convicted of manslaughter. This apparently was sufficient to disqualify him, and the Governor appointed Joe Quee-Nygua as PC despite the lack of widespread support for him. In retrospect, this proved a mistake, for his administration was characterized by constant controversy, including accusations that he at least tolerated the presence of ritual murder activities in Lower Bambara. The Speaker and a number of section chiefs made serious petitions against him, and it became clear that he did not have the confidence of sizeable portions of the chiefdom. The denouement came when an inquiry was held in 1947 to investigate his administration, resulting in his removal.

Deposition and exile did not bring an end to the dispute. Although banished to another district, his "presence" served to prevent the election of a successor for six years. In 1950 he was allowed to stand by proxy, and gained a slight majority over Dauda Farma but not enough for a successful election. The same thing happened in 1951. Finally in 1954 the administration decided to solve the problem by expanding the size of the TA from 75 members to 160. This gave Dauda Farma exactly the 60% majority support necessary for election.[32]

It took strong outside intervention to break the deadlock. Outside intervention also contributed to a resumption of the underlying conflict. The advent of African Ministers made the top levels of Government more accessible to men like Joe Quee-Nyagua who felt that they had been victimized by the British. His friend Albert Margai became Minister of Education, Local Government and Welfare. In April 1955 his banishment was lifted through Albert's explicit orders. As might be expected, this news was received with extreme distaste in Lower Bambara. Albert personally accompanied him to Panguma, where "he spoke to the TA's rudely and bruskly, saying that they had no choice but to accept Joe Quee because the Government had decided so."[33]

Not entirely providentially, his return coincided with the rise to prominence of diamonds in the public consciousness. Rich deposits had been discovered in Lower Bambara near the Tongo River. PC Dauda Farma and the chiefdom authorities were engaged in negotiations with Sierra Leone Selection Trust (SLST), the European company which had enjoyed a diamond-mining monopoly in Sierra Leone since 1935. SLST had agreed to renounce its monopoly in return for sole rights over two deposits, a major area in Kono District and a smaller core in Lower Bambara, which came to be called Tongo Field. At the same time, the Government was readying its plans to open up all other diamondiferous areas to individual African diggers under a licencing program known as the Alluvial Diamond Mining Scheme. Decisions made during those few years in the mid-1950s had vast implications for politics not only in the mining areas but in Sierra Leone as a whole. SLST—representing economic power—became a major source of income for the Government. African diggers—representing political power—reflected the growing legitimacy and influence of popular forces. Conflict between the two modes of mining has persisted ever since.

Lower Bambara found itself a focal point for intense concern from international cartels, from national politicians whose sense of public interest and private fortune was sometimes difficult to distinguish, from immigrants flocking from all over West Africa in search of quick wealth, and from its own citizens, who felt both the danger of exploitation and the opening opportunities for securing at last their own interests and goals. Hence it is not surprising that Ministers should seek leverage at the grassroots level by forging alliances with local potentates such as Joe Quee-Nyagua. Nor is it surprising that his faction should seize this opportunity to build its resources.

Security on the SLST leases fast became a gargantuan problem, larger in scale in Kono but hugely disruptive in Tongo Field as well. The two areas were linked because periodic police "stranger drives" to reduce illicit diamond mining (IDM) in Kono spilled hundreds of dispossessed diggers into Lower Bambara. By 1958

gangs of illicit miners 400-strong were attacking the diamondiferous swamps of Tongo Field.[34] Normally such raids on the
SLST reserves in Lower Bambara followed the rhythm of police
and army action in Kono: When "stranger drives" were being
conducted in Kono, IDM rose sharply in Tongo Field. Recently,
however, the intensity of IDM in Tongo Field has been not only
high but constant, indicating that chiefdom people as well as
"stranger elements" have become seriously involved. As one European employee of SLST put it:

> Normally the local people do not engage in IDM to any large ex-
> tent. However, lately the scale of IDM has been so large that
> everybody is involved, local people included. Each side in the
> political rivalry tries to blame the other for engaging in IDM. It
> has become so blatant that few people feel that they can afford to
> stay out of it.[35]

The scale of organized illicit mining has become so large that
gangs of 1,000 – 1,500 raid the SLST concession, dig numerous
huge pits, wash, sift, and extract their treasures, and dispose of
it—all in a night.

The full explanation of this recent turn of events is shrouded
in the mystery of illegal operations, but some general obser-
vations can be put forth.

1. The popularity of SLST within Lower Bambara has always
been contingent upon internal political factors. In co-operating
with SLST, Paramount Chief Dauda Farma and his successor,
A.M. Farma, opened themselves up to criticism from their rival
faction. Since the earliest negotiations with the company, the
Nyagua side has berated the lease arrangement as European exploitation of what properly belongs to Lower Bambara's
landholders. This has naturally attracted to their faction those
people and those chiefdom sections who feel deprived by the
alien presence and who have pressed, sometimes successfully, for
an extension of the diamond-mining licensing scheme into sections of the SLST concession. As long as the Farmas and their
supporters—prime among them being Section Cheif Samuka

Konoa, in whose section Tongo Field is located—have been in control, SLST has received the (albeit grudging) cooperation of chiefdom people in general. But since 1969 and the election of Joe Quee-Nyagua to Parliament, the ensuing power shift within the chiefdom has weakened the elements disposed toward protecting the company's interests. The more the opposition to Paramount Chief A.M. Farma is able to muster political support internally and externally, the less he is willing or able to interfere with IDM.

It is worth stressing the interrelationship between local and central factors in dealing with the problem of illicit mining. Unless troops are to be permanently deployed against illegal diggers, the only means of control is reliance upon chiefdom people to police their own area. This means that local people must be well-disposed toward SLST. Yet is is the Central Government with which the company must deal on important issues. Moreover, it pays taxes directly to the Central Government, relegating SLST contributions to chiefdoms to the still marginal realm of yearly grants and occasional development projects. With such meager economic incentives available to counter IDM at the local level, the only remaining restraint is political. Remove this last restraint and IDM becomes rampant. This is precisely what happened in Lower Bambara. In 1969, the APC ran openly on a "free diamond mining" platform in Kenema East: If the APC won, unfettered mining would be permitted on the SLST lease. This no doubt contributed to Joe Quee-Nyagua's victory, not only by promising what everybody wanted but also by attracting outside supporters, especially Temnes from the North, who were drawn to Lower Bambara by the prospect of lucrative mining and friendly politicians. It also no doubt weakened already-feeble restraints against IDM, even though the APC Government was in no way prepared to honor the extravagant promises of its grassroots campaigners in Kenema East.

2. Although diamond mining in Sierra Leone has always been associated with "floating populations" and "stranger elements," the problem became especially critical during the 1968-69 elec-

tioneering in Lower Bambara. The ardent miners are mostly Northerners, Temnes in particular. (Mendes are more disposed toward using their control of diamondiferous land as a source of wealth, rather than toward doing the actual digging.) The North is a core region of support for the APC, and its diaspora in the diamond areas was no less committed to the party. Indeed, between 1967 and 1969 the "stranger element" in Lower Bambara had established an APC branch that far surpassed all others in Kenema District in terms of organization and financial resources. Nonnatives, increasingly numerous, wealthy, and cohesive, became a threat to the SLPP supporters in the chiefdom, especially when Joe Quee-Nyagua joined the APC organization and became its candidate for the 1968 by-election. In essence, this represented an alliance between the opposition ruling house and the diamond-mining strangers.

In response to this threat to its incumbency and to its SLPP allies, the chiefly hierarchy set in motion *Poro* Society activities designed to intimidate non-members in order to expel all "foreigners" from the chiefdom. *Poro* initiation ceremonies were instituted in a number of important towns, and the order went out that all "strangers" should remove themselves immediately. This swift move was apparently highly effective, since informants have reported that almost all nonnatives were forced to evacuate. The Government's reaction, however, was equally swift. It declared a nationwide State of Emergency, postponed the by-election scheduled for November 1968, and placed in preventive detention most leading SLPP activists, including Paramount Chief Farma and Section Chief Samuka Konoa. Under the security of police and troops, strangers flocked back to Lower Bambara, swelling their original numbers and, with their political rivals incarcerated, free to campaign unopposed for the elections now scheduled for March 1969. This chain of events greatly increased the number of strangers—APC supporters—in the chiefdom; as well, it sharply reduced the authority of the Paramount Chief and his hierarchy. IDM rose dramatically in response.

3. The willingness of chiefdom elders to cooperate with the Government in the area of mining was undercut by an NRC decree which gave to the Central Government powers of allocating licenses which hitherto had been in the hands of landowners. NRC Decree #49 of August 17, 1967, invested in the Area Superintendent of Mines the authority to decide who would get a license to mine where. Previously, a prospective miner had to get the consent of each figure in the chiefdom hierarchy—PC, Section Chief, town chief, landowner, and landholder—before he could get a license for a plot. Each step cost him dearly. The system permitted outright extortion of miners on the part of local authorities. The new arrangement sidestepped this fleecing of strangers but introduced a different species of abuse. After the return of civilian rule, political affiliation became a major criterion for distributing mining sites. Since the APC has been in power, the effect has been to favor Northerners over the local people. Mendes have complained bitterly that they should have the right to release their land to whomever they want. As one mining official explained it:

If things continue like this, the [Alluvial Diamond Mining] Scheme will flop. About 75% of the people of this Province are dependent for their livelihood on diamonds. There will come a time when the weaker people [politically], the local people, will stand firm and say no. They will demand their rights to control their own land.[36]

The cumulative effect of centralizing such decisions will be to increase the influence of strangers and the APC in localities like Lower Bambara. This in turn adversely affects the willingness and ability of chiefdom leaders to control illicit mining in both the SLST concessions and the scheduled areas for licenses digging.

4. Finally, in Sierra Leone there is often a direct relationship between money and political influence. The mechanisms linking them range from outright ability to buy votes, to the respect and

personal followings which often attach to wealthy men. The sharp increase in wealth in the diamondiferous chiefdoms expanded the pool of political resources, not necessarily to the benefit of incumbents and the established order. It is this which worries Paramount Chief A.M. Farma. He is widely accused of ignoring IDM. He frankly admits that he considers this a Central Government problem and that if he were to interfere with illicit miners they would plot against him and accuse him of being a pawn of SLST. In other words, those who came to the chiefdom to make money would use it against him were he to work against their interests. IDM thrives upon such official neglect.

The Central Government has also been dilatory in Tongo Field. It set up a Residence Permit Board composed of the District Officer and a number of appointed local leaders, including the President of the APC constituency organization for Kenema East. A police drive against illicit miners has been contingent upon completion of the Board's task, which is to decide which nonnatives would be permitted to reside in or near the SLST lease. During the time of this research, the Board met frequently but worked slowly, so that by July 1970 it was still in session, thus forestalling a concerted effort to rid the area of elements ostensibly engaged in IDM.

To return to the 1969 by-election, in a chiefdom as large and complex as Lower Bambara, there exists a complicated interplay of factors which explain why Joe Quee-Nyagua was able to shatter the SLPP's monopoly.

As a former PC and leader of the opposition ruling house, he enjoys automatic legitimacy and support within a sizeable segment of the chiefdom. Polling stations 34 and 35 (Table 5.1) illustrate the pattern of ruling house competition and its links with party politics. Voting in Panguma (headquarters for both families) and its outlying towns coincided in general terms with ruling house associations. Panguma I is the section of town controlled by the Nyagua side, while Panguma-Kpengbayiema is the seat of Farma residence.

Equally instrumental, however, was Joe Quee-Nyagua's close alliance with the stranger element and its well-organized APC

TABLE 5.1
Lower Bambara Chiefdom, Results of Parliamentary By-Election, 1969

NUMBER AND NAME OF POLLING STATION	J. QUEE-NYAGUA (APC)	J. BORNIEA (SLPP)
1. Old Lalehun I	111	140
2. Old Lalehun II	55	72
3. New Lalehun	146	118
4. Deima	44	129
5. Semewabu	24	109
6. Giema II	40	41
7. Tokpombu I	67	67
8. Tokpombu II	60	49
9. Sandeyeima	83	36
10. Kundu Sandeyeima	57	112
11. Taninahun	52	183
12. Bomi I	27	78
13. Bomi II	45	137
14. Lowoma I	135	79
15. Lowoma II	190	44
16. Fayamawa	211	58
17. Giehun I	179	89
18. S.L.S.T. No. 9	183	33
19. Konia	226	33
20. Fayama I	129	13
21. Foindu I	160	142
22. Foindu II	125	51
23. Foindu III	140	85
24. Foindu IV	116	21
25. Komende Luyama	319	108
26. Guala	154	113
27. Guala Town	80	68
28. Konjo I	200	120
29. Konjo II	152	113
30. Saama I	82	173
31. Saama II	105	30
32. Gangama	132	47
33. Weima	118	150
34. Panguma I	166	156
35. Panguma-Kpengbayeima	79	185
36. Gbandiwo	194	82
37. Kamboma Oldtown	118	101
38. Kamboma	129	118
TOTAL	4633	3483

Source: Electoral Commission, Score Sheet, Kenema East By-Election, 1969.

branch. Polling stations 3-16 and 18 are located within the
Tongo Field lease. In most of these towns are located large
stranger communities, composed largely of SLST employees and
workers in related occupations. The organizational core of
Kenema East's APC branch is likewise associated with this area.
It is also, however, the region which benefits most directly from
SLST's presence, and therefore whose section chiefs most
strongly support the incumbent ruling family and SLST. Hence,
competition within Tongo Field was fierce, particularly in
Tokpombu, headquarters of Section Chief Samuka Konoa, who,
as we have seen, has been the most stalwart supporter of PC
Farma.

The diamondiferous areas *outside* of the Tongo lease also include significant collections of well-organized strangers.
Moreover, these sections are less well-disposed toward SLST
than those graced by geology and politics with the fortune to be
included within the concession boundary. Polling stations 20-27
and 30-32 are located just to the south of Tongo Field along a
riverine strip rich in diamonds. Not only is the stranger population relatively high, but the region has been intermittently
engaged in a political effort against SLST, occasionally successful,
to induce the company to release portions of its base for licensed
mining by individual Africans. Not surprisingly, then, the APC
call for "free mining" struck especially resonant tones within
these towns. In all these towns but one, the APC won by large
majorities. The exception was Sanama I, home of A.J. Musa, a
powerful trader long a close confidant of PC Farma.

In some towns strictly particularistic factors determined the
electoral outcome. Such was the case of Konia (polling station
19), where common dislike of Section Chief Sheku Jaiah united
the masses of section people with Joe Quee-Nyagua. When he
was Paramount Chief, Joe Quee had a long history of clashes with
this truculent section chief, and the antagonism has persisted.
Sheku Jaiah was suspended from office shortly after the by-
election, in anticipation of deposition proceedings.

Finally, the effects of official intimidation must be seriously
considered. SLPP-supporters are unaminous in offering this as

the explanation for their defeat in Lower Bambara. There can be little doubt that the preventive detention of over a dozen of the chiefdom's leading figures cast an ominous shadow over those politicos disposed toward opposing the Government party and its local allies. Among those detained for at least two months were the SLPP candidate, the Paramount Chief, a section chief, a section speaker, two town chiefs, the Court President and numerous traders.[37] Not only did the APC gain the advantage of campaigning with its opponents in prison, but its local activists had thrust upon them the prestige associated with the ability to incarcerate powerful men.

Joseph Borneia's election petition before the Supreme Court stressed the issue of intimidation. He charged undue influence on the part of authorities at both the central and local levels. A Cabinet Minister, he testified, threatened to depose and put into detention any chief who did not support the APC. Another Minister was alleged to have accompanied soldiers to various polling stations in an attempt to intimidate voters. (These charges were denied by the Ministers.) At the local level, he claimed, chiefdom authorities threatened to prevent him and his supporters from campaigning in all three chiefdoms if he did not step down so that Joe Quee-Nyagua might be elected unopposed. Moreover, local APC activists threatened and physically coerced voters at certain polling stations, according to his testimony.[38]

Amidst the fog of legal maneuvering and terminology, it is difficult to assess fully the charge that official intimidation had a decisive effect upon the election outcome. Some of the allegations appear to be accurate. Although the lower-court judge decided against the petition, he readily granted that chiefdom elders had influenced the electorate and that there was violence and harassment on the part of both sides. Indeed, it was, *inter alia*, on these points which led the Court of Appeals to dismiss this decision and grant a retrial.[39] And it is clear that a substantial portion of the electorate in Kenema East stayed away from the polls during the by-election; although it was a more intensely fought campaign, 20% fewer ballots were cast than in the 1967 election. This reduction probably favored the APC, but the precise effects are impossible to assign reliably. Suffice it to say that violence and intimidation comprised one among a number of significant factors which together determined the election outcome.

Official intervention in Lower Bambara's squabble did not cease with the end of the by-election campaign. In an apparent effort to induce Mr. Borniea to drop his election petition, the Government initiated an inquiry into the administration of Paramount Chief Farma. Before it had gone past the preliminary stage the inquiry was called off, most likely in return for Farma's promise to cease his support of Borniea and the SLPP in Lower Bambara. As part of the understanding, the Prime Minister is said to have been willing to lend his good offices toward reconciling the chiefdom.

DODO CHIEFDOM

In contrast to Lower Bambara, Dodo is rent by no important factions or issues. It is one of the few chiefdoms whose unity is not disturbed by ruling house feuding; although officially there are two ruling families, the Gegbais have experienced only negligible competition from their rivals. Divisive influences from without have been minimal as well: Roads are few; economic development is rudimentary; and the "floating population" is sparse. Diamonds have very recently been discovered in Dodo, so the subsequent influx of money and strangers may alter significantly the political complexion of the chiefdom within the next few years, but so far tranquility has been the watchword.

Interviewees are in agreement that the posture assumed by PC James Gagbai II was decisive in determining Dodo's preferences during the by-election. By an overwhelming majority, all but one of the chiefdom's polling stations supported Joe Quee-Nyagua and the APC. His detractors claim that he was intimidated by the threat of Government reprisal into supporting the APC. He himself attributes his endorsement of the APC candidate to two factors: his sense of duty to support the Government, and kinship obligations.

Quee was our official candidate put up by the Prime Minister.
That is why we supported him. In 1967 we also supported him.
We supported him because he is our relative. . . . Joe Quee and I
are the great great grandchildren of Faba. We are related to Joe
Quee. You can't leave your brother crying. You want to encourage
him.[40]

Note, however, that he is also related to a rival figure in Lower
Bambara, PC Farma, so there has been an element of selectivity
in his choice of kinship ties as an explanation for his alliance with
the Hon. Joe Quee-Nyagua. To be sure, memories of the great
warrior empire, when Dodo and Lower Bambara were united under Faba and Nyagua, no doubt lend support to the bonds
between them, but even more so contemporary political exigencies have activated them as historical justifications of a mutually
convenient coalition.

An additional factor may also have entered PC Gagbai's
alliance calculations. Dodo and Lower Bambara have been engaged in a minor "bush dispute" since 1961. He may have felt
that he was more likely to gain favorable treatment on this issue
from Lower Bambara's opposition faction than from the incumbent chiefly hierarchy, which was heavily supported by the
section allegedly engaged in the pursuit of *lebensraum*.

MALEGOHUN CHIEFDOM

Malegohun is an amalgam of three smaller chiefdoms brought
together during the latter colonial period in the name of efficiency and economic viability. Like most other amalgamations in
Sierra Leone, Malegohun suffers from inveterate opposition
among its component parts. The three original elements—
Horahun, Togboma, and Konjo chiefdoms—compete with each
other for economic and political prizes, prime among them the
Paramount Chieftaincy.

In the 1967 General Election, the son of the Paramount Chief
and the son of the Speaker were both Independent candidates.
James R.M. Gendemeh was backed mostly by voters in his own

section, the former Togboma chiefdom. Saffa Yajo received most of his support in Horahun. Each received a small percentage of the total votes cast in Kenema East, a direct reflection of the narrow electoral foundations upon which their campaigns were built; that is, each relied for his political base upon limited segments of an already tiny chiefdom. In addition, they competed more against each other than against the more powerful candidates from Lower Bambara, a larger and wealthier chiefdom by far. For the by-election, Gendemeh put his efforts behind the SLPP, while Yajo and his section supported the APC candidate.

As in the case of Dodo, most informants attribute Joe Quee-Nyagua's by-election victory in Malegohun to the position taken by its Paramount Chief. There seems little question that PC Musa Gendemeh actively supported Quee-Nyagua. Indeed, he worked directly against his own son, who had become a key member of Joseph Borniea's campaign staff. His critics, including his son, claim that he supported the APC out of fear of Government reprisal. As one SLPP activist put it:

> In Malegohun the Minister of Interior . . . just before the election called all the TA's together, and told them if they don't vote for the APC they will be taken to Mafanta. Then [the Paramount Chief] said, "You heard the Minister; vote APC or you will be put into detention."[41]

PC Gendemeh died shortly after the election, but had he lived longer it is likely that, on being interviewed, his justification for supporting Joe-Quee-Nyagua would have resembled that of PC Gegbai of Dodo. It is likely, too, that he would have mentioned kinship ties linking Malegohun and the Nyagua faction, since Joe Quee was reared by a ruling family in Konjo section.

In keeping with the prevailing pattern of political competition in Malegohun, the two major candidates for Paramount Chief are James Gendemeh and Saffa Yajo. The relative fortunes of each will turn largely on how well he is able to unite his own section behind him as well as on his success in bringing the remaining section, Konjo, into his camp. Since Malegohun is diamondiferous, mining will also be an issue in the chieftaincy campaign.[42] As part of his strategy, James Gendemeh wrote to SLST asking the company to begin operations in Malegohun. (The offer was declined.) He felt that a chiefdom as a whole benefits considerably more from the presence of SLST than from licensed mining by individual diggers. As a member of the District Council Committee of Management he was also in a position to encourage and withhold development projects within the chiefdom in order to enhance his own chances for becoming elected Paramount Chief. For instance, he delayed work on an important bridge to deprive Joe Quee-Nyagua of credit for its completion; a major plank in the latter's campaign platform in Horahun and Konjo was a finished bridge which would link these remote sections with the outside world.

Like Dodo, Malegohun chiefdom supported the APC in the 1969 by-elections, due in large measure to the inclination of the chiefdom hierarchy to support the party in power. Unlike Dodo, however, internal cleavages provided substantial opportunity for the SLPP Opposition to sustain a base of operations.

Kenema Central and Kenema Town Constituencies

Two chiefdoms of unmistakably unequal size and wealth comprise Kenema Central constituency. Nongowa is the largest and most cosmopolitan chiefdom in the district, the site not only of Kenema Town, administrative headquarters for the Eastern Province, but of a flourishing commercial and industrial network made especially active by extensive extraction and trading of diamonds. Koya chiefdom, on the other hand, is small and remote, with no significant enterprise other than farming.

Kenema *Town* Constituency is composed of one section— called Gbo section—of Nongowa. This renders its politics an integral part of chiefdom politics, compounding the distinctive character of Kenema urban affairs.

Since it was formed, Kenema Central has been the domain of *Kutubu I. Kai-Samba,* second son of Paramount Chief Kai-Samba I of Nongowa and an Oxford-educated lawyer. His major opponent, both in 1962 and 1967, was *James During,* Albert

Margai's private secretary. A minor opponent was *Mohammed Salamie Cole,* a Temne who ran as the APC candidate. The results of the 1967 General Election were as follows:[43]

KENEMA CENTRAL CONSTITUENCY, 1967

1. James During (SLPP)	6,477
2. M.S. Cole (APC)	2,821
3. K.I. Kai-Samba (Independent)	7,567 elected

There was no petition of this election, so the results have stood and Hon. K.I. Kai-Samba has taken his place as one of the most vocal members of the SLPP Opposition.

Note, however, that he ran as an Independent, despite the fact that he was Minister of Agriculture and Natural Resources and despite the long and intimate relationship between the Kai-Sambas and the SLPP. The estrangement between K.I. Kai-Samba and Albert Margai offers a fascinating episode illuminating not only the former's Independent candidacy but a whole complex of relationships linking central and local politics. This theme informs the accounts that follow.

Political fortunes in Kenema Town Constituency have also been intimately bound with the Kai-Sambas. The seat was first held by *B.S. Massaquoi,* remotely related to the family through his mother, and a political protege of Chief Kai-Samba I. Due to a split in the family, Massaquoi was displaced in the 1967 General Election by an Independent, *J.B. Francis,* who had married a Kai-Samba and whose allegiance embraced K.I. Kai-Samba and his challenge to the Prime Minister. A minor candidate was *Edward Lamin,* a Mende journalist from outside the chiefdom and an original founder of the APC. The results of the 1967 election suggest the intensity of the cleavage which split the constituency in two almost equal parts:[44]

KENEMA TOWN CONSTITUENCY, 1967

1. B.S. Massaquoi (SLPP)	2,063
2. Edward Lamin (APC)	1,013
3. J.B. Francis (Independent)	2,464 Elected

The two successful Independents from Nongowa, Kai-Samba and Francis, played a crucial role in bringing to pass Sir Albert's political demise in Sierra Leone.

NONGOWA CHIEFDOM

The year 1956 witnessed the death of PC Kai-Samba I, whose strong and even-handed leadership, as we have seen, achieved admirable results in terms of economic and political development in Nongowa and throughout Kenema District as well. He was succeeded by his eldest son, who was elected (and became known as Kai-Samba II) in honor of his father. Political consecration proved a mistake in this case, for the new chief's reign was soon despoiled by intermittent seiges of alcoholism and mental sickness. Lacking the highly competent leadership which had built it into an advanced chiefdom, Nongowa was plunged into intrigue and stalemate by a number of big men who sought to capitalize upon the void which PC Kai-Samba II could not fill. Had a strong and well man taken control, the contemporary history of Nongowa and of Sierra Leone would likely have been considerably different. As it was, the Kai-Samba family put forth its least able candidate, although it was well-stocked with men who were to achieve prominence at the national level—Kutubu became a Cabinet Minister and Idrissa became one of the Majors who formed the NRC.

The man who made the strongest and most persistent bid to fill this void was *M.M. Koroma.* His connections with the chiefdom were numerous but tenuous. Although the son of a Paramount Chief from a chiefdom *outside* of Kenema District, he was also the maternal half-brother of PC Kai-Samba I. This gave him a technical right to the chieftaincy. His full brother was H.V. Koroma, an MP from Pujehun District but a highly successful construction company owner in Kenema Town. M.M. Koroma in his own right was a wealthy man. Moreover, he was a Muslim leader. His most enduring claim to prominence in Nongowa, however, was simply that he was a bigman—capable, literate, well connected, crafty, and feared. He employed a whole array of aliases, the most common among them being "Saffa Guyu," which means schemer, a sly and crooked man. Koroma encouraged the widespread use of this name, believing that it would enhance the fear and respect accorded him. M.M. Marto was another alias; it drew attention to his descent from Madam Marto—or Mattolo or Matto or Mattru, depending on the English rendition—the first Paramount Chief of Nongowa following the dismantling of Nyagua's empire. Under this appellation he ran unsuccessfully for the chieftaincy, precipitating a crisis which not only shook Nongowa but threatened the stability of all Sierra Leone.

Slowly, and with occasional setbacks, M.M. Koroma had established himself as a bigman within the Kai-Samba family. His means were fundamentally political. For instance, he brought himself out of temporary exile and reinforced his reputation as a strongman by masterminding the campaign of a Kai-Samba ally in the 1962 election for Kenema Town Constituency. After that, he was awarded with responsibilities as custodian of Kai-Samba finances and royalties. His rise to prominence within the family coincided with a downturn in the Paramount Chief's health, and gradually, almost by default, he succeeded in grasping a good many levers of power, including control over sale of land in Kenema Town, a profitable perquisite indeed. His most effective resource, however, was extralocal, to wit, close connections with the man who had recently become Prime Minister, Albert Margai. It is difficult to avoid the conclusion that the Prime Minister supported and perhaps even encouraged M.M. Koroma in his campaign for power and position in Nongowa. The reasons for this center-local alliance resemble those motivating his behind-the-scenes support for A.M. Lansana in Kenema South. K.I. Kai-Samba, along with Jusu-Sheriff, was becoming increasingly independent and critical of his rule; although members of his Cabinet, Kai-Samba and Jusu-Sheriff were among the core of the articulate young Bo School graduates from both parties in Parliament who were most likely to challenge not only his policies but even his incumbency. As in both Kenema South and Kenema East, *the Prime Minister dealt with a national rival by undermining him in his constituency. Almost by definition in Sierra Leone, this meant intervention in chiefdom politics.* In the case of Kenema Central, the Prime Minister attacked K.I. Kai-Samba and his local base of support by removing from office the latter's brother, PC Kai-Samba II. This split the family and the chiefdom, and opened the way for M.M. Koroma's bid for the chieftaincy. In return, Koroma worked for candidates more congenial to the Premier.

In more detail, illness provided the opportunity for, first, appointing Koroma "Deputy Paramount Chief" in 1965 and then, in 1966, pensioning off PC Kai-Samba II as a chief incapable of performing his duties. Both these decisions ran contrary to precedent. Moreover, they infuriated the supporters of the chief, most vocal among them being Hon. K.I. Kai-Samba. He stumped the chiefdom galvanizing sentiment against M.M. Koroma and his powerful ally in Freetown. Koroma was physically beaten and thrown out of the chief's compound, as a signal to the Prime Minister. As one chiefdom protagonist put it:

> We saw that there was no alternative but to physically assault him, to disgrace him so that Albert would realize that he had backed the wrong horse. He was beaten on 25 December 1965, causing a great uprising here. We were waiting to see what his father Albert would do.[45]

But Sir Albert persisted in his support of the challenger for the throne. Opponents accuse the Prime Minister of violating Mende law for the sake of partisan politics, since, according to them, sickness does not constitute grounds for removing a chief. In addition, the opposition ruling family, Vangahun, was disturbed at what it claimed was the creation of a new ruling house at the instigation of the Government. As the leader of the Vangahun side put it in a letter of protest to the Prime Minister:

> . . . the name of Guyu cannot be adopted by any ruling figure in Mende land except in the country of the blind but not in Nongowa; and if your Nighthood should encourage this, we will be

convinced that Government is trying to establish a third ruling house in this chiefdom apart from the Vangahun and Kai-samba ruling houses.[46]

Swears, threats, and protestations—in addition to occasional skirmishes—became commonplace. The manipulation of rules and alleged abuse of executive discretion had created in Nongowa an atmosphere which corroded mutual restraint and bared the rough edges of political hostility as the chieftaincy election approached.

The campaign brought forth a novel pattern of local alliances. The Kai-Samba family split into those who supported M.M. Koroma and those who opposed him. Supporters included Mackie Kai-Samba, who stepped down as a candidate in favor of Koroma, her "uncle," as well as more peripheral elements of the family. Opponents, of course, were centered about K.I. Kai-Samba, and included a number of elders such as Mowai Kai-Samba, the head of the family. *This segment allied with the Vangahuns,* and supported their candidate. That is to say, the leading members of the leading ruling family preferred to work toward winning the chieftaincy for the rival ruling house rather than see it in the hands of M.M. Koroma.

Other factors entered into the alliance system. All six Section Chiefs supported M.M. Koroma. It is perhaps true, as critics claim, that he had bought their allegiance with money, but a more compelling explanation is found in the fact that not only had he become *de facto* Paramount Chief, with the power over subordinates that that implies, but also he was well connected to the highest national office, with its initiative over depositions more than implicitly understood.

Koroma was also able shrewdly to manipulate a major dispute over land ownership in Kenema Town to his financial and political advantage. It is worth investigating this issue in some detail, for it illuminates further the theme "kinship politics" which has run throughout these case studies; as well, it introduces land as an important stake in the political game. The protagonists in the dispute over ownership of Kenema Town are two families, the Kai-Sambas and the Ngombulangos. (When Kenema land affairs are being discussed, the Kai-Sambas are referred to as the "Kahunlas." This emphasizes their claim to descent from Boima Kahunla, a putative founder of the town.) Each of these is really a conglomeration of smaller families, held together by ties of marriage, wealth, and political prospects.

The administration has been reluctant to make a definitive settlement of the issue precisely for this reason. If it were to attempt to draw a boundary between the two families, it would be immediately inundated by the claims and counterclaims of not just the two original disputants but of numerous subfamilies which pay allegiance to the core groups in order to share the benefits of land. "A man who perhaps, at this time, is on the side of the Ngombulangos might well have changed sides by the time a demarcation is made. . . . The individual families will tend to split up and fight for their rights. So, instead of dealing with two families, we might well have to face from four to eight groups."[47] Indeed, in the days of Chief Kai-Samba I the two families were considered as one, united under his strong leadership:

> The Kahunlas and the Ngombulangos are very much related to each other. They were one family originally. During the time of PC Kai-Samba I, there was no palaver. He was the head of the family. He handled the land affairs and shared the money with all the important members. He was an influential man, and there was no grumbling.[48]

Just as the entire chiefdom lost cohesion after his death, so too the landowning family of Kenema Town broke into smaller parts. Ancillary elements of the family began to claim land in their own right rather than as tributaries. The Ngombulangos found in M.M. Koroma an influential leader willing to work for their cause. The crux of their campaign was the claim that their ancestor Ngombulango preceded his nephew Kahunla as a town founder, and therefore they were the rightful controllers of land in Kenema, since "a nephew can only have right to claim property subject to the Uncle's approval."[49] By championing their cause, Koroma gained not only important political allies—both the Town Chief and Town Speaker of Kenema were Ngombulangos—but considerable wealth from the sale of lands. As a family spokesman put it:

> The great part of the Ngombulangos supported M.M. Koroma in the Paramount Chief elections. . . . We supported him in the election, and he supported us in the land palaver.[50]

Rules of land tenure, especially in urban areas, are ambiguous and contradictory in upcountry Sierra Leone, providing ample opportunity for instrumental manipulation. Two factors contribute to this situation. First, there is conflict between Sierra Leonean and Mende law concerning land tenure. Sierra Leone's law says simply that ". . . all land in the Protectorate is vested in the Tribal Authority who hold such land on behalf of the native communities concerned. . . ." Mende law, on the other hand, clearly puts control of land in the hands of *families*. Moreover, it is against national law to sell land in the provinces. In order to avoid running afoul of the national law, landowners transfer land in surreptitious fashion, without records or deeds. Already sub-rosa, the system of land control is open to secret arrangements and behind-the-scenes manipulation.

Second, "family" is contextually defined. One unit might be considered a family for purposes of land *ownership,* while another for purposes of land *usage.* One family might be created out of many for political purposes, yet have no explicit function when marriage or landownership or initiation was concerned. But perhaps in time the overreaching family would partially assume these functions, or some of them, creating confusion and ambiguity especially in crisis circumstances. This is what happened in Kenema Town. During the reign of Kai-Samba I there was no doubt that the political leader was in charge of land controlled by an "umbrella" family, but uncertain leadership following his death invited an assertion of subgroup autonomy and squabbling over what were once considered collective resources. M.M. Koroma was able to capitalize upon the nascent disunity and uncertainty of the Kai-Samba family by encouraging an eminently divisive issue, land. Thus he derived considerable benefit from his temporary position as custodian over Kenema Town lands, and it can be anticipated that in the future similar strategies will prove profitable.

On the other side of the political fence, the leader of the opposition house, Foray Vangahun, in addition to his new affiliation with the Kai-Samba-Kahunla segment, was backed by most strangers, including a number of diamond miners whose financial help contributed to the campaign effort. What little APC presence existed in Nongowa at the time—mostly identified with strangers—was also associated with Vangahun.

To review, perhaps it would be helpful to list the elements which were arrayed behind each of the candidates for Paramount Chief by mid-1966:

Foray Vangahun	*M.M. Koroma*
Vangahun Ruling House	Mackie Kai-Samba (plus
Core of Kai-Samba Ruling	ancillary elements of
House (incl. Kahunla)	Kai-Samba house)
J.B. Francis	Sir Albert Margai
Strangers	Ngombulangos
APC	Section Chiefs
	B.S. Massaquoi

The Prime Minister had hoped for a successful chieftaincy election within three months, in time to consolidate resources for the 1967 General Election. Events did not conform to his wishes, however. In June 1966 the first attempt to elect was unsuccessful because neither candidate polled the required 55% of the Chiefdom Council votes:[51]

M.M. Mattolo (Koroma)	358
Foray Vangahun	388
Total	746

In preparation for the next attempt, each side engaged in widespread oath-swearing to recruit new votes and to prevent the erosion of already-existing support. Each side accused the other of force and intimidation in administering the swears. Tension was temporarily relieved by the Government, which brought in two Assessor Chiefs from outside to "pull" the swears. Foray Vangahun is said to have told the Prime Minister that if he continued to stand behind M.M. Koroma, the Vangahuns and their allies would no longer support the SLPP in national elections.

All these threats and accusations as part of the electioneering process seem to have influenced prevailing opinion very little, for in October 1966 the second attempt was unsuccessful, having again failed to provide a 55% majority for one candidate. Other than a violent clash which took place early in 1967 between the two sides, the only result was a decision to postpone a third attempt until after the General Election tensions had abated.

As the reader has no doubt anticipated, competition for the Kenema Central seat took place largely within the context of this imbroglio in Nongowa. The same is true of Kenema Town constituency. Since only one major party, the SLPP, was involved in the contest at that time, the chiefdom dispute manifested itself first in the nomination phase of the campaign. Early in the nomination process both Hon. K.I. Kai-Samba and J.B. Francis, his ally in Kenema Town, were denied the SLPP ticket. Instead the nominations went to James During, Albert Margai's private secretary, and to Hon. B.S. Massaquoi, the incumbent in Kenema Town Constituency and an ally of M.M. Koroma. Despite the demonstrated strength of the K.I. Kai-Samba faction, the SLPP was able to deny him and Francis party recognition for three reasons. First, SLPP nomination procedures are haphazard and ill-defined, in keeping with the *ad hoc* nature of its organization, causing them to be open to manipulation and rigging. Second, Albert Margai as the party leader was able to add weight for or against whichever candidate he preferred or disliked. Third, Albert Margai as Prime Minister had implicit influence over the chiefs and headmen who made up a large portion of the constituency nominating committee. Later, after much protest, the SLPP reversed its decision and attempted to give the party ticket to Kai-Samba and Francis, but they declined to accept it on the well-calculated grounds that it was impolitic to accept backing from an already discredited Sir Albert.[52]

As Independents, K.I. Kai-Samba and J.B. Francis won their respective Parliamentary seats in March 1967. Both were instrumental in defeating the SLPP Government and in allowing the installation of the former Opposition Leader, Siaka Stevens, as Prime Minister. The balancing role held by Independents at the national level can be seen from the overall results of the General Election:[53]

APC	32 seats
SLPP	28 seats
Independents	5 seats
Total Ordinary Members	65 seats

Had there been a swing of Independents toward the SLPP reminiscent of the 1962 election, there would have been no change of Government—and, most likely, no *coup d'etat*. But Albert Margai's intervention in Nongowa chiefdom affairs had alienated at least three of the five successful Independents, as well as Jusu-Sheriff who, although he ran under the SLPP banner, was sympathetic to their cause, since he had experienced similar undermining within his own constituency and chiefdom. Four Independents wrote the following letter to the Governor-General, whose task it was to appoint a new Prime Minister:

We would like it to be known to the People of Sierra Leone that we shall at all appropriate times co-operate in whatever measure may be deemed necessary in the national interest with any of the two Political Parties which commands the majority of members in the House, *provided that in the case of the Sierra Leone People's Party the present leader of that Party, Sir Albert Margai, resigns the Premiership and his leadership of that Party.*[54]

The letter was signed by K.I. Kai-Samba, J.B. Francis, L.A.M. Brewah (from outside Kenema District, but who had close connections with Nongowa), and Prince J. Williams (from Bo Town). The Governor-General, when presented such evidence, had no choice but to invest Siaka Stevens and the APC with the duty of organizing a new Government. (This excludes consideration of whether or not the Governor General should have waited until the 12 Paramount Chief members of Parliament were elected.)

It was at the confluence of the local Nongowa dispute and the national General Election that events concatenated to bring down the SLPP Government. This is not to say that his interference in chiefdom politics was the sole cause of Sir Albert's demise—there were numerous contributing factors, the most obvious of which was the rise of the APC in Freetown and the North—but had it not been for the disaffection he engendered in Nongowa, he probably would have been able to retain power, albeit by a slim margin.

The events of March 1967—the change of Governments and its military aftermath—did not ameliorate the tensions which had built up in Nongowa as a result of continuing crisis. Indeed, *the military Government became just as entangled in Nongowa politics as had its civilian predecessor.* Two members of the original NRC triumvirate were intimately linked by kin ties to the two factions in the chiefdom dispute. *Major B.I. Kai-Samba* was the full brother of ex-PC Kai-Samba II and Hon. Kai-Samba; however, he tended to side, although not openly, with the M.M. Koroma segment of the family. He attempted to play the role of family mediator, but he felt that his elder brother was simply too sick to assume the burdens of the chieftaincy. *Major S.B. Jumu* was weighed down by no such complications: His uncle was Foray Vangahun.

Evidently in the councils of the NRC Major Jumu won on this issue, because the effect of military overlordship was to favor the candidacy of Foray Vangahun. The NRC was anxious to hold the third attempt to elect a PC as soon as possible. Only a few days before the scheduled event, however, M.M. Koroma withdrew because of illness, and in his stead Mackie Kai-Samba declared her candidacy. Her request for more time to campaign was refused by the NRC. K.I. Kai-Samba, in the language of kinship politics, declared that Mackie was *not* a child of the late Paramount Chief and therefore was ineligible to run. (This was clearly untrue, since the late PC had listed her as one of his "right" children.) On the day of the election Mackie refused to contest on the grounds that insufficient time had been allotted. And in the face of charges that she was only the "foster child" of PC Kai-Samba I, she and her followers walked out of the court barri. Many of her followers claim that they boycotted the election also because it was held at night and the barri was surrounded by armed soldiers. Whatever, enough of the chiefdom Councillors stayed and voted to give Foray Vangahun slightly more than the 55% required for election:[55]

for Foray Vangahun	419
against Foray Vangahun	4
refused to vote	295
Total	718

After over a year of bitter campaigning, three election attempts, the bifurcation of its most prestigious family, and persistent external intervention, Nongowa had finally elected a Paramount Chief.

True to his instinct for political power, M.M. Koroma supported the party in power following the overthrow of the NRC; that is to say, he switched to the APC and became a staunch backer of Siaka Stevens. Ill-health kept him from actively campaigning for APC candidates during the by-elections, but his financial and organizational contributions were proffered, including the donation of a building which was to become the APC Branch Headquarters for Kenema District. His death in 1970 ended his political ambitions, supreme among them the desire to become Paramount Chief.

No longer harassed by Sir Albert, who had fled the country, K.I. Kai-Samba and J.B. Francis reentered the SLPP fold, this time as vocal members of the Opposition. Francis, who was the most pugnacious member of the Opposition, but whose instinct for political survival was strong, crossed carpet to the APC as part of a wave of SLPP defections which took place just prior to the 1973 General Elections.

Although very old, Paramount Chief Vangahun has proved himself far more shrewd and capable than most people—including his supporters—originally expected. It is likely that the Kai-Sambas sustained his candidacy in the hopes that he would soon die or all but officially abdicate through senility. Instead, he has strengthened the Vangahun position without committing himself too deeply to the APC. If the Kai-Sambas prove unable to reunify under strong leadership, it is within the realm of possibility that they have forfeited their claim to primacy in Nongowa.

KOYA CHIEFDOM

Koya is the smaller, less important component of Kenema Central Constituency. Yet its voters have played a crucial role in providing K.I. Kai-Samba the requisite margin for electoral victory in both 1962 and 1967. Had the chiefdom been unified against him, it is likely that he would have lost the seat. As it was, in 1962 the Paramount Chief was behind him, while one opposition ruling house affiliated with other candidates. In 1967, this pattern of alliances was reversed: The PC worked for James During (the Prime Minister's candidate), while the chiefdom opposition arrayed itself behind Kai-Samba. Hence, ruling family rivalries offer the basic explanation for the character of center-local relations extant in Koya.

There are three ruling houses in Koya: Kane, Komei, and Sellu, each headquartered in a separate town. Since 1927 the Kane house has dominated the chieftaincy. In response, increasingly the other two families have agitated against the incumbents, contending that the Kanes have ruled long enough and that it is now the turn of another house. Antagonism came to a head in 1955 with the death of PC Mohammed Kane. The opposition families demanded a complete revision of the TA list before the upcoming election; when the central administration declined to do this, they swore in the *Poro* bush not to allow the election to take place. They also refused to pay taxes, as a protest against the Government. Finally, after five years and imminent collapse of local government finances, they lifted their boycott, agreed to pay taxes, and allowed the election of M.M. Kane, brother of the former PC.

The Kanes had established "diplomatic relations" with ruling houses in Nongowa during the days of Madam Humonya, and PC Kai-Samba had greatly strengthened ties through a close friendship with PC Mohammed Kane. M.M. Kane and K.I. Kai-Samba were friendly as children, so perhaps it was natural that in the 1962 election Koya was closely aligned with the Kai-Samba candidate. Even one of the opposition houses was persuaded, through its leader, the chiefdom Speaker, to lend its tacit support.[56] PC Kane, with some exaggeration, claims that Koya held the balance in that election:

> It was us who allowed Kai-Samba to win in 1962 against Alhayi Ngegla ... Nongowa supported Ngegla. It was only in Koya that he was strongly supported. ... Hon. Kai-Samba asked us to support him out of friendship.[57]

Ties of friendship had to compete with the power of Government during the 1967 election, however. Since Kai-Samba had been denied (and then had refused) the SLPP nomination and was running against the Prime Minister's personal candidate, Paramount Chief Kane had to choose between this fomer affiliation and what he interpreted as his duty to remain loyal to the Government. His decision to back James During was based entirely on his notion that it was not only their obligation but the lesson of practical wisdom for Chiefs to support the party in power:

> In 1967 Kai-Samba refused to take the SLPP symbol and I vowed to support the Government. Otherwise the Government will humbug me. I felt that I should *always* support any Government in power. Because he had the Government symbol, I supported

During. I asked all my people to support the Government in
power. Had Kai-Samba taken the Government symbol, I would
have supported him.[58]

What he meant by the "Government symbol" was the SLPP
emblem, a palm tree. Note the constant substitution of "Government in power" for "party in power." This inability to dis-
criminate betweey the two is in part the result of confusion about
national institutions among rural chiefs and people, and in part
their shrewd realization that in the "West Africa party-state" it
is less than discreet to insist on a strict separation between "party" and "Government."

Sensing that they could profit from this rift between PC Kane
and Hon. Kai-Samba, the opposition ruling houses placed
themselves behind the latter's candidacy. It was their hope that a
victorious Kai-Samba could induce the Government to depose or
at least discredit the chief, so that their chances of winning the
office might be enhanced.

Their expectations however, proved empty. With the installation of the APC in the seat of power, PC Kane held true to his
strategy of supporting the Government of the day, no matter
what the party. He became a staunch supporter of the APC. Indeed, he married PC Madam Theresa Vibbi of Kandu-Leppiama
chiefdom, a widow of M.M. Koroma (who, it will be remembered, switched parties to become an important APC leader in
Kenema District shortly after Siaka Stevens took office in 1968).
Together they have more than any of the older chiefs in Kenema
District overtly worked on behalf of the APC. Chief Kane's
marriage, to the APC and to Madam Vibbi, has proved profitable
both politically and financially. Not only has he neutralized the
opposition in his own realm, but he has taken to mining in his
wife's 'diamond-rich chiefdom.

NOTES

1. Interview.
2. *The Sierra Leone Gazette,* April 23, 1968, p. 403.

3. (KPA) KNA/391/1/1, Ex. PC Siaffa Kebbi, p. 126.

4. (KPA) KNA/391/1/3, PC Vandi Dassama, p. 3.

5. Interview #84. March 2, 1970.

6. Adapted from Electoral Commission, Score Sheet, Kenema South, By-election, 1969.

7. (KPA) KNA/391/1/3, PC Vandi Dassama.

8. Interview #81. Feb. 23, 1970.

9. (KPA) KNA/393/1, Gaura, Death and Election of Paramount Chiefs, p. 41.

10. William Riker, *The Theory of Political Coalitions* (New Haven, Yale Univ. Press, 1962).

11. All data presented here are found in (KPA) KNA/393/1, Gaura, Death and Election of Paramount Chiefs, p. 76. The data in the files was incomplete and had to be filled in by simple extrapolation.

12. (KPA) KNA/392/2, Tribal Authorities, Speakers and Sub-chiefs, p. 118.

13. Interview #89. March 6, 1970.

14. Interview #85. March 2, 1970.

15. T.J. Alldridge, *The Sherbro and Its Hinterland* (London and New York: Macmillan, 1901), pp. 244-45.

16. Interview #143. June 17, 1970.

17. Adapted from Electoral Commission, Score Sheet, Kenema South, By-election, 1969.

18. Interview #83. February 25, 1970.

19. (KPA) KNA/391/3, Dama, Boundaries and Bush Disputes, pp. 11-14.

20. A persuasive example of the instrumental relationship between politics and kinship, the following account of the Njavombos was provided by a maverick member of the family: "In the days before colonialism there were no ruling families. A group of bigmen (elders) would choose a leader, and *then* would consider him a father of that family. In other words they created a family by choosing a leader. This happened . . . in Upper Tunkia. . . . Bockari was chosen as leader by a number of elders, Senesi Ngunya, Temeh, and Kpaolelema. Later Njavombo came from Malema and was absorbed into the group. . . . After Sama died, there was a prediction by a Muslim soothsayer that the next PC would die within seven years. So [the others] did not run. Bockari was dead by then. Njavombo, a relative

stranger, stepped forward. He was backed by Temeh. Since then, the others have called themselves Njavombo or Temeh."

Interview #91. March 9, 1970.

21. *Soi* is the Mende word for Bundu mask. The Bundu Society, or *Sande,* is a female secret society, the membership of which is almost universal among Mende women and girls.

22. (KPA) KNA/115/2, Tunkia Chiefdom Council, p. 65 (Feb. 18, 1960).

23. Adapted from Electoral Commission, Score Sheet, Kenema South, By-Election, 1969.

24. See article entitled "Activities of Paramount Chief M. Karmoh of Nomo and His Henchmen," *Daily Express,* March 16, 1970, p. 4.

25. (KPA) KNA/361/2, Nomo Tribal Authorities, Speakers, Sub-chiefs, p. 30.

26. Interviews #91 (March 9, 1970) and #144 (June 16, 1970).

27. (KPA) KNA/361/1, Nomo, Death and Elections of Paramount Chiefs.

28. Adapted from Electoral Commission, Score Sheet, Kenema South By-election, 1969.

29. *The Sierra Leone Gazette,* April 23, 1968, p. 404.

30. Adapted from Electoral Commission, Score Sheet, Kenema South, By-election, 1969.

31. (KPA) EP/108/1, Lower Bambara, Death and Election of Paramount Chiefs, p. 136. Letter from Paul Quee-Nyagua.

32. (KPA) KNA/389/1/vol. 1, Lower Bambara, Death and Election of Paramount Chiefs, pp. 33-67.

33. (KPA) CONF/INT/6, Monthly Intelligence Reports, April 1955.

34. (KPA) CONF/INT/7, Monthly Intelligence Reports. Oct/Nov. 1958.

35. Interview #80. February 21, 1970.

36. Interview #106. April 7, 1970.

37. From Julius Cole's list of detainees in Mafanta Prison, in *Daily Express,* Nov. 21, 22, and 24, 1969. Since the Government has never disputed this list, I have accepted it as accurate.

38. From the Supreme Court Justice's judgment, Sept. 19, 1969, reproduced in *Daily Express,* Sept. 29, and Oct. 3, 1969.

39. From the judgment of the Judge of Appeal, reproduced in *Daily Express,* November 24, 1969.

40. Interview.

41. Interview #111. April 13, 1970.

42. Diamonds have been a divisive issue in Malegohun ever since they became prominent during the boom era of the mid-1950's when—"neocolonial" is inappropriately used here only because of its prematurity—a number of international syndicates were attempting to make exclusive lease arrangements with certain chiefdoms in order to preempt SLST. One such company was the Sierra Leone Mineral Syndicate, which persuaded Paramount Chief Musa Gendemeh not to allow SLST into Malegohun. Bribes from the company's engineer, a South African, leavened its persuasiveness. It was financed from European sources, but the roster of syndicate members read like a *Who's Who* of high politics in Sierra Leone, including A.M. Margai, Siaka Stevens (then Minister of Lands, Mines, and Labour), A.J. Demby (a Cabinet member), and G.S. Panda (a high civil servant).

In his own version of neocolonialism, PC Gendemeh attempted to turn over to Syndicate mining the land within the two chiefdoms which came under his rule at the time of amalgamation, while at the same time retaining his own section for licensed mining. In this way he favored his own original chiefdom at the expense of the other components of the amalgamation, which, needless to say, was bitterly resented.

The Syndicate was soon closed down by the Government when it was discovered that it had sold a valuable diamond to a Belgian who had attempted to smuggle it.

43. *The Sierra Leone Gazette,* April 23, 1968, p. 404.

44. *The Sierra Leone Gazette,* April 23, 1968, p. 404.

45. Interview #105. April 2, 1970.

46. (KPA) C/111/1/01, PC Kai-Samba II. p. 184. Letter from Foray Vangahun to P.M. Jan. 24, 1966.

47. (KPA) EP/111/10, Kenema Land Affairs, p. 22 (May 29, 1968).

48. Interview #100. March 26, 1970.

49. From a mimeographed sheet signed by Saffa Mambu Ngombulango, a young spokesman ("warrior," as he put it) for the family.

50. Interview #101. March 29, 1970.

51. (KPA) EP/111/1/vol. II, Death and Election of Paramount Chiefs, Nongowa. p. 51.

52. Interview #105. April 2, 1970.

53. Sierra Leone. *Report of the Dove-Edwin Commission of Enquiry into the Conduct of the 1967 General Elections.* (Freetown: Government Printer, 1967), p. 19.

54. *Ibid.,* p. 24. Emphasis added.

55. (KPA) EP/111/vol II, Death and Election of Paramount Chiefs, Nongowa, pp. 145-49.

56. This account comes from Interview #110. April 11, 1970.

57. Interview.

58. Interview.

Chapter 6

Center-Periphery Alliances

This chapter uses the preceding case studies as a source of information for dealing with four fundamental questions. (a) What is the basic pattern of center-periphery alliance which prevails in Kenema District? (b) Which model, identity or utility, more economically accounts for this pattern? (c) What are the consequences of this pattern for political development and political integration? (d) To the extent that this pattern entails links embedded in traditional local units, how effective is party organization in mitigating the trade-off between development and integration predicted by the identity and utility models?

Patterns of Alliance

Perhaps the most economical mode of investigating the structure of alliances is, paradoxically, to search for patterns of conflict. Alliances do indeed bring together diverse elements into larger groupings, but in a prior sense they are based upon cleavages. They are most often combinations of people and groups which have formed *against* something, frequently other alliances. Thus, in order to discover the pattern of alliances and potential alliances which aggregate the various segments of society, it is first necessary to know and assess the cleavages which divide it. This is hardly an original insight; it derives directly from the "conflict theories" of Simmel and his intellectual descendants who stress the integrative implications of crosscutting lines of conflict.[1]

Since our concern is with alliance as one species of center-local linkage, it is necessary to specify two sets of cleavages, those at the national level and those at the local level. Viewed from local perspective, cleavage at the *center* appears as simply a rivalry between the two major political parties, the APC and the SLPP. Although parties are themselves alliances, from the grass-roots standpoint the boundary between the two parties was *the* distinctive and meaningful fault line of national political competition during the time of research. Naturally this is a simplifying assumption. Intraparty conflicts did indeed exist, but the initiative for fission and splintering came from above, from conflicts within the national political elite. It was not within the realm of feasibility for strictly local groups to precipitate splits within the national parties; they had to accept the party system as a given environmental conditon. At the *local* level a more complex pattern of cleavages was relevant. As we have seen, a fairly complicated blend goes into the making of chiefdom politics; and chiefdom palavers, as they are called, are a composite of several types of conflict. But the individual ingredients seem to be based on the following cleavages:

1. between ruling houses;
2. between strangers and indigenes;
3. between youngmen and elders;
4. between major personalities;
5. between historically-determined rival groups; and
6. between chiefdoms themselves.

1. Ruling house rivalries provide the major source of conflict in Mende chiefdoms. In most cases, no matter what other cleavages exist, this cleavage fashions the broad outlines of political competition. Structurally, the semblance of a two- or multiparty system is built into chiefdom politics because (almost) every chiefdom has at least two ruling families. In fact, local people often use the terms "ruling party" and "opposition

party" to describe the factions and antagonists active in their chiefdom. Of the sixteen chiefdoms in Kenema District, only three have no overriding tendency for local politics to be strongly influenced by ruling house rivalries. Simbaru (not included in the case studies) is the only chiefdom in the district boasting only one ruling family; as might be expected, its politics are characterized by widespread consensus and little overt conflict. In Dodo and Nomo, family rivalries are muted, resulting also in unusually high intrachiefdom unity. At the other end of the spectrum, Nongowa, Gaura, Tunkia, and Lower Bambara are examples of intense ruling house conflict; all other aspects of local political interaction are rendered subordinate to the demands of this basic cleavage in these chiefdoms.

Most often the opposition ruling houses support the national party which opposes the one favored by the incumbent family. That is, if the Paramount Chief supports one party, then the likelihood is that his rivals will support the other. For the whole array of reasons discussed in Chapter IV, Chiefs and the SLPP in the past enjoyed a long and mutually profitable alliance, and many Paramounts have continued to identify with the SLPP, while, in keeping with the consistency of local disputes, their opponents have turned to the APC. This has been obviously the case in Dama, Gaura, Tunkia, Lower Bambara, and Gorama Mende chiefdoms. Since 1968, when the APC came to power, this pattern has produced an apparent paradox: The local incumbents are allied with the national Opposition, while the local oppositions are allied with the Government party.

This tendency, however, has run counter to an equally powerful current, the lure of the party in power. Chiefs especially have an incentive to identify with the Government of the day. Since 1968, in Nomo, Koya, Malegohun, and Dodo, the Paramount Chiefs have made public by word and deed their overt support of the party in power, that is, the APC. In most of them the reaction of the opposition houses has been to lean toward the SLPP.[2]

Prior to 1968, the rivalry between the APC and the SLPP in Kenema District was colored mostly by the stranger vs. indigenes cleavage. In the 1962 and 1967 elections only minor candidates—almost all of them strangers from the Northern Province—ran under the APC banner. Those Mende candidates unable to win the SLPP nomination simply stood as Independents. After 1968, however, a signal change took place: The APC became the Government of the day. Only since then have important ruling houses allied themselves with the APC. Indeed, in the 1969 by-election, three of the five APC candidates were Mendes who had run strongly as Independents during the 1967 election. All of them (Joe Quee-Nyagua, A.G. Lappia, and A. M. Lansana) were closely affiliated with "out" ruling families in their constituencies. In other words, once the APC had something concrete to offer, these ruling houses did not hesitate to join, despite its erstwhile reputation as a "strangers" or "Northern" party. From local perspective, the Central Government possesses above all the ultimate power over the chieftaincy. In their anxiety to further their own interests, grassroots factions scramble to latch onto the source of that power, granting the incumbent political party a quantum increment of acceptability and support.

Not only have ruling houses been the most important source of candidates for Parliamentary seats, but electoral success has been directly related to strong connections with important ruling houses. From Table 6.1 it can be seen that almost two-thirds of the total number of candidates for Parliament from Kenema District in three elections were tied directly or indirectly to ruling families. (Category *b* in the table is self-explanatory; category *c* includes those individuals whose ties with a ruling family have been close and long-lived, through marriage, friendship, or historical affiliation. Under this category would come such candidates as S. Jusu-Sheriff, whose family of Muslim scholars has been long associated with the Samas of Tunkia; A.M. Lansana, who is married into the Dakawa family of Dama; and B.S. Massaquoi, who is distantly related to the Kai-Sambas and enjoyed the favor and friendship of PC Kai-Samba I for many years. Excluded are ties concluded through short-term, political alliances where expedience appears the prime motivating force.) Moreover 83% of the *victorious* candidates in the three elections were connected

TABLE 6.1
Candidates for Parliamentary Elections, Kenema District

	1962	1967	1969*	TOTAL
a) Total No. of Candidates	25	23	10	58
b) No. of direct members of ruling houses	7	7	2	16
c) No. indirectly connected to ruling houses	8	7	5	20
d) No. of winners from categories b) and c)	5	7	3	15
e) Total no. of seats	6	7	5	18
f) % of winners from ruling houses	83%	100%	60%	83%

*By-Election

Adapted from: Sierra Leone House of Representatives. *Ordinary Members and Paramount Chief Members, Election Statistics, 1962; Sierra Leone Gazette,* April 23, 1968, pp. 404-5; and Electoral Commission, Score Sheets for 1969 House of Representatives By-Elections.

either directly or indirectly to chiefdom royalty. This corroborates evidence presented by both Kilson and Cartwright documenting the strong association throughout Sierra Leone between membership in the ruling families and electoral success.

Throughout the case studies, we have had cause to note the politically instrumental nature of kinship ties. Kinship groups comprise the basic units of political competition within chiefdoms. But they are not simple and easily identified groups determined largely by biological and cultural factors. That is to say, their size and membership is apt to vary according to political expedience as well as to more commonly recognized criteria such as birth and death rates, marriage and residential patterns. From the point of view of the individual, both patrilineal and matrilineal avenues open opportunities and obligations within the Mende kinship system. "In addition to inheritance of his father's property, a person is also entitled to share in, and use, his maternal uncle's [*kenya's*] belongings and has certain traditional perquisites. . . . Reciprocally, the uncle is entitled to full use of his nephew's services on his farm and other ways."[3] A politically illuminating example of the choices open to an individual is this interview statement:

> Mendes usually include both their father's side and their mother's side in their family. Usually the father's side is more important, for many things, but in certain situations the mother's side becomes important. If your mother's side is the family of a PC and your father's side has no chief, naturally you will look to your mother's side.[4]

Moreover, residence is likely to have a large impact on an individual's kinship affiliations, extending his range of alternatives even beyond strict patrilineal and matrilineal calculations. *Ndehun-bla*—the family people—"may even include . . . someone originating in the same town as himself with whom there is no biological or affinal relationship, but with whom there has always been a close social connection."[5] This is why Little prefers the term "kindred" rather than the more strictly defined terms "family" and "lineage" to describe Mende kin groups. And we have already noted how occasionally an individual will place himself in a position of deference to a more powerful person by positing a kinshiplike relationship between them. (See Chapter 3, note 17.) In sum, the Mende kinship system is unusually flexible. Ties among persons can be established in a variety of ways; obligations and perquisites can be evoked from a number of sources; and loyalties are, within fairly generous boundaries, determined by situational and utilitarian considerations.

In similar fashion, from the point of view of the group, kinship units are not immutable. To give some examples, in Gaura chiefdom groups which were considered families have undergone fusion and fission depending upon the peculiar political circumstances of the time. Mostly as a result of shaky and divisive leadership, the powerful Kai-Samba family of Nongowa chiefdom has split into a number of conflicting groups, at least one of which has established its claim as an autonomous family. In this case, not only did a number of peripheral elements break away when the distribution of spoils became disappointing to them, but the core of the family itself bifurcated over the issue of who would become Paramount Chief. Moreover, groups and individuals are likely to offer kinship explanations for political behavior; whether true or not, family relationships are put forth to explain, or rationalize, or emphasize political relationships. Kinship can be manipulated, invented, imagined. It is an idiom, a kind of ideology, by which politics is understood and through which it takes place. In literate societies organizations are formed from written constitutions, guidelines, and sets of rules. Preliterate societies, however, must rely upon other idioms, such as kinship or ritual, to "underwrite" their organizations. Thus, particularly in societies like the Mende where kinship is somewhat loosely structured, it is a built-in vehicle for alliance formation and political competiton.[6]

Kinship can be envisioned, following Cohen, as an *articulating principle* by which groups gain and maintain their identity. It is a symbolic framework within which groups arise, conflict, and adjust in competition for power and other valued goods. It determines the broad outlines of political behavior, not its detailed structure. Political ambition and goalseeking play an important role in constituting the concrete groups in the Mende political arena. Utilitarianism and the kinship system act in reciprocal fashion: Instrumental behavior affects the composition of kin groups just as the latter channel the energies of political competition.

2. A second type of cleavage pits strangers against indigenous Mendes. Kenema District is by and large an economically active area, and many people have migrated there from poorer sections of Sierra Leone—and from other West African countries—in search of wealth and livelihood; the glitter of diamonds has been especially alluring. As might be expected, the bulk of these

"strangers" comes from the Northern Province or from related regions in Guinea.

Since its core area of support is in the north, it is not surprising that there is a strong tendency for people of northern origin to vote for the APC. Towns with large concentrations of strangers are likely to be APC strongholds. Blama, Konta, Baama, Foindu, and Levuma are diamond towns with large stranger communities—and all polled heavily in favor of the APC.[7] The numerous towns located within the SLST lease have absorbed quantities of northern immigrants, and it is in this Tongo Field area that the APC has built the most durable and well-organized party structure in the entire Eastern Province. Likewise, the cosmopolitan diversity of Kenema Town provides a congenial breeding ground for APC activity.

As long as the APC was a "stranger's party" in Kenema District, it fared poorly. Cartwright estimates that it "succeeded in attracting some southern [Mende] support" in the 1962 election,[8] but neither in 1962 nor in 1967 did it win a seat in the district; the APC candidates in almost all cases received only tiny percentages of the total votes cast.

But in the 1969 by-election the APC, by then in power at the national level, was able to ally with significant indigenous local groups, most notably ruling houses. As mentioned above, in three of five constituencies, former candidates of Northern origin were replaced by Mendes who were closely identified with "out" ruling families. The APC's electoral performance in the district improved dramatically in response.[9] *Strangers plus opposition ruling houses form the core of the APC alliance in Kenema District.*

3. Attached to that core, however, are other elements spawned by additional cleavages. For instance, there exists in most Mende chiefdoms a latent rivalry between youngmen and elders. This is really another way of stating that there is always potential friction between those who have and those who do not have power and influence. This is less a conflict between generations than an interaction between those who lead and those who follow.

Youngmen naturally have an interest in limiting the claims made upon them by their elders, in restricting the amount of communal labor required of them, in reducing the fines leveled upon them, and in curtailing the various other exactions demanded from time to time. Thus, to improve their bargaining position they are often prepared to offer their support to whatever bigman promises to better their relationship vis-a-vis the elders. A common technique for reducing the power of a competitor—say a Paramount Chief from a rival ruling house—is to undermine him by sowing dissatisfaction among his youngmen. As they shift their allegiance away from him, he is left without votes, without finances, and in danger of deposition. On occasion youngmen can be stirred to demonstrations and violence, but it should be recalled that they rarely act on their own. There is almost always an elder behind them, directing their movements for his own benefit.

Dama chiefdom offers the most visible example of this phenomenon. Ever since A.M. Lansana became Speaker, he has steadily weaned the youngmen away from the Paramount Chief, rendering him ineffectual and isolated. This has enhanced Lansana's own chances for a seat in Parliament as well as the probability of deposition proceedings being initiated against the chief. Lower Bambara provides another example of this type of cleavage, although it is manifest to a lesser extent than in Dama. Here, PC Farma is supported by most of the bigmen in the chiefdom, particularly his Section Chiefs, but his major rival, Hon. Quee-Nyagua, has gradually attracted to his side youngmen anxious to exploit the mineral wealth of their locality. In both cases the APC has profited from the support of dissident youngmen, whereas the SLPP remained associated with the chiefdom establishment.

This is not to imply an *automatic* pattern whereby elders support the SLPP and youngmen the APC. Rather, a tendency is postulated: If a number of youngmen are chafing under the reign of a particular ruling house, there is a distinct probability that they can be persuaded to support an opposition ruling house, and in turn the APC. But in cases where the Paramount Chief is an

APC adherent, the likelihood is that dissatisfied youngmen will turn towards the SLPP. The youngmen-vs.-elders cleavage simply adds another level of complexity to our analysis of center-local alliances, compounding the effect of ruling house cleavages. Youngmen are only partially independent of the ruling house rivalries that stir them to action. Recognizing this requires us to qualify the generally accepted accounts which present the SLPP as the "establishment party" and the APC as the "commoners' party."[10] In most of Mendeland the APC has lacked the strong, autonomous party organizations which have served it so well in Freetown and the North. Thus, in Kenema District it has resorted to alliances with the same species of local faction which has been the mainstay of the SLPP. Its appeal to commoner elements (i.e., youngmen) lies not so much in its "leveling" ideology as in the grass-roots alliances it has entered. *If there is a tendency for dissentient youngmen and the APC to align, it is a consequence of their common affiliation with opposition ruling houses, not the radical expression of a mobilized rural mass.*

4. A fourth source of cleavage at the local level—personality conflicts—needs little explanation. Perhaps a Chief and his Speaker have become disaffected with each other (as in Dama); or a Chief resents the ambitions of a local headmaster (Gorama Mende); or a longlived struggle for office has alienated rivals beyond the norm for ordinary political competiton (Small Bo); or family leaders resent a distant relative who has seized control of their kinship group (Nongowa); or a crisis escalates in such a way that individuals become singled out for purposes of punishment or protest (Tunkia). Whatever the original cause, if such a conflict is personally bitter enough it will take on a life of its own; the five such major conflicts I have identified have all taken the same course.[11] One man will almost automatically oppose what the other stands for. If one is associated with the SLPP, then the other will ally with the APC, in search of outside—especially Government—support.

Naturally, it is difficult even analytically to separate this from other types of cleavage. Personal animosities build on other forms of conflict, or else result from them. But it is important to isolate personality as a separate variable, since *personal animosities make it less likely that local factions can compromise and more likely that they will ally with rival camps at the national level.* An illustrative example of the obstinancy fostered by personal embitterment is the case of Boima Temu, who was humiliated and deposed as Speaker of Small Bo chiefdom as a result of political maneuvering. He was reinstalled after the APC assumed power, but his unwillingness to compromise on terms other than those which would in turn humiliate his rivals has meant not only perpetuated unrest in the chiefdom but quaranteed minority status for the APC in Kenema West constituency. Tunkia is another case in point. If the SLPP Government has not punished Moinina Kallon so severely for his opposition to PC Sama, the chiefdom would perhaps not be so irreconciliably divided as it is today.

In contrast, where personal animosities have been kept to a minimum, chiefdom reconciliation and compromise have been more easily effected. Nongowa under PC Kai-Samba I and Simbaru under PC Gamanga have been generally acclaimed for their ability to adjust peacefully and without accumulated grievances the conflicting demands of opposition groups. The explicit policy of chiefdom leadership in both cases was to co-opt opposition spokesmen by absorbing them into the local administration, thereby satisfying aggrieved or ambitious individuals before bitterness could build to disruptive proportions. "Power sharing" discourages a politics based on personality conflicts.

5. For want of a better term, the next category has been labeled with a rather protean phrase: "historically-determined" cleavages. Like personality conflicts, these have accidental as well as structural causes; they develop a life of their own; and they are only partially independent of other forms of cleavage.

The most common example is the amalgamated chiefdom. During the 1950's the colonial Government often combined two or more chiefdoms, creating new and larger chiefdoms that were presumably more viable economically and capable politically. But the component parts of these amalgams have tended to retain their original identity, and now compete with one another. Most of the amalgamations took place in the Northern Province. In Kenema District only two of sixteen are amalgamated chiefdoms, so the effects of decisions taken by the colonial authorities do not weigh heavily upon that part of Sierra Leone. Nevertheless, in these two cases, Malegohun and Kandu-Leppiama, there is a tendency for competition among the original units to become expressed in party political terms. Each party enjoys concentrated support in one element of each amalgam. However, this simple relationship is complicated—and thus weakened—by ruling-house rivalries which take place *within* each component part. Especially in Kandu-Leppiama, crosscutting cleavages not only contribute to the integration of the chiefdom but reduce the strength of association between party affiliation and original identity. Amalgamation expanded the structure of strategic choice, widening the arena in which local actors (e.g., ruling houses) could compete by increasing the number of potential allies.

Another example falling under this rubric is more particularistic. In Tunkia a bitter, ten-year dispute arose because a number of religious articles were removed from the chiefdom under false pretenses. The "*Soi* case" reinforced with religious fervor already-existing cleavages, hardening into intransigence what in other chiefdoms would have been the normal—flexible—lines of everyday political competition. A spiral of violence further insured that the chiefdom would remain divided along congruent cleavages. As expected, the side centered about the Paramount Chief has allied firmly with one party, the SLPP, while the opposition side affiliated first with Independents and then, since 1968, with the APC.

Issues like the "*Soi* case" are often kept alive by individuals who profit politically from continued turmoil and financially from intermittent exactions for lawyers fees and other services. The element of deliberate manipulation is also often noticeable in ostensibly highly emotional issues such as *Poro* offenses, ritual murder, and oath-swearing. It is difficult for an insider, much less an outsider, to determine which of such cases have been manufactured and which result from genuine indignation, but there is no doubt that they are used as instruments to promote factional interests.

These emotional issues, entwined as they are with the Mende cosmology, generally tend to polarize a chiefdom. Land disputes, on the other hand, usually are more particularisitic in scope and effect. "Bush palavers" have become increasingly common since the advent of diamond mining, which reinforced land pressures stemming from population growth and soil erosion. Ordinarily, land conflicts involve individual villages squabbling over small plots of terrain, so that politically their consequences are confined to limited areas. Occasionally whole chiefdom sections become involved, but generally land issues cut across other cleavages, further fragmenting the elements which enter the orbit of factional politics.

6. Finally, interchiefdom conflicts comprise an additional source of local cleavage. This is implied in Cartwright's claim that during the 1962 General Election, "Most candidates clearly drew their strongest support from their home chiefdoms; conversely, each chiefdom tended to favor its own candidate."[12] Our data, however, suggest that this factor operates in a more complicated way than Cartwright would have it. *Candidates draw support from segments of their home chiefdoms, but rarely from the entire unit. Therefore, they are obligated to link with factions in the other chiefdoms of their constituency in order to build a winning coalition.* Data from Kenema South (Table 6:2) is illustrative. Here the winner, Jusu-Sheriff, actually received fewer votes in his home chiefdom than Njavambo, who as we saw in the case study, was heavily backed by one section of Tunkia. Jusu-Sheriff's key support came from Gaura chiefdom, which by a 2:1 margin rejected its own candidate in favor of the one allied with its incumbent ruling house. The table at first glance seems to indicate a general "friends and neighbors" pattern reminiscent of V.O. Key's description of Southern U.S. politics.[13] But the data

TABLE 6.2
1962 Election: Results in Kenema South Constituency by Chiefdom

CANDIDATE	HOME CHIEFDOM	VOTE IN EACH CHIEFDOM BY %				
		Dama	Gaura	Tunkia	Nomo	Total %
S. Jusu-Sheriff (Ind.)	Tunkia	19	42	35	6	31
A. M. Lansana (Ind.)	Dama	54	18	5	30	28
O. A. Njavombo (Ind.)	Tunkia	4	15	46	49	22
J. K. Taylor (SLPP)	Dama	17	4	10	7	11
B. S. Bunduka (Ind.)	Gaura	7	21	4	6	8

Source: Cartwright, p. 160.

hide the crucial influence of conflicts *within* chiefdoms. Cartwright's formulation is more appropriate for Temneland than Mendeland, since (nonamalgamated) Temne chiefdoms demonstrate greater internal unity than their Mende counterparts.

It is difficult to test his hypothesis further with information from Kemena District because in most cases all the major candidates have come from the same chiefdom. This stems from the fact that a home base in a large chiefdoms is almost essential for election. Not that large chiefdoms vote *against* small chiefdoms; rather, origin in a large chiefdom assures backing from a faction which is apt to be larger than all the small-chiefdom factions put together. What *does* happen on occasion is that a small chiefdom will unite against the "chief's" candidate from a threatening large chiefdom. Border disputes and fears of amalgamation seem to be common causes of this phenomenon. Such fears in 1969 helped induce at least two small chiefdoms (Nomo and Dodo) to vote solidly in favor of the APC, against an SLPP candidate who was allied with the Paramount Chief of the threatening big chiefdom.

It should be emphasized once again, however, that *intra*-chiefdom cleavages are far more important than interchiefdom cleavages in determining patterns of alliance formation in Mendeland.

We are now in a position to identify the pattern of center-periphery alliance which prevails in Kenema District. Pattern V can be eliminated forthwith: Alliance activity is vibrant and there is no evidence of widespread alienation from the central system on the part of local actors. Likewise, Patterns I and III do not approximate the situation in Kenema District, since it is internal cleavages which dominate the alliance considerations of chiefdom people. (Pattern III characterizes behavior in two minor chiefdoms, Nomo and Dodo, each of which acted as a unified whole in the face of perceived threats from larger neighbors.) The real choice is between Patterns II and IV. Do chiefdom actors ally at the central level in systematic fashion, or is their alliance behavior random with respect to the sociopolitical groupings which stratify the larger society?

Pattern IV characterizes the behavior of Mendes in Kenema District. Their alliances stem from intrachiefdom rivalries in which situational and *ad hoc* factors condition the actions of both

Figure 6.1
Patterns of Center-Periphery Alliance

Model

Local Politics		Identity	Utility
	No Internal Conflict	Pattern I: Alliance among neighboring communities	Pattern III: Alliance among non-neighboring communities
	Internal Conflict	Pattern II: Systematic Alliance	Pattern IV: Random Alliance
	Hostility to Center	Pattern V: Alienation	

incumbents and their opponents, who affiliate at the higher level in order to gain advantage over each other. Because of the various cross pressures which push them in different directions, not all chiefs support the same party. This became especially true once the APC replaced the SLPP as the party in central power. This in turn introduced a random factor into the alliance behavior of opposition groups: some switched to the APC, some stayed in the SLPP coalition, and some played a waiting game, depending on the special set of incentives present in each local situation. Other chiefdom categories, such as youngmen, likewise determined their external alignments on the basis of their relations with the chiefs. In short, the most salient cleavage is between local incumbents and oppositions, but there is no consistency in the manner by which they affiliate at the higher level.

The presence of strangers, however, introduces a systematic element into what otherwise would have been an alliance system based almost entirely upon situational considerations. Northerners almost invariably support the APC, whereas the SLPP receives nearly all of its backing from the indigenous Mendes. This ethnically-based behavior on the part of strangers reflects Pattern II. But this represents only a minority of the district's population. For the great majority, Pattern IV prevails.

If we accept Pattern IV as the predominant mode of center-periphery alliance formation—at least during the time of research, and with the significant exception of northern strangers—then we are led to prefer the utility model in favor of the identity model. Utility maximization accounts in a more complete and economical way for the particular characteristics of alliance in Mende localities than do more commonly accepted concepts based on identity considerations. Ideology, ethnicity, likeness, class, party identification—none proves so serviceable as utility in laying bare the mechanisms of affiliation between grass-roots groups and actors in the wider arena. This is not to say that the concept of rational choice in pursuit of self-interest provides an exhaustive explanation, but as a first approximation it exposes most essential characterisitcs of political behavior in Kenema District.

Before turning to the consequences of utilitarian politics for the Sierra Leonean system, we should attempt to explain more completely this pattern of interplay between conflicts within the central and local arenas, what one interviewee characterized as "double politics."

Double Politics

What accounts for the peculiar features of center-local alliance behavior in Kenema District? Perhaps an effective way of dealing with this question is to compare politics in Mende chiefdoms with the politics of segmentary societies. M.G. Smith has claimed that "political action is always and inherently segmentary," in the sense that ultimately rivals at one level become coordinated against outsiders at a higher level.[14] This corresponds to Pattern I. Yet the Mende pattern seems to contradict this sweeping—though intuitively attractive—statement. Not only in contemporary partisan politics but also in the precolonial era of war alliances, Mendes have had a tendency to externalize internal cleavages by seeking allies from rival camps in the wider world. What accounts for the differences between the segmentary and Mende patterns?

The instrumental relationship between politics and kinship among the Mende seems at first glance reminiscent of the fusion and fission common among "segmentary" or "acephalous" societies. Such peoples as the Nuer, the Ibo, the Tiv, and the clans populating the Somali Republic demonstrate a similar tendency to use kinship as an articulating principle.[15] And even more than the Mende, their political responses are situational in nature. But there are crucial differences between segmentary societies and the Mende. First, there are no principles of "equivalence" and "balanced opposition" among the segments of Mende chiefdoms. Groups vary in size and composition; fusion and fission occur relatively infrequently and take place in an *ad hoc* manner, not along strict structural lines as in segmentary societies. Secondly, and more important, the Mende response to outside forces runs counter to the segmentary principle of fusion against aliens. In a segmentary society, rival groups at the local level will unite at a higher level under an umbrella of putative kinship ties in order to compete in a wider arena. Ideally, the entire society can achieve "mechanical solidarity" to confront an external presence. Evidently modern politics is not exempt from this process. Party politics in Somalia apparently evoked a pattern whereby small-scale kin groups fuse into larger units in order to compete in an expanded political field:

> [T]he effective lineage interests now represented on a national basis are mainly those of the clan-families. Party politics in Somalia are dominated by the conflicting demands of the [various] clan-families. This represents an expansion of political action, an enlargement of the politically significant group, since in the traditional sphere the clan-families are generally too vast, too unwieldy, and too widely scattered to act as effective political units. . . .

> Thus in a national struggle for political power through the new channels of municipal councils and the Legislative Assembly, and through an increasingly dominant control in the Executive functions of government, men from widely scattered clans of the same clan-family see themselves as allies against those of other clan-families in a way which previously had little significance.[16]

And unity has been the watchword among the traditionally acephalous units of Iboland. Outside political parties found few fault lines in Ibo society which would permit challenge to the NCNC monopoly in the Nigerian east.[17]

Mende chiefdoms manifest no such unity in the face of outsiders. External forces further divide them, whereas they induce segmentary societies to expand the boundaries of unity. In gross measure, these contrasting patterns fashion the manner by which the respective "tribes" respond to the exigencies and opportunities of contemporary politics.

Still, we have yet to account for the difference between them. Barth has shown that it is not axiomatic that segmentary-type societies necessarily conform to the commonly-accepted pattern whereby rival local units unite in response to outsiders. His study of Swat Pathans in Pakistan documents a contrary pattern, one akin to the Mende tendency for local rivals each to seek separate allies beyond the locality. The explanation for the difference between the Swat Pathans and other segmentary societies like the Nuer lies, he claims, in the *structure of strategic choice*. In ordinary segmentary societies, unilineal descent groups unite for specific purposes, not the least of which are political; in other words, the individuals of a lineage have a fusion of interests in specific political contexts, though they may have conflicts of interest in other spheres. Among Swat Pathans, however, the rules of inheritance and land tenure create a situation whereby intense rivalry emerges *within* lineages over rights to land, which is secured basically through politics. In other words, there is no fusion within segments for political purposes. Rival kinsmen mobilize political resources against each other by searching for allies outside the primary group:

> In a meeting of a [lineage] council of a wide area, there is *not* the fusion of interests of smaller, related segments of a minor council vis-a-vis larger segments which one would expect in a lineage system. . . . On the contrary, the opposition between small, closely related segments persists in the wider context, and these segments unite with similar small segments in a pattern of two-party opposition, not in a merging series of descent segments.[18]

The particular structure of choice for individual Pathans leads to a society-wide system of two blocs, which cut across the patrilineages of each community.

In a like manner, the structure of choice in Mende chiefdoms encourages internal competitiors to seek rival camps in the wider context. There is no fusion of interests because the rules of the game encourage diversion in the political sphere. The prominent features of the game are as follows. (1) The grand prize is the Paramount Chieftaincy. (2) The rules require two or more kin groups to compete for it; only one can win at a time. (3) There is no rule of cooperation by which competitors can rotate the prize among them. (4) There is no way to abandon one game in order to join another; that is, the chiefdom boundaries laid down by the colonial regime preclude secession. (5) The rules are enforced and interpreted from the outside, by the Government. (6) Important resources for game playing (e.g., money, manipulation of rules, party support, deposition) are obtained outside the chiefdom. In short, the stakes and the resources of the game include a significant external element. The choice of allies is channeled away from mutual cooperation toward external powers. Put in similar terms, the rational actor bent on maximizing its chances for winning the Paramount Chieftaincy must recognize the exoteric features of the game and their importance. Moreover, there is little incentive for "out" groups voluntarily to stress internal unity. Precolonial Mende wartowns adopted quite similar strategies: In an environment of hostile neighbors, alliances were formed with powerful warriors further afield. The modern analogue finds one chiefdom faction linking with the SLPP, the other with the APC.

Utility maximization thus offers an economical explanation for alliance behavior in Mendeland. No identity assumption need enter the explanatory process. The utility model rather than the identity model serves to account for the essential features of "double politics" in Mendeland.

Development

To what extent does the pattern of center-periphery alliance which we have dubbed "double politics" contribute to political development? How resilient are the links thus formed? How stable are parties which are based on such alliances?

The factional nature of political support in this system of alliance renders it unstable and thus a poor contributor to the developmental side of linkage politics. The factions upon which Mende chiefdom politics is based are typical of factions generally.[19] They are not corporate groups, but rather their membership fluctuates and is recruited according to diverse criteria. Even the ruling families which form the core of chiefdom factions are not true corporate units, since on occasion they attract and repel members for strictly utilitarian reasons. Attached to this core with varying degrees of cohesion are individuals and groups who anticipate enhancing their welfare through factional politics. Indeed, factions exist almost exclusively for political competition. They are vehicles for advancing the interests of their members; there is little beyond this to attract membership, since as noncorporate groups factions have no other durable relationship with the wider society. Their behavior is characterized by pursuit of self-interest against rival but similar factions.

Political parties which enter this arena are likely to gain immediate grassroots support as long as they have something to offer one or another local faction. The relationship between party and faction is reciprocal: In exchange for votes and partisan support, grass-roots groups anticipate favor from the central actor with whom they are allied. From local perspective, the party has become attached to the faction—just as, from the central perspective, the faction has joined the party. Continued support is, however, contingent upon continued benefit; the alliance is viable only so long as it proves advantageous in the local factional struggle. Large numbers of people will climb aboard when an alliance is enjoying good weather but they are likely to abandon ship when the sailing gets rough.

Central authority is a major resource available to political parties, giving the incumbent party a weighty advantage in attracting local factions to its side. This results in large fluctuations in the support accorded a particular alliance, depending on whether or not it is in power. Carpet crossing is a problem which has plagued all opposition parties in Sierra Leone. Table 6.3 shows the composition of four Parliaments and the reshufflings which have taken place. In all cases there has been a steady surge toward

TABLE 6.3
Party Reaffiliations in the 1957, 1962, 1967, and 1973 Parliaments

1957		
SLPP	25	
KPM	1	
UPP	5	(of whom 2 crossed to SLPP)
Indep.	8	(all crossed to SLPP)
1962		
SLPP	28	
APC-SLPIM	20	(of whom 7 crossed to SLPP)
Indep.	14	(all crossed to SLPP)
1967		
APC	32	
SLPP	28	(of whom 15 went to the APC in 1968-9*, and at least 6 went to the APC in 1973)
Indep.	6	(of whom 4 went to the APC and 2 to the SLPP)
1973		
APC	84	
SLPP	0	
Indep.	1	

*By-election results.

the ruling party, particularly on the part of those successful candidates who had run as Independents. The attrition of opposition in the 1967 case is somewhat unusual, since the 15 SLPP seats which went to the APC were the result of election petitions and the by-elections which ensued. Just prior ot the 1973 elections, at least half of the remaining 12 SLPP Members of Parliament switched to the APC, avoiding what they interpreted as certain defeat in the face of determined government harassment through official violence, legal intimidation, and partisan manipulation of rules such as nomination procedures.[20] Independents, too, felt the heavy hand of governmental power, since a rule was imposed in 1971 penalizing a Member of Parliament with the loss of his seat if it were determined by the Speaker that he had changed party affiliation. Thus by 1969, once it had become the government of the day, the APC was able to reduce the once-dominant SLPP to a minority opposition of only 12 members from its heartland in Mende country, and by 1973 even that hard core had been reduced to nil, creating a *de facto* One-Party State.

What is the probability that the APC in the future could be simclarly reduced to its core area in the North ? If the pattern of center-local alliances we have described brings quick benefits to a party during good times, the obverse is that it will rapidly disintegrate when it has less to offer. President Siaka Stevens is fully aware of this phenomenon:

> Party in the ideological sense of the word doesn't exist in Africa. We never have been divided into classes. So people jump from one party to the other depending on the benefits they can get. People see the immediate benefits of supporting the Government party—rice, loans, and so on. It was only through my determination and perseverence that the APC did not fall apart [when it was the Opposition].[21]

Most of the chiefdom factions in Kenema District—and *a fortiori* in all of Mendeland—now allied to the APC are unlikely to remain with the party if it should lose control of the national Government. The localism and opportunism which underlie its alliances do not bode well for the stability of APC strength outside its Northern core, just as the SLPP alliance system rapidly collapsed in upon its core area once it had lost national power.

Seen from a nationwide perspective, however, the APC does have an advantage. The APC stronghold in the North is more stable than the SLPP's core of support among the Mende. This stems first from the organizational network which the APC has elaborated throughout the North, which was born out of adversity and will not be easy to eliminate; and second, from the fact that Temne and Limba chiefdoms are more likely to be internally unified than their Mende counterparts. This apparently is the consequence of a practice common in Northern chiefdoms whereby succession to the chieftaincy rotates among ruling houses in a predetermined order, rather than the uncertain, competitive system prevalent among the Mende. Thus, struggle for chieftaincy among Northerners tends to take place *within* not between families, cutting across the cleavage which, above all, sows disunity and invites outside penetration into Mendeland. Ruling house rivalries in Mende chiefdoms constitute the major opportunity for non-Mende political parties to reduce the SLPP's core strength. Retaliation on the part of the SLPP cannot take place with equal ease, however, due to the greater cohesion of Northern chiefdoms. Put differently, the rule requiring rotation in Temne chiefdoms affects the structure of strategic choice for local actors, rendering them less likely than their Mende counterparts to engage in intransigent competition with each other.

In sum, this system of center-local alliances is not stable, involving as it does a potential for large, rapid fluctuations in the size and composition of political parties. The APC does have a somewhat more durable foundation than the SLPP, which relies almost entirely upon chiefly factions in Mendeland, but outside its core area it is likewise dependent upon the vicissitudes of local issues and their local spokesmen.

Such instability contributes to the extreme sensitivity with which party leaders view dissent and splintering. Recognizing the fragility of the constructs they have patched together, they are reluctant to tolerate even a minor departure from the fold, lest it initiate a process of cumulative depletion which could seriously weaken if not destroy the party. Perhaps this explains Sir Albert's bald manipulatory stance toward those members of his own party who disagreed with his plans for a one-party state. It likely also explains Siaka Stevens' heavy use of official coercion against members of the National Democratic Party, a vocal dissident group which had broken away from the APC in 1970 and which enjoyed a potential stronghold in certain Temne chiefdoms, since a number of its members were from royal families. What appeared as an overreactive and indiscriminate trampling of civil rights can be interpreted as a reasoned effort to forestall a reverse snowball effect, in which initial minor dealignments if they are successful may provide incentives for local factions throughout the alliance network to raise their demands, with threats to defect if they go unmet. In the absence of links no more reliable than utilitarian alliances, violence is one of the few means available to prevent such a run on the political bank.

Violence—official or otherwise—is a logical extension of utilitarian politics. In Sierra Leone it serves elites as an instrument for intimidating and eliminating opponents, for intimidating voters, and for galvanizing local support. From grassroots perspective, it is also a means for gaining the attention of the central government. Given its effectiveness in producing short-term results, it is not surprising that Sierra Leone has experienced a trend of increasing coercion, intimidation, and official force. From one level of analysis—the periphery—rational calculation may point to violence as an effective technique for promoting factional goals. But at a higher level of analysis—the system as a whole—a series of such acts takes on a significance far greater than the sum of its individual parts. Intended to serve only discrete, limited aims, violence often escalates, vitiating its original purpose and expanding force to systemic proportions, with unintended consequences. Central actors are provoked into protecting their clients—setting into motion a whole chain of action and reaction. Local strife induces intervention by national actors, which precipitates a new level of local violence, which in turn invites intensified retaliation from the center. Events in Kenema District since 1967 illustrate this sequence. Minor SLPP harassment of strangers in the General Election convinced the APC that cadres imported from outside were necessary to protect the party's power base during the by-elections. Local chiefdom establishments, anticipating invation by northern "thugs," mobilized the *Poro* and other community machinery against strangers and their APC supporters. In response, the Government took stringent martial measures. The State of Emergency imposed coercive conditions far more severe and widespread than the isolated incidents which led up to it. This process of escalation has not been confined to Kenema District. Intensified interaction between center and periphery has abetted increased violence throughout the country.[22]

Faction-based violence has not been confined to chiefdom politics and its central ramifications. Pervasive factionalism within the military contributed significantly to the spate of coups and foiled coups which burst upon the Sierra Leonean scene between 1966 and 1971.[23] Cliques formed and reformed, each stitched together by much the same threadwork that runs through chiefdom politics—home ties, family, marriage, friendship, clientship, and simple expedience. Built as it was upon a variety of relationships, a faction was likely to cut across such military distinctions as rank, schooling, unit, or function. Indeed, factions sliced the very boundary between the military and civilian realms, uniting in alliances of convenience soldiers who sought protection and promotion with politicians who needed assurance that the *ultima ratio* would be applied in their favor. In 1967 Sir Albert Margai and Brigadier David Lansana were the leaders of a faction fabricated from dovetailing interests: the Prime Minister needed support from the army to withstand the APC onslaught; the Commanding Officer in turn needed help from high politicans to meet the challenge of younger, better-educated, and more professional officers who wished him to step aside and who were playing their own factional game within and without the army. At the same time, a group of northern officers who resented what they perceived as a Mende plot to dominate the military, aligned with APC politicians to promote their mutual interests in advancing the northern cause.

Since the ultimate weapon of each faction was the coup, and since each had an incentive to strike first in order to preempt the others, the probability of violence was high in 1967—especially when the election produced a close and ambiguous outcome. Two coups in rapid succession reversed the election results. The first was the handiwork of the Margai-Lansana faction. The second was centered about the clique of young Mende officers (a number of whom were from Kenema District) who wanted to displace Lansana. A third coup a year later put into power Colonel John Bangura, leader of the northern faction, who very quickly installed his APC allies in the seat of civilian power.[24] None of these factions was stable. The Margai-Lansana group had originally included at least some of the young Mende officers— who dealigned at the crucial moment, and who fell to squabbling among themselves during their year in power. Colonel Bangura, soon promoted to General after assuming command of the army, remained loyal to Siaka Stevens and the APC only until March 1971, when he launched an abortive attempt to kill his ally and to assume control of the state. Perhaps he feared betrayal once the highly-politicized second batallion became operational, but whatever his motives, his deadly caper forced Prime Minister Stevens into virtual dependence upon a foreign country for the security of his life and his regime. A army detachment from Guinea was flown to his rescue and remained in Freetown as his bodyguard until the 1973 General Election, at which time disagreements between Sierra Leone and Guinea apparently caused the troops to be removed. (Rumors intimate that Stevens has since then engaged military missions from Cuba and the People's Republic of China for his personal security.) Factionalism has rendered the Sierra Leonean army so volatile an instrument of governance that the Prime Minister (now President) has had to resort to alliance in the international arena as a key domestic resource—"double politics" at a higher level.

Were politics constructed on a foundation built of deeper loyalties, violence would have less appeal. Yet violence itself militates against building stronger structures. Its use in politics discourages the long-term commitments the very lack of which makes it an effective tactic in the first place. The result has been a "shift from power to force as a technique of Government. . . ."[25]

Corrosive violence is not the only adverse effect which "double politics" has upon the developmental dimension of center-periphery linkages. Due to their tentative nature, utilitarian alliances mesh the two arenas in a manner which preserves discontinuities between them, for grass-roots people participate in national politics primarily on the basis of local issues. Localism is actually enchanced by the intervention of central actors seeking to exploit chiefdom cleavages for electoral advantage. Debate on the broad problems of economic policy, foreign policy, taxation, education and most other national issues, becomes restricted to the relatively narrow circles of Parliament, the Cabinet, the press and its largely Freetown-based audience. Rarely is such debate taken to the hustings. A notable exception involves constitutional issues, which do receive articulation at even the lowest grass-roots level in Sierra Leone. Debate over Sir Albert's One-Party State and his attempt to write Republican principles into the Constitution was widespread and contrary to his expectations. Similarly, Prime Minister Stevens' campaign for Republican status received wide attention at the local level—and, in Kenema District at least, little enthusiasm. Fundamental changes in the Constitution could radically alter the national political structure and, with it, the complexion of local politics. Local people view with protective sensitivity the entrenched clause confirming chieftaincy as a basic institution of government. So it is not surprising that constitutional controversies breach the normal tendency for grass-roots people to concentrate on local problems to the exclusion of national issues.

In ordinary circumstances, "double politics" links the central elite and the peripheral masses in a manner which diminishes the probability that broad, collective interests will gain expression and acceptance on a population-wide basis. The system is predisposed to deal with diverse particularistic demands from the separate local arenas rather than to develop the general political resources requisite for policy aimed at collective problems. We will return to this theme shortly in our discussion of party embeddedness in local structures; the point here is simply that a localistically-based system of alliance quite unsurprisingly imposes powerful constraints on the authority which can be exerted from the center. As the utility model anticipated, the politics of expedience bodes ill for development.

Integration

To what extent does "double politics" serve to integrate the various tribes, regions, and status groups of Sierra Leone into a unified entity? Is this pattern of alliance formation favorable or unfavorable to meshing the central political system with the out-lying localities? Many people in interviews felt strongly that such pentration of national politics into chiefdom affairs has been disastrous, that central interference on a partisan basis has sown division and distrust, and that nothing good has come of it. They are perfectly accurate in one sense: It is undeniable that party competition has reinforced and exacerbated local disputes; in almost every chiefdom of Kenema District, outside interven-tion has augmented internal dissension. But viewed from a wider perspective, this structure of center-local linkages does con-tribute to national unity and is indeed in many ways more desirable than alternative patterns of aggregation.

For instance, there could be a pattern by which all northern chiefdoms ally against all southern chiefdoms (Pattern I). That would be "tribalism" in its most blatant form, reminiscent of the cleavages which have rent Dahomey and Nigeria. Sierra Leone came dangerously close to such a distribution of allegiance as a result of the 1967 General Election, when the vast majority of successful SLPP candidates was Mende, and the new APC parliamentary group was composed largely of Temnes and related northern peoples. Or, put differently, the SLPP won only one northern seat, the APC only one southern seat. Once it managed to assume power—following the military coups—the APC was, however, able to penetrate Mendeland by exploiting the inherent disunity within its chiefdoms. Had the south been invulnerable to penetration by a northern regime, it is likely that politics in Sierra Leone would have hardened into outright tribal confrontation, with popular recruitment into national system conditioned by unmoderated ethnicity and little else. As it was, cleavages within the separate chiefdoms allowed the APC access to Mendeland: From a central standpoint, the APC was rendered a national, not tribal party; from local perspective, party com-petition was invited to take place *within* Sierra Leone's largest and most powerful tribal group. Both aspects encouraged national integration.

Or, we can envision another pattern of alliance, by which the rich elements of the population combine to protect themselves against the poorer elements, and vice versa (Pattern II). This is the familiar model of class competition. Had the APC remained true to its original radicalism, perhaps political participation in Sierra Leone would have followed class lines, with the APC aggregating workers and farmers throughout the nation against the chiefs and their wealthy brethren, who in turn would have turned to the SLPP. This—had it materialized; indeed, had it been politically feasible—would have contributed to *horizontal* integration in Sierra Leone. That is, such a pattern would have cut across tribal, regional, and local distinctions, with both parties operating on a territorial basis. However, it would have had a deleterious effect on *vertical* integration. Discontinuities between elite and mass would have become pronounced. Sierra Leone is ruled by an elite characterized by its blend of Western education, wealth, and traditional status. Were politics to assume strictly class features, this elite would be pitted against the masses, since there exists no alternative elite with the capabilities and educational qualifications requisite for running the state machinery.[26] Class politics does not enhance *rapport* between elite and mass when the upper class and the ruling elite largely coincide.

In contrast, the existing system of locally-oriented alliances forges links along both the horizontal and vertical dimensions. The system is territorial in scope; the ruling party in particular operates on a national not a tribal or regional basis. And by allying with local factions—each of which includes both an elite and a mass—parties aggregate in a manner which does not threaten the entrenched social structure of chiefdoms in rural Sierra Leone. Each party elite has a strong localistic component. Indeed, the national political elite and local elites largely overlap, in the sense that each Parliamentarian and Cabinet member has a political base embedded in the chiefdom rivalries of his home constituency; and in the sense that a member of the national elite is also likely to be member of a particular local elite. Through the intermediacy of local elites, the masses and the political center are connected.[27]

A third alternative would array "modern" against "traditional" elements of society (Pattern II). Here, educated, urbanized, Westernized, and "progressive" actors would coalesce against the forces of rural conservativism entrenched in the chiefdom hierarchies. The difficulty with such a formulation, however, is that the two categories are not at all mutually exclusive in Sierra Leone. Traditional and modern blend along myriad dimensions to such an extent that they are far more appropriate for polemics and scolasticism than for description of Sierra Leonean society. Even if it were possible to separate them analytically, competition between them would be counterproductive from the standpoint of not only practical politics but of political integration. By any measure the vast preponderance of the population falls into the "traditional" category: in 1963, over 90% of Sierra Leoneans lived in chiefdoms; less than 10% lived in urban areas of 10,000 or more; 43% lived in villages of 200 or less; and 77% worked in such "traditional" occupations as farming, fishing, and hunting.[28] This is a political fact of life which cannot be ignored; in a democratic era—when popular votes mean something—the masses cannot be discounted, whether "unmobilized" or not. If politics were to take on an unmistakable modern-versus-tradition cast in a country as ill-developed socioeconomically as Sierra Leone, surely the modernizers would be swamped. Moreover, such politics would entail competition between the urban areas and the countryside, between center and periphery. National integration is hastened by fostering links between rural and urban areas, hindered by drawing a sharp line of cleavage between them.

"Double Politics," on the other hand, diffuses whatever distinctions actually exist between modernity and traditionality. Aggregation takes place in two phases of alliance formation. First, at the local level, each chiefdom faction is composed of members from a variety of groups and categories, all clustered about a ruling house; by attracting adherents from both sides of more fundamental cleavages, factions help knit society together. Second, at the constituency level, alliances centered on individual Parliamentary candidates further randomize tradition-versus-modern discriminations by lumping together local factions in a fashion based much more on expedience than on ideology or sociological compatibility. Rural and urban, rich and poor, royalty and commoner, literate and illiterate—all constitute the ingredients of each party alliance based on "double politics."

A utilitarian alliance pattern promotes national integration in a manner more effective and less disruptive than alternative patterns. At least in Kenema District, center-periphery alliances cut across tribal, class, regional, and residential distinctions. Rather than reinforcing such cleavages, they slice through them, reducing their potential for disunity and aggregating people along novel lines of division. This is the insight of Simmel and his disciples: the more the *cross-cutting* lines of conflict, the greater the level of integration. The alliances which link grassroots groups in Kenema District with the central system are neither strong nor enduring but—paradoxically—they serve the cause of national solidarity by randomizing the issues which fracture its constituent localities.

Embeddedness

As the utility model predicts, an alliance pattern based on localism and expedience promotes integration but hinders development. Party structures embedded in local groups through utilitarian attachments can link many points along the social topography, but such links are a weak basis for generating the political resources necessary for exercising central authority and promoting coherent policies. In Eisenstadt's terms, embedded ties limit the "free-floating resources" available to central institutions. In Kilson's terms, the *quid pro quo* premise inherent in such arrangements invites breakdown in systems underwritten by poverty and economic uncertainty. The question here is whether party organization offers an escape from this dilemma. If embeddedness is reduced by forging autonomous party structures at the local level, does the trade-off between integration and development relax, allowing an increase in central political capacity with no corresponding reduction in unity?

Kilson predicts breakdown of the Sierra Leonean system because increases in the exercise of authority will outstrip the economy's ability to produce the material resources necessary to procure compliance. In essence, he posits a primitive exchange relationship between political support and wealth. There is no doubt that money and material favors represent common means for mustering political resources in Sierra Leone, but in the rural areas the relationship between wealth and politics is not so strong as Kilson would have it. Most of his examples derive from the urban context, where he describe the relationship between support for the SLPP and payments to such urban-based groups as tribal unions, the Ex-Servicemen's Association, sports associations, students' unions, and co-operatives.[29] The typical medium of exchange in the countryside, however, is less tangible but no less significant than wealth—outside support in chiefdom rivalries. Political support at the local level is reciprocated for political support at the central level.

This mitigates the harshness of Kilson's conclusions. Rather than a constant-sum relationship between wealth and political capacity, as he implies, other resources are available for conversion into power at the national level. The most readily available reservoir of power is the chiefdom, home of the vast preponderance of Sierra Leoneans and the site of persistent internal feuds, most of them easily convertible into electoral sustenance.

If the constraints upon the growth of political capacity are less severe than Kilson contends, this pattern of center-local alliances does, however, impose distinct limitations upon national actors and institutions. In the absence of autonomous grass-roots organizations, political parties in particular become the prisoners of small-scale squabbles.

The SLPP has been almost devoid of an organizational structure separate from the chiefdom hierarchies upon which it has so long depended. As Jusu-Sheriff put it:

> The SLPP never has been organized. It is more a movement than a party. We have never had anything like the organization the APC has.[30]

Every aspect of party electoral activity, from nominations to fund-raising to vote-getting, has been inextricably intertwined with the affairs of the separate chiefdoms. Furthermore, without an intervening structure to act as buffer, intraparty disputes and chiefdom disputes have interpenetrated one antoher, fractionating its power base whenever differences of opinion divided its leadership, and splintering the leadership whenever local issues threatened their home bases. The most obvious instance of the SLPP's propensity to resist orderly coordination and central discipline was Sir Albert's abortive attempt to exert control by undermining in their home constituencies those SLPP members, including Cabinet Ministers, who were not congenial to his way of thinking. During the 1967 election, "there were at least nine seats in which sitting SLPP members were being opposed by men known to be close to Sir Albert."[31] His method was to exacerbate existing or dormant chiefdom disputes, hoping to excite sufficient support from awakened chiefdom oppositions to elect the candidate he favored. In the end, however, he succeeded not in gaining adherents but only in stirring up local unrest, the effects of which persist today. Indeed, resentment against arbitrary intervention into chiefdom affairs contributed significantly to the bifurcation of the SLPP and the downfall of his government.

Not surprisingly, the SLPP when in power demonstrated little willingness or ability to act in the field of local reform. In the early days of SLPP rule the momentum of the colonial "reform era" was allowed to continue, albeit at an ever-slowing pace. Additional Court Presidents were appointed, Tribal Authorities expanded, and Chiefdom Committees instituted, but in general, especially by the time of Sir Albert, local administration suffered from severe neglect. The District Councils were allowed to degenerate; chiefdom finances became even more corrupt and inept; the marketing boards were abused for self-serving reasons; and local taxes, perhaps out of fear of the northern tax riots of the 1950's (or even the Hut Tax War of 1898), remained ridiculously low. Indeed, it is difficult to think of one bold initiative undertaken by the SLPP regime at any level of analysis— local, national, or international. For the most part, it perpetuated the patterns of policy which had evolved under the British during the reform era.

For long the national Opposition, the APC, in order to survive had to build a party organization independent of the chiefdom structures within which it had to operate. In its core areas of support, the Northern Province and Freetown, the APC boasts strong branch and constituency organizations capable of raising funds, votes, and candidates without extreme reliance upon chiefdom factions. On the other hand, in Mendeland it has undertaken serious competition only recently. Hence its autonomous organization initially was minimal in areas like Kenema District. As a consequence it too relied heavily upon chiefdom cleavages for electoral backing. Only since the APC concluded alliances with important segments of important chiefdoms has it been able to contend seriously in Mendeland. This has reduced by several degrees of freedom its capacity and willingness to carry out the programmatic goals at the local level which once characterized its ideology. What started out as a radical "class" party voicing the grievances of commoners against their chiefs, now speaks the language of the SLPP and the colonial regime which preceded it: Respect and obey your chiefs; make your complaints through proper channels; the Government will back natural rulers against unjustified troublemakers.[32] Of course part of this conservative drift can be attributed to the onus of administering the countryside which the APC assumed with the mantle of Government, but it is due as well to increased dependence upon the contentious factions of chiefdoms and the Parliamentarians they have elected.

Without organizational penetration of the countryside, a party can relegate itself to permanent minority status simply by dint of the local alliances it has forged. An extreme case is found in Small Bo chiefdom, where the APC is closely tied to an unpopular Speaker. Embeddedness inhibits the growth of power. This is clearly recognized by Siaka Stevens:

The divisions between ruling houses is something that can help a party get votes. There is no point in rejecting such an alliance. But it can be a disadvantage. I see organization as a way of avoiding such dependence. However, we will not reject ruling house support. We can use both forms of support.[33]

In other words, local alliances and local party organizations are not mutually exclusive; but the latter permits a degree of maneuverability unavailable through reliance upon the former alone.

With this in mind the APC launched in Kenema District and other Mende areas an organization-building effort which gradually distinguished the party from its SLPP rival. Building on already-existing enclaves of organization centered in stranger communities, the APC worked to institute regular procedures, regular funding, and regular membership. A district office (corresponding to the branch offices of many European parties) was opened in 1969, staffed by a permanent paid official, William Smith, a young educated Mende from Bo District. Smith was given some financial backing from headquarters in Freetown and was instructed to build further his resources through the sale of membership cards and through money-making functions such as dances. Constituency offices were established in Kenema East, Kenema West, and Kenema Northwest. A membership drive was undertaken in 1970, the success of which unfortunately cannot be ascertained, since the party was unwilling to reveal whatever records it had available.

While the organizational apparatus of the APC in Kenema District far surpassed the SLPP's meager efforts, its accomplishments should not be overestimated. At the time of research it was plagued by two deficiencies. Its day-to-day resources were skimpy, consisting of only one full-time organizer, no vehicles, a supply of APC lapel buttons, very limited funds, one mimeograph machine, and minimal use of propaganda media such as handouts, skits, and social events. On the other hand, resources were intermittently made available from above in the form of speeches by national personalities and, at election time, an influx of young activists ("thugs" to the SLPP) ready to take on party tasks. The second deficiency brings us back to our consideration of embeddedness. A significant portion of what has just been itemized as the APC's autonomous organizational resources in reality originated from chiefdom factions allied to the party for their own local reasons. The district office was donated to the party by M.M. Koroma of Nongowa as part of his effort to court the Prime Minister. The Kenema West constituency office is actually Speaker Boima Temu's house; the only thing which distinguishes it from any other house in Small Bo chiefdom is the red APC sign which hangs over the front door. The "mass" membership drive was actually undertaken by a handful of people most of whom were temporary recruits linked inextricably to one chiefdom faction or another. In Small Bo, for instance, the effort to sell party cards was assumed largely by Smith, Temu, Keitell (the APC candidate from Kenema West), and Lansana Kellah, a local rice merchant identified with the Temu faction. Their efforts consisted largely of attempting to pursuade the Paramount Chief to legitimize or at least to tolerate their campaign. Little time was actually spent in the villages. The same pattern obtained in most of the other chiefdoms, the major exceptions being APC strongholds rooted in stranger concentrations, representing in reality another form of embeddedness.

The APC, then has achieved mixed results in its effort to reduce dependence upon chiefdom factions, rendering ambiguous the "independent variable" of our embeddedness hypothesis. Furthermore, no clear-cut trend regarding central capacity has emerged. On the one hand, in terms of national and foreign policy, the APC regime has departed in a number of significant areas from patterns which prevailed during the colonial, military, and SLPP regimes. A Republic was declared; a "leftward" shift in foreign policy was signalled by the recognition of Communist China and by establishment of intimate links with Guinea; the government negotiated a 51% nationalization of SLST; a second army batallion was created, dedicated to community-oriented rather than to military-oriented goals; and a *de facto* One-Party State was established through the APC's overwhelming victory in the 1973 election, although the impact of party organization is difficult to determine due to the heavy use of coercion. These examples have been listed not to demonstrate their desirability or undesirability but merely to illustrate the capacity of the APC government to formulate and execute bold policies, in contrast to its predecessor.

On the other hand, however, at the subnational level, the line of continuity with past precedence has remained firm under the APC. Its policies have departed in no significant manner from those of the three prior regimes, suggesting that the political arrangements it has made with chiefdom factions continues to constrain its ability to make concerted demands upon local folk. Perhaps it will translate its recent electoral victory into a mandate to induce deliberate change at the grass-roots level through new institutions, closer central supervision, more comprehensive development schemes, and higher local taxes; but until now it has channelled its reform energies to the more tractable and less fundamental national and international policy arenas. This confounds our ability to draw even tentative conclusions about the embeddedness hypothesis. But it is certain that the chiefdom administration remains the bedrock of governance in Sierra Leone; that the chiefdom faction survives as the most essential political unit; and that the boundary between society and party is tenuous, rendering the party system a poorly-institutionalized link between center and periphery.

NOTES

1. Georg Simmel, *Conflict and the Web of Group Affiliations,* Trans. Kurt Wolff and Reinhard Bendix (Glencoe, Ill.: Free Press, 1950); Lewis Coser, *The Functions of Social Conflict* (New York: Free Press, 1956); Ralf Dahrendorf, *Class and Class Conflict in Industrial Society* (Stanford: Stanford Univ. Press, 1959); and Max Gluckman, *Custom and Conflict in Africa* (London: Basil Blackwell, 1956).

2. Nongowa offers an ambiguous case. The bifurcation of the major ruling house, Kai-Samba; the shifting in and out of parties on the part of the most visible protagonists, M.M. Koroma and Hon. Kai-Samba; and the ambivalence, probably deliberate, of the old man, PC Vangahun—all have made neat categories and clear-cut regularities at best ephemeral in this most kaleidoscopic of chiefdoms.

3. Kenneth Little, *The Mende of Sierra Leone* (London: Routledge and Kegan Paul, 1951), p. 110.

4. Interview #78. Feb. 16, 1970.

5. Little, *op. cit.,* p. 109.

6. I am greatly indebted to Abner Cohen, who in conversation alerted me to these characteristics of kinship. For further elaboration, see Abner Cohen, "Political Anthropology: The Analysis of the Symbolism of Power Relations," *Man,* IV (June 1969), 215-35; and *Custom and Politics in Urban Africa* (London: Routledge and Kegan Paul, 1969).

7. Electoral Commission, Score Sheets, 1969 By-Elections.

8. John R. Cartwright, *Politics in Sierra Leone* (Toronto: Toronto Univ. Press, 1970), p. 159.

9. Cooptation of Mende candidates into the APC does not, however, completely explain its improved performance. Of five candidates, two were considered strangers; one of these (Peter Keitell) lost by a large margin, but the other (Abibu Sackor) won with relative ease. SLPP supporters are quick to point out that officially-condoned intimidation was widespread, especially in Kenema Northeast, where Sackor was victorious. There is some basis for these accusations, but it is difficult to assess with even passable accuracy the degree to which the constituency outcomes were influenced by force and threats. The issue of undue influence during elections should not hide the fact that the APC established itself as a major party in Kenema District by linking up with indigenous factions.

10. Cartwright, *ibid.,* dwells on the APC's initial "class" appeal to common people:

> "More than any previous opposition party, the APC maintained a marked ideological tone. Its leaders professed to be socialist. . . . It regarded itself as the party of the 'common people' as opposed to the privileged elite, particularly the chiefs, and some of its leaders seemed to believe that the potential for class struggle existed in Sierra Leone." (p. 132)

Cartwright also stresses the shift from this "class" appeal toward a "regional" (i.e., Northern) orientation. (See pp. 262-67.)

11. Speaker A.M. Lansana (APC) vs. PC Vandi Dassama (SLPP) in Dama; A.G. Lappia (APC) vs. PC Kanja (SLPP) in Gorama Mende; Speaker Boima Temu (APC) vs. ex-Speaker James Kougbaka (SLPP)

in Small Bo; M.M. Koroma (APC) vs. Hon. K.I. Kai-Samba (SLPP) in Nongowa; and Moinina Kallon (APC) vs. PC Madam Sama (SLPP) in Tunkia.

12. Cartwright, *op. cit.*, p. 160.

13. V.O. Key, *Southern Politics* (New York: Alfred A. Knopf, 1950), esp. pp. 37 ff. and pp. 82-105.

14. M.G. Smith, "On Segmentary Lineage Systems," *The Journal of the Royal Anthropological Institute,* 86 (July-Dec. 1956), 48.

15. E.E.Evans-Pritchard, "The Nuer of the Southern Sudan," in M. Fortes and Evans-Pritchard (eds.), *African Political Systems* (London, N.Y., Toronto: Oxford Univ. Press, 1940), pp. 272-96; I.M. Lewis, *A Pastoral Democracy* (London, N.Y., Toronto: Oxford Univ. Press. 1961); M.M. Green, *Ibo Village Affairs* (London: Sidgwick and Jackson, 1947).

16. Lewis, *op. cit.,* pp. 284-85.

17. For an explanation of the few exceptions see Richard Henderson, "Generalized Cultures and Evolutionary Adaptibility: A Comparison of Urban Efik and Ibo in Nigeria," *Ethnology,* V (Oct. 1966), 365-91. For two case studies of politics in Iboland, see Audrey C. Smock, *Ibo Politics: The Role of Ethnic Unions in Eastern Nigeria* (Cambridge, Mass: Harvard Univ. Press, 1971).

18. Fredrik Barth, "Segmentary Opposition and the Theory of Games: A Study of Pathan Organization," *The Journal of the Royal Anthropological Institute,* 89 (Jan.-June 1959), 9. Also see *Political Leadership Among Swat Pathans* (London: Athlone, 1959).

19. Ralph W. Nicholas, "Factions: A Comparative Analysis," in *Political Systems and the Distribution of Power,* ASA Monographs 2 (N.Y.: Praeger, 1965), pp. 26-61. Fortunately, factional politics has received recent attention from political scientists, ending a long period of neglect; e.g., Rene Lemarchand and Keith Legg, "Political Clientelism and Development: A Preliminary Analysis," *Comparative Politics,* 4,2 (Jan 1972), pp. 149-178; and Norman K. Nicholson, "The Factional Model and the Study of Politics," *Comparative Political Studies,* 5,3 (Oct. 1972), pp. 291-314.

20. *West Africa,* 5 March, 1973, p. 354; 7 May, 1973, p. 614; 21 May, 1973, p. 681. *Africa Report* (May-June 1973), p.6.

21. Interview.

22. For a more detailed treatment of violence in Sierra Leonean politics, see chapter VII of my unpublished dissertation, "Local-Level Politics in Sierra Leone," Yale University, 1971.

23. The following account is based on Thomas S. Cox, "Civil-Military Relations in Sierra Leone: A Case Study of African Soldiers in Politics," unpublished dissertation, Fletcher School of Law and Diplomacy, 1973; and Barrows, "La Politique de L'Armee en Sierra Leone," *Revue Francaise d'Etudes Poltiques Africaines,* No. 36 (Dec. 1968), pp. 54-64.

24. This actually resulted from what I have called in *Ibid.* "the sergeants' *coup,*" a takeover by the rank-and-file led by noncommissioned officers who arrested all their officers and *then* invited Bangura to form a government. There is evidence that Bangura and Siaka Stevens operating from sanctuary in Guinea were engaged in fomenting discontent especially among northern elements of the rank-and-file.

25. Aristide Zolberg, "The Structure of Political Conflict in the New States of Tropical Africa," *American Political Science Review,* LXII (March 1968), p. 77.

26. Cartwright contends that in 1962 the "APC leaders and members of Parliament constituted a 'new class' entering the political elite for the first time. Relative to the SLPP oligarchy, the APC members came from lower-class occupations, had more limited formal education, were younger, and had fewer links with ruling families." (p. 166.)

However, the evidence he presents regarding the attributes of *successful* candidates for the 1962 Parliament demonstrates no radical difference between the APC and the SLPP, other than age. *All* APC candidates combined (successful and unsuccessful) did as a group differ significantly from their SLPP counterparts, though. This suggests that those who had the characteristics of the prevailing elite (wealth, education, chiefdom status) had a greater chance of election than those who did not. (Compare his tables on p. 148 with those on pp. 163-66.)

27. These comments are neither so obvious nor so trivial as they appear at first glance. It is not axiomatic that a member of the central elite will also be a member of a particular local elite. Witness much of Southeast Asia, where the state apparatus is apt to be the preserve of

an urban-based culture (Redfield's "great tradition") quite removed from the "little traditions" of the rural priests and headmen who comprise the local elites. Similar comments can be made about colonial regimes, which by definition impose an alien central elite upon indigenous local elites.

28. *1963 Population Census of Sierra Leone* (Central Statistics Office, Freetown, 1965).

29. Kilson, *Political Change in a West African State,* pp. 259-265.

30. Interview.

31. Cartwright, *op. cit.,* p. 235.

32. See Cartwright, *op. cit.,* pp. 262-64 for a discussion of the shift within the APC from a "class" to a "tribal" (or regional) party.

An example of the APC's present approach to chiefdom affairs is a speech given by Prime Minister Stevens in Kenema. "Speaking on the question of Chieftaincy, he said that the Government fully supports [the] institution of Chieftaincy. Government, he said, expects people to respect their chiefs. . . . Continuing, he said, 'you may not like your chief, you may hate him, but if you don't take care you will spoil the chieftaincy not for the chief you don't want but for the future of Paramount Chiefs.'" *Daily Express,* March 24, 1970, p. 3.

33. Interview.

Chapter 7

Conclusion

We have been led in our examination of linkage politics in Kenema District to prefer the synthetic to the displacement model of social change. Similarly, the patterns of center-periphery alliance distilled from the Mende experience indicate that the utility model is a more serviceable analytical device than the identity model. Preference for the synthetic and utility models should not be construed as a claim that the explanations they offer are pure and plenary accounts of politics in Sierra Leone. As models they are only approximations of reality: They embrace the view that Mende politics is *essentially* synthetic and utilitarian, and that important consequences for development and integration issue from this fact.

The instrumental nature of politics in Mendeland has been stressed throughout this study. The precolonial era was marked by fluidity and strife to such an extent that few deep-seated political traditions evolved. A battle-torn age, it encouraged leaders who were warriors rather than priests. The slight religious content to his role allowed the Mende chief a greater range of permissible action than most of his West African counterparts. Such built-in flexibility enabled Mende societies, in the political sphere at least, to adapt easily to the new conditions brought by colonial rule.

The penetration of the Sierra Leonean hinterland by Western influences was accomplished by no sharp clash of opposites, no direct confrontation between the "modern" and the "traditional." "[P]eople do not simply adhere to tradition in a vacuum, but only in the contemporary context of the struggle for interests and rights and privileges, and in defense of those they already have."[1] Traditions, like all rules, can be manipulated for partisan purposes. They are altered to suit new circumstances and called forth when they further the interests of competing groups and individuals. The Mende especially have been adept at absorbing the requisites of colonial rule into their body of traditions. Interaction between the "encapsulated" communities of Mendeland and their political environment has been characterized by a ready willingness and ability to utilize external structures for internal aims. In reaching for allies further afield, however, chiefdom factions have become dependent upon the outside world and compelled at least partially to accept its premises.[2] To a significant extent, the self-interested behavior of local actors has energized this mechanism by which Mende societies have adjusted to Western-style forms and practices. The process of change initiated by colonial overlordship has been distinguished less by displacement of the old by the new than by a synthetic interaction between them.

The Paramount Chieftaincy played a key linkage role during the colonial era. In the twilight years of colonialism, when popular participation and nationalism had entered the political nexus, and when democratic reforms had widened the scope of political protest, chiefs came under considerable attack. But especially in Mendeland, these attacks cannot be interpreted as an effort on the part of new groups and interests to eliminate an obsolete role. Most of the political heat was generated by local oppositions who were anxious to fill the role, not destroy it. Furthermore, those members of the new elite who from time to time clashed with chiefly interests did so on the basis of particular issues, not from wholesale condemnation of chiefdom institutions; adjustment and compromise in most cases easily dealt with the disputes. During the decade of advance towards Independence, chiefs did not represent a countercurrent against the main flow of Sierra Leonean history: they were among the leaders of the nationalist movement; they comprised a key element in the SLPP coalition which was leading Sierra Leone towards Independence; and they maintained myriad socioeconomic links with the new educated elite which was inheriting central power from the British. The role of Paramount Chief outlived the colonial regime which did so much to shape it because—essentially—an inherent instrumental premise has allowed it to adapt sufficiently to changing conditions.

The Paramount Cheiftaincy has endured as a linkage role since Independence, but the controversy surrounding chiefs has continued apace; if anything, it has heightened in tempo. Again, however, the presence of conflict should not be interpreted necessarily as a clash between modernizing forces and a traditional institution. Much of the turmoil regarding chiefs since Independence stems from contradictions among the expectations about chiefly behavior which issue from the central system. From central perspective, chiefs are expected at one in the same time to be dignified figureheads, removed from the hurly-burly of everyday political events; agents of the party in power, prepared to seize partisan advantage; and civil servants, disinterested instruments of rural administration and development. In short, the Sierra Leonean national elite has failed to define a consistent role for chiefs to play in the central system. It is not a question of conflict between modern and traditional traits since it is the modern sector alone which calls for cross-purposeful behavior. Faced with this "trilemma" chiefs become easy targets for local opposition factions whose own utilitarian premise leads them to draw central attention to chiefly departures from norms to which conformity is almost impossible.

Political development implies among other things the emergence of linkage roles which are capable and resilient. They must be "institutionalized"—coherent roles around which a firm consensus has been built. At the peripheral level, coherence and consensus regarding the Paramount Chieftaincy are both very much in evidence; conflict will always exist of course, but generally the strictly local aspect of the chiefly role forms a consistent whole about which there is deep consensus. At the central level, however, there is neither coherence nor consensus regar-

ding the chieftaincy. Since the central role expectations contradict each other, consensus necessarily cannot crystallize.
Hence, in its linkage capacity the role of Paramount Chief is no
more effective now than it was during the latter years of the
colonial era; indeed, in relative terms it has declined in importance, since politicians, parties, bureaucracies, and modern communications have in the meantime increased their effectiveness
in tying center to periphery. If the Sierra Leonean elite wishes to
exploit the full potential of the chieftaincy for linkage purposes,
it must redefine its role in the central scheme of things.

Political alliances comprise another key mechanism for linking center with periphery in Sierra Leone. The factional nature
of Mende politics provides entry for national political parties to
compete at the local level; parties can in fact be envisioned as
networks of factions linked to a central leadership by utilitarian
and localistic considerations, prime among them being control of
the Paramount Chieftaincy. "Double politics" connects the local
and central arenas through a complex interplay among chiefdom
actors anxious to secure their interests and national politicians
attempting to build and consolidate power. Neither ideology nor
ethnicity, religion nor region, class nor party identity serves as
the basis for interaction between the two levels. The political
currency which underwrites the transactions of "double politics"
is self-interested reciprocity: Factions support parties in return
for local favors.

Factionalism is not confined to Mende chiefdoms alone. It is
characteristic of politics throughout Sierra Leone, including such
central institutions as political parties and the army. No full-
length study has yet been made of politics within the civil
bureaucracies, but it is a plausible inference that factions represent an important vehicle for competition within the administrative apparatus as well. Impressionistic evidence regarding the mode of advancement within the Ministry of Interior
lends support to this speculation. Such politically critical civil
servants as District Officers and Provincial Secretaries rose and
fell during the 1961-71 era less according to their competence or
incompetence than as a function of the influential patrons they

had cultivated inside and outside the ministry. The demise of Albert Margai was accompanied by sudden deceleration of the career advancement of more than several key civil servants; the NRC favored a particular set of officials, especially those out of favor during the Albert Margai regime; and with the consolidation of APC power at the center, other officials saw their careers suddenly blossom. This suggests that interpersonal networks—factions—perhaps based upon old-boy ties, ethnic affiliation, friendship, and kinship, as well as upon strategic calculation of interests, provide one mechanism for bureaucratic politics. This should not be construed as a claim that civil service norms have disappeared in Sierra Leone; they have not, by any means. But since Independence, as part of a systemwide politicization process, partisan ship and its attendant factionalism have become more characteristic of behavior in the administration, complicating the role of civil servants in much the same manner as divergent expectations from the center entangle the role of Paramount Chief.

Studies of local-level politics elsewhere in Africa lend comparative support to the themes developed here. For instance, Hopkins in his study of Kita, a middle-range town in Mali; Owusu in his examination of politics in Swedru, a mid-sized town in Ghana; and Vincent in her investigation of Gondo, a backwater parish in Uganda—all three are notable for their fundamental agreement on the relative unimportance of such oft-used categories as tribalism, rural-urban rifts, traditional-modern cleavages, and ideology.[3] Instead, they stress the instrumental behavior of ambitious leaders and followers and the groups—such as factions—that emerge as agents of political competition. Put in our terms, they suggest that utility serves as a more powerful device than identity for analyzing the politics of their respective localities. Like the Mende, the people of Kita, Swedru, and Gondo are energized by self-interested motives centered especially upon the tangible side of life.

Utilitarian politics has distinctive consequences for integration and development in the African context. This can be illustrated by comparing the nature of factions in Kita and Swedru.

Hopkins in his study of Kita offers a systematic and theoretical analysis which traces two decades of factionalism from the colonial days through the era of modern party politics.[4] The rise and fall of individual groups was matched by the vicissitudes of ambitious leaders and their fickle followers, but the overall pattern of competition between two factions was stable—a line of continuity between the old colonial politics and the new Malian Socialism. Hopkins explores the positive functions which factions performed in Kita. First, they provided the mechanism by which competition among ambitious individuals integrated society; by drawing elements from *all* sectors of Kitan society into utilitarian alliances, factions helped bridge fundamental socioeconomic cleavages. Second, the network of factions extended beyong Kita's borders, linking the town with smaller networks in its rural hinterland and, at a higher level, with factions operating in the national arena. Third, political participation was facilitated by the reciprocity and bargaining inherent in utilitarian politics; both individual and group demands gained expression in the give-and-take of factional competition. Finally, the distribution of resources and patronage was conducted largely within the framework of factions vying for central favor in pragmatic fashion, despite the strictures of a puritanical national ideology and the rigidities of an ever-present state bureaucracy.

In contrast, Owusu stresses the negative consequences of factionalism for Swedru. As in Mali, the veneer of one-party unity in Ghana was thin—barely concealing an inner reality seething with personal ambition and partisan competition. With the decline of Ghana's economy in the early 1960's, factionalism in the Congress Peoples' Party (CPP) took firmer hold as politicians sought to secure for themselves the benefits of power and position won in an earlier era marked by less scarcity. At the national level, and at the grassroots in localities like Swedru, the consequences were disastrous. CPP politicians became more arbitrary, more unresponsive, more self-centered, and more monopolistic; and the masses, increasingly alienated, became more inclined to withdraw their support. In other words, a utilitarian style of politics underwritten by an underdeveloped economy rests on a fragile foundation. A period of poor economic performance can set in motion destructive rivalry among factional leaders and a withdrawal of support among followers. The ties which bind leaders to followers lack the durability to survive hard times.

The differences between Hopkins and Owusu are less contradictory than might first appear; their arguments really represent opposite side of the same coin. Links based on converging interests make for easy association among individuals and groups. It is this *integrative* side of utilitarian politics which Hopkins emphasizes. On the other hand, by virtue of the ease with whlch such links are made and unmade, instrumentally-based alignments are weak, tentative, and inelastic. Except under conditions of sustained material abundance, they are unable to gain strength and mature beyond the conditions which gave rise to them in the first place. It is this negative consequence for *development* which Owusu emphasizes. As in Kenema District, political linkages in these two communities form a widely-dispersed network of cross-cutting ties, but, as.in Kenema District, they provide an unreliable basis for the expansion of central authority.

Factionalism need n t emerge as an inevitable outgrowth of utilitarian politics. As described by Vincent, the Gondo elite is much less given to pervasive competition within itself than are the elites of Kita, Swedru, and Mendeland. She emphasizes the corporate features of Gondo's leadership. What she calls its "strategic elite" came to prominence largely in response to a hostile environment: More than a century of alien overlordship imposed first by neighboring kingdoms and then by the British has habituated the people of what is now Gondo parish of Uganda to choose their leaders according to their ability to deal with outside forces and to hold them at bay. One of the key tasks undertaken by the elite involves settling disputes *before* they become so serious that outside agencies intervene. As a buffer between the community and its environment, the elite acts to minimize internal conflict in order to deflect external involvement.

But at the same time, utilitarian competition is the prime mechanism for recruiting the elite in Gondo. Rivalry for prestige leads aspiring men to exploit social and economic resources in order to accumulate power. They manipulate the agricultural cycle to maximize support from work groups, which in turn provides the material wherewithal (tools, food, beer, etc.) to attract future work teams from the community. In Vincent's words, local politicos must "compete for cooperation" in order to gain elite status.

Put succinctly, utility *and* identity considerations interact to shape the particular nature of Gondo's politics. Unlike the other localities we have considered, in Gondo a distinct community identity vis-a-vis the outside world serves to temper what otherwise would be near-unlimited internal competition for tangible resources. A preference for closing ranks against outsiders to preserve local identity exists alongside the kind of utilitarian materialism with which we are so familiar. The principle of segmentary politics—"I and my brother against my cousin; I and my cousin against the world"—operates in Gondo, while it does not in Kita, Swedru, and the chiefdoms of Kenema District. This is not to say that the people of these localities lack a sense of community identity, for they refer to themselves as Kitans, Swedrufo, and Mendes (or, at a lower level of analysis, as natives of, say, Dama chiefdom). But identity values are not powerful enough to overcome the utilitarian impulse to invite outside elements into the internal fray. Factions compete for external allies; a faction's success in building a body of supporters depends in part on its ability to tap sources of largess and prestige that lie beyond the community's boundaries. It is not true that "*all* politics is segmentary"[5]—where rivals at one level become allies at a higher level. Much depends upon the relative influence of utility and identity values. If utility preferences dominate, then "double politics" or some variant is likely to emerge, as in Kita, Swedru, and Kenema District. But if identity and itility preferences coexist in more or less even balance, then "segmentary politics" of the sort observed in Gondo will in all likelihood prevail.

A dramatic case of lively interplay between identity and utility values is described by Cohen in his account of politics in the Hausa quarter of Ibanda, Nigeria.[6] During the 1950's the Hausa of "Sabo," as the quarter is called, felt their distinctive identity threatened by two major developments: the approach of Independence was forcing an end to indirect rule, which during the colonial era had bolstered the autonomy of groups such as Ibadan's Hausa by officially sanctioning them and by administering them as units through their traditional leaders; and the spread of Islam among the Yoruba, Ibadan's majority group, was eroding the religious exclusivism upon which Hausa identity was in part based. Moreover, the rise of party politics undermined unity and the authority of the Chief of Sabo in a manner reminiscent of "double politics" in Mendeland, whereby internal factions aligned with competing national parties in their efforts to promote parochial goals.[7] But this represented more than a challenge to community identity. The material basis of Sabo society depended directly upon its ability to draw firm boundaries between members and nonmembers. The long-distance trading networks that provided livelihood to most of Ibadan's Hausa could not operate except on the basis of trust, credit, identifiability, easy communications, and discipline—qualities which only a tightly-knit community could furnish. Hence, utility and identity considerations became inseparable parts of an interrelated whole; blurring the distinction between Hausas and outsiders imperiled the intimate bond between a way of making a living and a way of life.

But a new "articulating principle" arose to replace indirect rule as a custodian of group identity. The Tijaniyya, a Muslim order, spread quickly among the Hausa of Ibadan during the 1950's, differentiating them from the Yoruba population and, more important, turning their attention inward upon their own community. The special features of Tijaniyya beliefs, emphasizing collective worship conducted by malams (learned holy men) as well as the unique power of malams to divine earthly fortunes, refocused Sabo society by reshaping the conceptual lens through which people perceived the world. Businessmen especially became closely associated with the malams, whose blessings was thought to be indispensable backing for any risky venture. But laymen in general—landlords and clients, chiefs and commoners, politicians and traders—became linked to the malams and to each other through the growth of belief in the ritual powers of mystical men. "The new structure of power has become routinized, institutionalized, and legitimized by the development of new ideologies, myths, values, loyalties, and attitudes."[8]

The impact of this rejuvenation of Sabo identity upon political development and integration is clear. *Within* Sabo, political links grew stronger and more dense. The intensification and collectivization of ritual activity greatly increased the interaction of Hausa with one another. But, correspondingly, links with the outside world diminished in frequency and intensity. "The Hausa of Sabo are today more socially exclusive, or less assimilated into the host society, than any other time in the past. They thus seem to have completed a full cycle of 'retribalization.'[9] By converting "double politics" into "segmentary politics" through the stimulation of religiously-based community identity, Sabo was able to dampen the impact of factional activity. Like Gondo, Sabo closed ranks against external forces, curtailing the penetration of national institutions and containing the competition of political parties. In Kita, Swedru, and Kenema District, center-periphery links were easily established because local actors were anxious to make use of external resources for their own purposes, factions being an especially apposite agency for the grass-roots articulation of party movements. But in Gondo, where internal conflict was muted, and in Sabo, where community exclusiveness was cultivated, such access was confined to narrow official channels. As predicted by our models, utility hastens and identity hinders the integration of peripheral groups into the central system.

Interplay between identity and utility values helps to account for the close association between northern Sierra Leoneans and the APC. At first glance it appears that the APC's ethnic stronghold in the north contrasts radically with the utilitarian politics of the Mende south. Solidarity among the Temnes and related peoples of the north seems grounded in a sense of close identity rather than the result of studied comparison of costs and benefits. But this is only partially correct. What seems to have occurred is a convergence of the two forms of association. Northerners by 1960 became increasingly aware of their region as a neglected area in contrast to the south, which appeared to be favored by the Mende-dominated SLPP government:

> The "tribal" discontent which arose among Temnes, Limbas, and other northern tribes was largely a by-product of social mobilization. These areas had been backward long before the APC appeared in 1960. Their discontent arose . . . from their becoming aware of their backwardness, an awareness brought about by the spread of information through the migrations of diamond miners, the opening of new roads and new jobs, and the growth of schooling opportunities and towns. The growth of "tribalism," of the common identity of all Temnes as against the rest of the world, occurred not in the remote villages but among the transitional individuals who had been drawn part-way into the modern world.[10]

Similar comments apply for the Susu, the Limba, and the Kono peoples.[11] Indeed, not only was there a growing sense of "tribal" identity within each group but at the same time their common posture vis-a-vis the south led to the emergence of a "northern" identity. A new ethnic group had evolved, its sense of identity fragile and heavily contingent upon the vagaries of national politics, but a self-conscious grouping of like-minded peoples just the same.[12] The APC was born as the "northerners' party" amidst this sense of regional deprivation. Its electoral success stemmed to a significant extent from its ability to convert into political consciousness this diffuse demand for reallocaton of public benefits. In our terms, common identity vis-a-vis Mendes dovetailed with utilitarian calculation of interests, out of which emerged a sense of northern ethnicity and a substantial political base for the APC.

Thus, the APC rests on a firmer foundation in the north than it does in the south. We have dubbed the north a "core area" upon which the party can rely despite oscillation of support elsewhere in the political system. To the extent that northerners do indeed extend long-run allegiance to the APC, these well-developed links provide a basis for further expansion of central authority. But our treatment of emergent ethnicity in the north sensitizes us to some features of the APC Monopoly which may in the future become "unstuck," threatening the stonghold from which the party controls the center. First, the relationship between the APC and the north is not entirely visceral. Were the party to fail in its mission to supply tangible benefits to deprived regions, the marriage between utility and identity which now underlies northern ethnicity may weaken or even dissolve. Political support is not as contingent upon the provision of tangibles as in Mendeland, but the utilitarian element is present and its failure to reinforce identity-based linkages threatens them with eventual extinction. Second, emergent northern ethnicity is rooted in unfavorable comparisons with the south. Were the situation to change so that regional contrasts were perceived to be diminishing, northern identity might recede into the social backdrop as a category no longer relevant for contemporary events. In other words, the APC's very success in equalizing regional welfare may in the long run dry up a major reservoir of support.

Third, "emergent" suggests the tenuousness of northern ethnicity. It competes with other identities—Temne, Limba, Susu, Kono, as well as "Sierra Leonean"—which have been established longer and which may reassert themselves in the minds and emotions of individuals. We need not—nor should we—think in zero-sum terms, whereby an increase of, say, "Temne" identity occurs at the expense of "northern" identity, in order to envision the possibility of competition for scarce resources among the elements which make up the northern camp. For instance, there have been recent reports of friction between Temne and Limba components of the APC over the distribution of power within the party. Particularly if perceptions of the Mende bogeyman fade, intranorthern rivalries are likely to render the APC more a coalition of separate ethnic groups than the organizational embodiment of regional—or national—identity.

Fourth and finally, the APC is only slightly less susceptible to factionalism than other political structures in Sierra Leone. At the local level, northern chiefdoms are given to the same kind of competition for the Paramount Chieftaincy which divides their Mende counterparts,[13] although the Temne practice (when it is followed) of rotating the chieftaincy among ruling families, mutes internal differences and diminishes but certainly does not eliminate a major incentive for forming factions. The existence of rival factions at the local level signifies a potential source of support for opposition groups at the central level—within or without the APC—were they to demonstrate a capacity for supplying tangible resources. And there is no dearth of APC factions at the central level. One group centers on S.I. Koroma, now Vice-President and Prime Minister of Sierra Leone; another revolves about C.A. Kamara-Taylor, Secretary-General of the APC; a third, composed of younger, better educated northerners like Ibrahim Taqi and former Finance Minister Sembu Fornah, broke away to form the short-lived National Democratic Party. With a youth wing and a women's auxiliary, militia units and businessmen, Creoles and Paramount Chiefs, Bo School graduates and old boys from Freetown, northerners and southerners—with all these groups seeking shelter under the APC umbrella, it is not surprising that factions have become an integral part of its inner workings.

Thus, center-periphery links between the APC and the north are likely increasingly to parallel the southern pattern. This is not to say that the future will see a virtual return to past practices; especially in an era of rapid social mobilization and growing political consciousness, it would be foolhardy to expect former patterns to repeat themselves as if no fundamental changes had taken place. But if this analysis is valid, there is a strong probability that "double politics" will increasingly characterize affairs in Sierra Leone, despite a *de facto* One-Party State and despite the APC's present stronghold in the north. Comparison with other African systems lends support to this proposition. In both Ghana and Mali, as we have mentioned, behind a one-party facade factionalism and an instrumental style of politics breathed life into, and in turn was supported by, grassroots factionalism in localities like Swedru and Kita. The competitive, uncertain nature of such center-periphery links dispersed the downward flow of power, vitiating two prime justifications for one-party authoritarianism—central direction and unencumbered ties between the regime and its public. In much the same fashion, we can expect utilitarian politics increasingly to fractionate the APC monopoly of power in Sierra Leone.

Is there any escape from the dilemma implied by the utility and identity models, in which development is purchased at the price of integration an vice versa? Can development *and* integration grow in Sierra Leone?

We have suggested that organizational elaboration is one avenue of escape, although our confidence in the strength of this factor is tenuous because the data at present support only ambiguous interpretations. Party building is a slow and laborious process, a long-term investment whose profits are uncertain. Hence, before-and-after comparisons are able to assess the effectiveness of organization only after a considerable period has elapsed. The APC has a long way to go before it can match the organizational adaptability, complexity, autonomy, and coherence—Huntington's four dimensions of "institutionalization"[14]—of the model it has lately attempted to emulate, the *Parti Democratique de la Guinee*. Too many of the party's resources have been embedded in the cleavages of local communities, hindering its ability to mobilize the requisite skills, motivation, and sustained central direction for rapidly extending a permanent apparatus throughout the countryside. Organization can probably contribute to ameliorating the trade-off between development and integration, but the organization must first be built, a process which requires support from other sectors of the polity. Unless the regime can afford to allow an autonomous party-building effort to proceed slowly and incrementally over a long period of time, other strategies are necessary to supplement and sustain organization, and to provide additional mechanisms for escaping the development-integration dilemma.

One such strategy is simply to expand the supply of tangible resources available to the system through economic development. This "neomercantilist" strategy has been adopted by the Ivory Coast, so far with success.[15] The scarcities which sharpen utilitarian competition can be reduced by assuring constant increases in the income that each actor receives. Continuous prosperity purchases sustained support from those sectors which share in it. A regime which performs well economically can not only devote material resources to organizational efforts but can also shift scarce entrepreneurial talents from the short-term task of simply staying in office to the more long-term investment in party building.

The political benefits which derive from economic rrowth should never be underestimated, but there are limits to the extent to which it can soften the harshness of political choice in systems such as Sierra Leone. First, some key resources are not expandable. The most important example of this in the Sierra Leonean case is the chieftaincy; there is a fixed supply of such offices and they are usually filled on a lifetime basis. Since "double politics" rests heavily on this factor, its transactions are underwritten by a relatively inelastic source of supply. Second, economic growth is likely to be accompanied by widening inequalities—both regional and class-based—which have disintegrative potential. While all sectors may be enjoying increasing incomes, some sectors (usually the richer ones) are likely to grow faster than the others, aggravating rather than moderating perceptions of deprivation.[16] The north-south cleavage in Sierra Leone is especially susceptible to this malady. Third, and perhaps most important, *sustained* economic growth is unlikely to be achieved in small low-income countries like Sierra Leone, dependent as they are on the vagaries of international demand for primary products, and deficient as they are in planning and entrepreneurial skills. Growth usually proceeds in fits and starts, interspersed with periods of stagnation or recession. Under such conditions, political links fall prey to the difficulty highlighted the utility model—instability. Except in the unlikely case of continuous increases in real income, political development suffers from a strategy of exclusive reliance on economic development due to the contingent nature of utilitarian affiliations.

A final strategy lies in the realm of belief. Political symbols, myths, and ideologies can be manipulated to create an "identity of the whole"—a sense of Sierra Leonean nationalism. The identity model pointed to the integrative deficiencies of a politics based on ethnic, regional, religious, or class loyalties. But if the relevant identity group were the society itself—a "nation"—then there would be no necessary trade-off between the strength and distribution of center-periphery links. Political development and integration could proceed together, their mutual growth dependent upon the range and intensity of national identity relative to less inclusive forms of identity. (Naturally we are referring to development and integration *within* a society; national identities impede integration *between* societies in the same way that, say, ethnic identities impede integration within a society.)[17] Nation building is an escape from the dilemma.

It is easy to claim that building national identity offers a solution; the problem, of course, is how to do it. The problem bulks especially large in Sierra Leone because the anticolonial "struggle" was so mild, leaving in its wake no powerful myths of national origin, no panoply of emotive symbols, heros and villains, and no widespread and deep-felt sense of being tied to all other Sierra Leoneans by common fate. In short, the base for nation building is feeble. Moreover, the ideological content of Sierra Leone's style of politics has always been low. The SLPP during its fifteen-year reign promoted beliefs about society and politics which could be called ideology only in the remotest sense. The APC in its early years did work out a class-oriented reform philosophy which demonstrated some concern for applying general concepts to the particular situation in Sierra Leone, but by 1968 when it took power it had already undergone the "deradicalization" which afflicts incumbent parties throughout Africa.[18]

What Sierra Leone needs is the functional equivalent of Tijaniyya Islam in Sabo—a powerful new ideology which quickly strikes deep roots, heightens identity vis-a-vis outsiders, institutionalizes the role structure of society, and charts past, present, and future with a set of beliefs attuned to the existing culture and capable of inspiring men and women to both action and sacrifice. These are ambitious goals, perhaps beyond reach, but our examination of the synthetic model of change suggests that at least in Mendeland new ideas and arrangements are easily absorbed; to the extent that the model applies throughout Sierra Leone, innovations do not receive wholesale opposition for being new; they are accepted when necessity beckons and welcomed when they promote welfare. The kind of ideology which stands the greatest chance of widespread adherence is one which responds to the day-to-day needs and anxieties of ordinary people. But to be effective in promoting a common identity it must rise above petty matters to articulate a collective cause. In other words, the ideology should be rooted in the materialistic, utilitarian political culture of Sierra Leone—but at the same time it should strive to change it.

Following LaPalombara we can define ideology as a more or less coherent set of beliefs which involves "a philosophy of history, a view of man's present place in it, some estimate of probable lines of future development, and a set of prescriptions regarding how to hasten, retard, and /or modify that developmental direction."[19]

Creating a sharper, stronger sense of identity is a prime function performed by ideology. This is a process which works simultaneously at two levels, the collective and the individual. For the collectivity, ideology can define boundaries and evoke visions of social solidarity. Socialism in developing countries— whether the radical, mobilization socialism of Nkrumah's Ghana and Toure's Guinea, or the communitarian socialism of

Senghor's Senegal and Nyerere's Tanzania—is an example of an ideology employed (in part) for integrative purposes:

> The distinctive implications of the ideal of social solidarity in the various [socialist] movements . . . should be appreciated. Socialist "togetherness" means one thing in the mobilization regimes, where the effort is to galvanize the populace into a single-minded dedication to the development of the nation and a total responsiveness to the intentions of the modernizing elite. In the more moderate systems, the ideal of socialist harmony and brotherhood summarizes the good society to be achieved through development.[20]

Socialism may or may not be an appropriate doctrine for engendering national identity in Sierra Leone; perhaps a more "traditional" set of beliefs, analogous to Tijaniyya mysticism in Sabo, would prove more receptive and effective. The point is simply that a coherent stock of ideas about society, packaged and distributed by a self-conscious elite, can serve to expand popular identity attachments beyond the "primordial" group. The content of the ideology is not so important for our analytical purposes as its contribution to an emergent nationality.

At the individual level, ideologies can confer a sense of personal identity to people undergoing the insecurities and uncertainties of transition amidst rapid change.[21] From the welter of confusing facts and conflicting demands which confront him, an individual imbued with an ideology can select the important from the unimportant, good from evil, allies from enemies, truth from deception. He has a personal system for appraising political objects. Moreover, with an ideology he can locate himself in the grand scheme of things—discover his place in history, as it were. The historical consciousness of ideology is transferred to the individual who internalizes it, delineating his part in the social drama. It is as a couple between collective and individual identity that ideology commands attention as a linkage mechanism whose potential for political development and integration needs to be thoroughly explored by thinkers and practicioners alike.

Ideology can also function to institutionalize key political roles. The two elements of role institutionalization—coherence and consensus—can be advanced by the wide dissemination of a systematic set of beliefs about society. An essential feature of ideology is the attention it directs to the roles of specific groups, organizations, and individuals in shaping present society as well as their designated roles in unfolding the future. In other words, ideology deals with the normative component of roles. Consensus is promoted by an ideology to the extent that its norms are internalized by role holders. Likewise, coherence is advanced by systems of thought disciplined at least in part by logic and consistency. Greater attention to ideological matters seems a proper prescription for polities like Sierra Leone where both consensus and cohesion are low with regard to key political roles.

An ideology appropriate for Sierra Leone could hardly fail to confront the problem of the chieftaincy. Are chiefs to play a role in the future and, if so, how can their role be clarified to avoid the ambiguity and conflict which has hitherto sapped their linkage capacities? What shall be their relation to the state, to the party, to their subjects? Similarly, the roles of party activist, civil servant, and soldier could be articulated and coordinated by an ideologically-oriented elite. Perhaps most importantly in Sierra Leone's case, the role of "citizen" could gain expression and acceptance as a means for redirecting popular energies. The overriding drawback to the utilitarian style of politics which now characterizes Sierra Leone is that it knows no limits. In the absence of cultural restraints, maximizing actors escalate competition into violence and factionalism into Hobbesian rule by force and fraud. This is the "Prisoners' Dilemma" known to game theorists: rational actors pursuing self-interest make choices which leave everybody worse off than they would be if a modicum of restraint, internally or externally imposed, were applied to encourage a cooperative solution. Norms which stress the obligations of citizens to the collectivity are characteristic of ideologies. They are a source of self-restraint, an internalization of the "public interest" which checks the excesses of self interest. An ideology which contributed to institutionalizing the role of citizen would espouse norms demarcating the bounds of acceptable behavior in the political arena. As Owusu put it in regretting the destructive consequences of instrumental politics in Ghana: "What Africa needs . . . is a new ideology of sacrifice."[22]

Ideology alone, however, is not a sufficient strategy for overcoming the integration-development dilemma. It can contribute to engendering a collective identity and it can temper the license of utilitarian politics, but extreme reliance upon doctrine is more debilitating than no doctrine at all. Ideology arouses expectations, entailing as it does a kind of promise that present sacrifices will be rewarded in the future.[23] If the promise is not eventually realized, mass alienation and hostility against the regime are likely outcomes. Hence, ideology is most effectively employed in conjunction with other strategies, as part of a grand design for engineering a self-reinforcing cycle whereby promise is matched with performance, which in turn enhances the potency of future promises. In particular, ideology can complement organization building and economic growth as strategies for promoting political integration and development. It can be envisioned as one part of a three-pronged effort to establish stronger, more widely distributed links between center and periphery. Ideology can direct and energize the party-building campaign, providing a resource to substitute for heavy reliance upon embedded ties. It can also act as an emergency fund during economic downturns, a reserve of political support from which the regime can draw to counteract the utilitarian impulse to defect. Similarly, organization and economic growth lend substance to ideology, backing symbols with action and promises with their satisfaction. This mutual reinforcement is the inner meaning of institutionalization, "the process by which organizations and procedures acquire value and stability."[24]

The most pressing challenge to political creativity in Sierra Leone is the problem of devising a set of symbols and ideas which can accommodate yet overcome its distinctive style of politics by tempering materialism with morality and utilitarianism with utopia. Development and integration depend ultimately upon the inventiveness of political elites.

NOTES

1. P.H. Gulliver (ed.), *Tradition and Transition in East Africa: Studies of the Tribal Element in the Modern Era* (Berkeley and Los Angeles: University of California Press, 1969), p. 12.

2. For a related discussion of the way in which "encapsulated political structures" adjust to their environment in one area of rural India, see F.G. Bailey, *Stratagems and Spoils: A Social Anthropology of Politics* (Oxford: Basil Blackwood, 1969), pp. 144-185.

3. Nicholas Hopkins, *Popular Government in an African Town: Kita, Mali* (Chicago and London: University of Chicago Press, 1972); Maxwell Owusu, *Uses and Abuses of Political Power: A Case Study of Continuity and Change in the Politics of Ghana* (Chicago and London: University of Chicago Press, 1970); and Joan Vincent, *African Elite: The Big Men of a Small Town* (N.Y. and London: Columbia University Press, 1971).

See my review article of these three books, "Comparative Grassroots Politics in Africa," *World Politics,* XXVI, 2 (Jan. 1974), pp. 283-297. Material in this and following paragraphs is adapted from this article.

4. His research ceased just prior to the November 1968 military coup which abolished party politics in Mali.

5. Abner Cohen, "Political Anthropology: The Analysis of the Symbolism of Power Relations," *Man,* 4,2 (June 1969), p. 220. Emphasis added. For another view that all politics is essentially segmentary, see M.G. Smith, "On Segmentary Lineage Systems," *The Journal of the Royal Anthropological Institute,* 86 (July-Dec. 1956), pp. 39-80.

6. Abner Cohen, *Custom and Politics in Urban Africa: A Study of Hausa Migrants in Yoruba Towns* (Berkeley and Los Angeles: University of California Press, 1969).

7. *Ibid.,* pp. 142-150.

8. *Ibid.,* p. 175.

9. *Ibid.,* p. 186.

10. John R. Cartwright, *Politics in Sierra Leone 1947-67* (Toronto and Buffalo: University of Toronto Press, 1970), pp. 263-4.

11. For analytical purposes, Kono District can be considered part of the north, even though officially it is in the Eastern Province. On

regional deprivation in Kono District, see Fred M. Hayward, "Some Generalizations About a Progressive Political Organization in the Bush: A Case Study in Sierra Leone," paper delivered to the African Studies Association annual meeting. New York, 1968.

12. On emergent ethnicity see Immanuel Wallerstein, "Ethnicity and National Integration," *Cahiers d'Etudes Africaines,* I (July 1960), pp. 129-139.

13. See, for instance, Victor Minikin, "Indirect Political Participation in Two Sierra Leone Chiefdoms," *Journal of Modern African Studies,* 11,1 (March 1973), pp. 129-135. Minikin's account of politics in a Temne and in a Kono chiefdom describes the same *pattern* of faction-based "double politics" that we have discovered in Mendeland. However, he departs from our interpretation in his central thesis, which maintains that the pattern derives from the deliberate attempt on the part of elites to limit mass political involvement. "[N]ational leaders in Sierra Leone *feared* the implications of mass participation in politics." (p. 129; emphasis in original.) Minikin gives no direct evidence that the elites feared mass participation; he simply infers that interpretation from the structural relationships between local actors and central parties which we have dubbed "double politics." A more compelling interpretation stems from our rational-actor approach. In the absence of elaborate party machinery, alliances with local factions were the most effective means for mobilizing votes and other forms of support necessary for power in central politics.

14. Samuel P. Huntington, "Political Development and Political Decay," in Claude E. Welch, Jr. (ed.), *Political Modernization* (Belmont, Calif.: Wadsworth, 1971, second ed.), pp. 238-277.

15. See Philip Foster and Aristide R. Zolberg (eds.), *Ghana and the Ivory Coast* (Chicago and London: University of Chicago Press, 1971), especially the chapters by Richard E. Stryker and Elliot J. Berg. The term "neomercantilist" is from David E. Apter, *The Politics of Modernization* (Chicago: University of Chicago Press, 1965).

16. This seems to be the greatest danger in the Ivory Coast. See Richard E. Stryker, "A Local Perspective on Developmental Strategy in the Ivory Coast," in Michael F. Lofchie (ed.), *The State of the Nations* (Berkeley, Los Angeles, and London: University of California Press, 1971), pp. 141-164.

17. Note that we are not postulating a zero-sum relationship between ethnic and national identities. It is perfectly possible for them to grow together, as is often the case in African politics or, for that matter, in the United States. But the relative strengths of national and subnational identities is an important determinant of integration. System integration is impeded if, say, ethnic identities become stronger and there is no compensating increase in identification with the overall society—the "nation."

18. See Henry Bienen, "Political Parties and Political Machines in Africa," in Lofchie, *op. cit.*, pp. 195-213.

19. Joseph LaPalombara, "Decline of Ideology: A Dissent and an Interpretation," *American Political Science Review*, LX, 1 (March 1966), pp. 5-16.

20. Charles W. Anderson, Fred R. von der Mehden, and Crawford Yound, *Issues of Political Development* (Englewood Cliffs, N.J.: prentice-Hall, 1967), p. 198.

21. This is emphasized by Erik H. Erikson, *Young Man Luther* (N.Y.: Norton, 1958). Erikson focuses on the efforts of leaders to solve their own identity problems during times of stress through ideological innovation. His ideas are applied by Lucian Pye, "Personal Identity and Political Ideology," in Dwaine Marvick (ed.), *Political Decision-Makers* (Glencoe, Ill.: Free Press, 1960). Clifford Geertz stresses the importance of ideology as a conceptual road map for individuals during periods of cultural disorientation, in "Ideology as a Cultural System," in David E. Apter (ed.), *Ideology and Discontent* (N.Y.: Free Press, 1964), pp. 47-74.

22. Owusu, *op. cit.*, p. 329.

23. See John R. Nellis, *A Theory of Ideology: The Tanzanian Example* (N.Y.: Oxford University Press, 1973).

24. Huntington, *op. cit.*, p. 246.